TEACH ME IF YOU CAN!

Dr. David Lazerson

National Teachers Hall of Fame Inductee – 2008

"This book is a must-read for anyone interested in education. It really works. For any teacher, any parent, any student — for any subject!"

Blair Gardner, Teach.com

TEACH ME IF YOU CAN
Dr. David Lazerson

INTRO

"If your plan is for one year, plant rice.

If your plan is for ten years, plant trees.

If your plan is for one hundred years,
educate children."

Confucius

This book is not about complaining or griping about the changes, for better or worse, taking place in the very wide and often murky world of education. Like Bob Dylan sang, "The Times They are a'Changin," and this certainly seems to be the mantra echoed from the halls of capitol hill, to our state lawmakers, to our local school districts. They eventually impact, in profound ways, our schools, teachers, parents, and children.

What this book is about is proactive solutions, some practical and others, perhaps, a bit out there — outside the box — the four walls of the classroom. (And the four walls where little Johnny and Julia spend most of their time, their private TV/computer/digital/social networking room). This book is also written with the parent in mind and more specifically, it is about amazing techniques that can be adapted and utilized on the home front as well.

All of the strategies referred to in this book have been tested and put to use during my 34-year tenure as a full-time teacher in special education. This timeframe has given me many opportunities to fine tune things and to see what really works with my students, both in and out of the classroom. It is my sincere hope that the book will ignite some fires within you, and help generate ideas on how better to reach and teach your children and students. So before you open up your own one-room school house, or begin homeschooling, or start pulling out some hairs, (assuming there's still some left), and before you make the move and quit your teaching job please read on and become inspired. By the way, many of the techniques discussed in this book are remarkably simple to initiate, and in fact, dirt cheap to implement. Teaching and parenting individuals with special needs can be remarkably rewarding, and quite fun.

The entire "system" might seem to be at the point of saying to an educator, "teach me if you can." One can almost see all the involved parties — standing with their arms folded over their chests, heads turned a bit sideways, clad in smug expressions...saying to the parent or teacher, "Go on... I dare ya!" This book is the positive affirmation, the ammunition that today's educator and parent need in order to respond to them with a gentle smile and say; Yes, I will teach you. And yes... I can.

The dynamic community and spiritual leader, known as the Rebbe Rashab, often remarked, "we should actively contemplate the education of our children for at least 30 minutes every day." He compared the importance of education to that of any other directive, such as honoring one's parents or helping the needy. Forget the temporary, "band-aid" solutions to education. We need a healthy, balanced, long-term plan. It's my hunch that to achieve the 100 year model of Confucius, (mentioned above), we begin by taking the small, daily proactive steps that have direct, positive impact. Try to put one or more of the ideas discussed in this book to practical use for 30 minutes each day. I'm hoping you'll be more than just pleasantly surprised.

I thank all my superstar teachers who inspired me along the way, many who are mentioned in this book. I even have to thank the teachers who bored me nearly to death as I made my way through the tumultuous middle and high school years. They tried. At the very least, they taught me what techniques not to use with my own students. My deepest gratitude to my parents and siblings for giving me an absolutely wonderful childhood, on so many levels. Somehow, from my adolescence through early college years, they stuck with me and showed me love and guidance, when all I wanted to do was rebel against the status quo. My profound gratitude, respect, and love, to my wife and children. They are a tremendous wellspring of inspiration and goodness, and are all amazing educators in their own unique way. Thanks so much to my dad, Mr. Richard Lazerson, for suggesting the title for this book. It is both profoundly simple and incredibly deep, at the same time. I think it hits the nail right on the head. I also want to thank all of my awesome students throughout the years. Yikes, 34 years and still at it! You are all truly special — in the most positive sense of the word. It has been a privilege and honor for me to be part of your lives and I look forward to hearing wonderful things about you always. Finally, I want to thank my son, Dr. Aharon M. Lazerson, and editor, Chris McCorry for their careful proofreading.

Peace, blessings and happy educating.

Dr. Laz, January 2012

TEACH ME IF YOU CAN!
BOOK DEDICATION

(L-R: Zak Betesh, President of King David Bikers of South Florida; Paul Chandler, assistant director of Project CURE; Author's dad, Mr. Richard Lazerson; & Dr. Laz)

This book is dedicated to my superstar mom, Tillie Lazerson,

and to my beloved father,

who was also my best friend, mentor,

guide, and life-long role model,

who passed on after a brief illness in January 2011.

This picture was taken when my dad,

(84 years young here - sitting on the Harley),

attended my 2007 Arts Teacher of the Year ceremony

of the Broward County Public Schools.

His love for life, affection for people, keen intelligence,

and wonderful sense of humor, were nothing short of contagious.

He suggested the title for this book and is deeply missed.

TEACH ME IF YOU CAN!
CHAPTER 1

What's So Special About Special Education?

"I'm not a teacher but an awakener."

— *Robert Frost*

I've often wondered about the use of the word "special" and its connection to education. After all, I've devoted much of my life to this field. I've been a full-time special education teacher, (and occasional administrator), for more than 34 years. I started teaching students with learning disabilities (LD) when the field was brand, spanking new. That was the late 70's. There weren't too many books or materials available for my special students, and much of my time was spent trying to find something that worked for them. I was in desperate need of books, supplies, and workbooks; but more importantly, ideas about things that would click with my students. It was the first year that Buffalo, New York public schools offered LD self-contained classes. My students ranged in age from 11 — 14 years and I soon discovered that LD is not some nice, neat convenient label. Rather, it includes all sorts of interesting secondary conditions, such as behavioral problems, psychological & emotional issues, and more. I spent many sleepless nights that year racking my brain for ways to reach and teach them.

Then one day, Keith, my childhood buddy and lifelong friend, reminded me — ever so sweetly — that I would have been in an LD class myself, except for one thing: they didn't have them back when I was a kid! "C'mon," he said, "you could barely sit still for a moment!" Ever so politely, he continued, "And you still turned out okay."

Later that day, I wrote down what my interests were, what areas I had developed skills in, and what my goals were. To my surprise, (and many others for that matter), I've written some books, made some music CD's, learned to play drums, guitar, some piano, and banjo, and have even participated in, and help run, some very inspiring community projects. Perhaps even more surprising, I was holding down a respectable full-time job and had become a husband and father. The light bulb went off. If it could work for me, quite frankly, it could pretty much work for anyone. I simply had to look into my own experiences and see what clicked inside me...what motivated me to want more. This book is an elaboration of these ideas, an accumulation of special approaches or events that made me connect with learning and more importantly, with life. Things that inspired me to grow, develop, learn, and take risks. They worked wonders for me and they can for you and your kids and students, as well. The techniques in this book have been put to the test on the frontlines of special education, from the moderate to the most profound special needs.

I have been fortunate enough to direct experiential music and expressive arts programs for students with autism, Downs-syndrome, cerebral palsy, and medically fragile conditions. I think Robert Frost, (quoted above), would be very pleased with the results. We've had some real awakenings.

Throughout the years, I've personally experienced some of these eye-opening events. One of those "ah-ha!" moments, (where the bulb suddenly came on to shed some light), involved my very own field of work. I soon realized that special education is nothing but good education. It contains all the elements that make education really work. In a nutshell, good education is not rocket science. I call it:

The 7 Basic Commandments of Really Special Education:

- *Student (not teacher) centered*
- *Utilizes real-life experiences*
- *Provides for hands-on events and manipulatives*
- *Takes the student from passive observer to more-active participant*
- *Keeps things on the fun-oriented side*
- *Taps into the individual's strengths & interests*
- *Uses built-in reward systems that catch the student(s) being good*

Back in those early days of the LD field, I often heard this expression: Every special child deserves an education. It was used as a rallying cry to drum up support for this rather new area of special needs. I think, however, the slogan should be changed to read: Every child deserves a special education! While the ideas and practices contained in this book are intended for both parents and professionals who work with special needs individuals, they are simply the backbone of any decent educational program. In other words, they work in "regular" educational settings as well. Special education is indeed nothing but good education. Period.

From those early days back in my hometown of Buffalo, I went on to direct, (and teach), special ed programs for some large, private schools. I also pursued a personal dream and opened my own alternative high school program. At first it was known as Beth Rafael, named after my father-in-law. It later was named after my daughter Devorah Leah, who unfortunately, passed on at the young age of 25 from a seizure disorder. She was, and continues to be, a tremendous source of inspiration for me and all who knew her. She was an amazing individual who fought courageously against her illness. She went through all sorts of medication therapy and even had brain surgery. Eventually it was a special diet, known as the Ketogenic Diet, which helped her most.

During her last eight years with us she became totally independent, had her own car and apartment in Brooklyn, NY, and emerged as an extraordinary teacher. Her students and colleagues loved her so much. Devorah used many of the techniques discussed in this book with her students. Her classes were exciting, filled with all sorts of motivational, hands-on activities; her lessons filled with joy, song, and drama.

The Devorah Leah Alternative High School ran successfully for seven years. While I initially believed this program would cater to individuals with special needs, our seats were soon filled with teenagers who were, in a nutshell, alienated from the "system." They were basically good kids who had never quite made it in their regular schools, and simply didn't fit the mold. Besides some direction and TLC, (Tender Loving Care), I knew from the start that my program was not only a second chance for my students — for many it was a 5th, 6th, and 13th chance. They had been kicked out of so many other programs that mine was in fact, their last chance. Some called my special high school "Custer's Last Stand." Even better was "Custard's Last Stand," since we used to go out for lunch every day. More specifically, this school was, for many of these teenagers facing rough challenges, Laz's Last Stand. They either made it in my program or went to rehab. Or jail. While a few students did end up in such facilities, close to 95% of my students finished high school, got their GED's, and moved on to bigger and better things.

The principles and techniques discussed in this book were the very backbone of my alternative high school. In other words, these strategies have been given the "litmus test" with my special needs students, whether they were alienated and frustrated teens, adolescents with Downs-syndrome, or non-verbal individuals confined to wheelchairs. The principles work, and many are astoundingly simple to implement. They're gold mines, waiting for you to tap into and put to good use.

We need to bring up two more important points, before we sink our teeth into the meat of the book. Time for a word or two on who has special needs, and a few thoughts on the use of those pesky labels, so rampant in the field of special education.

We're All Special... Needs!

In order to appreciate this concept of "special" needs, I take you back to one of my first graduate-level courses at State University College at Buffalo, known affectionately as Buff State. I was working toward a Master's degree in Learning & Behavioral Disorders, (LBD), and had the pleasure of being a student of the amazing psychologist, psychiatrist, educator and mentor, Dr. Bernie B. Yormak. It was an ongoing joke with my fellow colleagues about how perfectly I fit into the LBD program. My middle name is Brian and thus, my full initials are DBL. One of the conditions we studied thoroughly was dyslexia, or reading difficulties. Individuals with dyslexia often read things backwards. They read was for saw, bat for tab, stop for pots, etc. My entrance into the program meant that DBL was LBD; thus, a match made in special education heaven.

Dr. Yormak was known as Dr. BBY, and his classes were always eye-opening experiences. Since it was a graduate class, Dr. BBY was challenged to keep us awake. But nobody ever slept in his class. The evening class was a good four hours long. Most of us came straight from our full time, day jobs. But BBY somehow had a way of keeping us on the edge of our seats. Our first class with him was no exception. It would be a lesson I would never forget.

FID & GOK

"These goodies," he said, turning to write two words on the board, "are all you need to get started and stay in this wild and wacky field of special education. It will help maintain your sanity and just as importantly, your perspective."

The board had two words written on it: FID and GOK.

He looked back at us with that sort of "well?" expression on his face. I was as dumbfounded, as was the rest of the class. We had no blooming idea what FID or GOK meant.

He then asked us to look out the window and describe what we saw.

Across the campus road stood an imposing, tall iron fence. Each bar of this fence came to a sharp point. Clearly, nobody was climbing in or out. On the other side of this barrier stood something even more intimidating: Buffalo State Hospital. It was a lock-down psychiatric facility and to my surprise, I would often see the stereotypical guys in white coats moving about. The large, dark stone building had bars over all its windows. This facility was using shock therapy during a time when it was neither popular nor condoned in professional circles. Simply put, it was a scary looking place, and my imagination went wild whenever I gazed upon its cold exterior. I could only thank my lucky stars that I wasn't on the other side of the fence being held behind those bars.

"Now tell me," BBY continued, "what's the difference between you in here and them in there?"

He pointed out the window to Buffalo State Hospital.

No one dared offer an answer. The class became very quiet. "Oh gimme a break," I thought to myself. "There are probably 16 million differences between them and us. We're productive, trying to make positive contributions to society. We're on the ball. Got our act together. We're graduate students, man! We're winners and they're, well..."

"FID is all that separates you from them," BBY smiled, interrupting our thoughts. "We all have hang-ups and idiosyncrasies and strange things we engage in. We are all a bit neurotic and rebellious and anti-social. Only, they do these activities, F — more frequently, I — with greater intensity, and D — for a longer duration of time."

BBY stood there, just kind of nodding his head, while this little bombshell of an insight hit us. FID. Frequency. Intensity. Duration.

This was no instant light switch. More like the slow-but-steady coming of the dawn after a long, dark night. About two minutes went by before any of us even breathed. By then, we were all nodding our heads. The bottom line is that we are all special needs. There is no "perfect specimen" amongst us, and thank the Good Lord for that. We're all works-in-progress. I guess the main thing is that we, at the very least, try to improve ourselves and the lives of others.

"You all have heard of the fear factor," the good doctor continued. "Now you know one of the most important notions in all of special ed. And in life. The FID Factor!"

BBY turned and pointed to the strange term "GOK" written on the board. Around this acronym he drew a bunch of small circles. "Let's fill in the small circles with the care providers and the significant others who interact with our students," he said.

Soon all the circles were filled with word descriptors like parents, teachers, doctors, therapists, psychiatrists, psychologists, siblings, principals, assistant principals, and more. He drew arrows from the smaller outer circles to the word GOK in the middle.

"GOK," he explained, "refers to our special needs child. When all these significant others have had their say, when they've all picked apart our troubled little Junior, analyzed him, labeled him regarding what he can or cannot do, what he will become, and what he, (or she), is capable of doing right now... it's GOK. Nothing more. Nothing less. GOK!"

He turned to us, put his hands on his hips and uttered three simple, yet deeply profound words:

"God Only Knows!"

These three amazing words of wisdom, alongside the FID Factor, have become the backbone of my entire approach to special education. And indeed, just when I think I have some kid all figured out, he or she does something that totally surprises me. Our job is not to label and thus, automatically limit a child. Our job is to inspire and provide as many opportunities as possible to help each and every child. You never know what might click and make some magic happen. The bottom line is that they're usually capable of doing a lot more than what we think they can.

Labels, Labels & More Labels

I t always boggles my mind when I read my students IEP's. Don't let that little innocuous title of "Individual Education Plan" fool you. Many of these IEP's folders are well over three inches thick. They're stuffed to the gills with all sorts of goodies, reports, documents, legal proceedings, test results, and jargon that would give Einstein a run for his money. They're also filled with lots and lots of labels, the various "innocent" letters we so quickly attach to kids. In special education we were always taught to be flexible, to think outside the box, to be creative, to individualize; and that labeling is, in fact, disabling. For a field that pretends to dislike labels, we sure have lots and lots of 'em floating around and making their way from the diagnostic tests to a nice, fat stamp on the kid's foreheads — often in permanent marker.

Here's a very brief list of some of the cute little labels used in our labeling-is-disabling field, which has, of course, its own cute little acronym of ESE. That's, Exceptional Student Education. I'm limiting this list to the labels that I've encountered in my 30-plus years as a career professional. Trust me on this — there are lots more where these came from:

LD — Learning Disabilities

LBD — Learning & Behavioral Disabilities

ADD — Attention Deficit Disorder

HD — Hyperactivity Disorder

AD/HD — combo of the two above

ASD — Autism Spectrum Disorder

PINS — Persons In Need of Supervision. (No joke, folks. This is one of my favorites. Who doesn't need helpful supervision at some point in life?)

JD — Juvenile Delinquent

EBD — Emotional & Behavioral Disorders

ED — Emotionally Disturbed

GE — Giftedness Education

GWD — Giftedness With Disabilities

GWD — Giftedness Without Disabilities. (I guess when you see these three letters you get to decide whether it's with or without).

GTC — Gifted & Talented Children

AS — Asperger's Syndrome

MR — Mental Retardation

EMR — Educable Mentally Retarded

TMR — Trainable Mentally Retarded

BD — Bipolar Disorder

DD — Developmental Disabilities

DD — Developmentally Delayed

TBI — Traumatic Brain Injury

OHI — Other Health Impaired

VE — Varying Exceptionalities

CI — Cognitive Impairment

HI — Hearing Impairment

EI — Emotional Impairment

ECDD — Early Childhood Developmental Delay

DB — Deaf Blindness

SMI — Severe Multiple Impairment

SLD — Specific Learning Disability

VI — Visual Impairment

PI — Physical Impairment

SLI — Speech & Language Impairment

SCI — Severe Cognitive Impairment

SWSCD — Students With Significant Cognitive Disabilities

MCI — Moderate Cognitive Impairment

And hey, let's not forget that old time favorite, the overused-and-abused three little letters that convey so much — OCD. That's Obsessive Compulsive Disorder.

I'd like to add one more term to this rather lengthy list, but I think it's absolutely necessary. The label is:

TLSRCWFTLIDAWAHPIDAC

In case you're not familiar with this one, it simply means: These Labels Stink Royally Cuz We Forgot That Labeling Is Disabling And We All Have Problems, Issues, Difficulties, And Challenges!

With all the labels out there, (and the above list is a drop in the bucket), I think the labelers are the ones with OCD! If a label must be used then I suggest we use the letters WIP and apply it to every member of the human species. They stand for "Work In Progress."

We have become quite obsessive and compulsive about labeling kids as soon as we get our paws on them. Straight from the womb we test them, compare them, and ultimately label them if we feel it's necessary. If we could, we'd give them labels while they're still in the womb. The problem is, of course, that another phenomenon quickly enters the picture right along with the label. It's known as the "self-fulfilling prophecy," and it often spells disaster for the labeled child. Once Johnny is marked as LD or AD or AD/HD or ED or OCD or whatever two or three or four letters we supposedly wise adults use, it's nearly impossible for Johnny to ever make the great escape from this designation. His label has, in effect, become a locked box with the key nowhere in sight. It's not just a scarlet ribbon hanging around his neck, but a blinking neon light right across his forehead.

Teachers quickly internalize this label and often, from the get-go, relate to this child in a lower-expectation-mode. After all, he or she is LD or AD/HD or OCD or, gulp, PINS, and thus can only do so much...can only go so far. The real problem, however, is when the child internalizes this label as his or her identity. Then it all seems like a losing battle. These kids often give up, or use the label as an excuse to never tap into their real potential. Both the significant other and the child internalize the label and respond accordingly. No one rises to low expectations.

On one occasion this notion really hit home. It happened when I was directing a special education program at a private K-8 school in Margate, Florida. This school, by the way, is a wonderful, warm, professional, and caring school. As I entered the school office, one of our special needs students was there, obviously in trouble for what was probably the 10th time in as many days. Linda was quite a firecracker, full of energy, with a really short fuse. She was quite smart, probably too smart for her own good; and for some strange reason, she always came to school in rather bizarre outfits. She loved to wear cowboy boots and wool vests, even when the mercury was hitting 95 degrees in that wonderful South Florida humidity. She was in our special ed program for behavioral and emotional issues. Academically, she probably could have taught all the courses.

"I don't care what you say," she screamed to the school's assistant principal, who was doing his best to keep things on the cool, calm side. "You don't know me, or understand me at all!"

"It doesn't matter, young lady," he responded. "You're not allowed to use cursing or bad language to a teacher, or even another student, for that matter."

"Yes I can!" she hollered back defiantly.

"No you can't!" he answered back, fighting to keep his voice on the quiet, subdued side.

"Yes I can!"

"No you cannot!"

"It's not under my control!"

"Yes it is!" he said, only this time his voice had gone up several decibel levels. "And I have the final..."

"Yes I can!" she interrupted, about to demonstrate who truly had the final say. "I have OCD and ADHD and you don't understand me! And I am on medication. And I will have my therapist call the school. You're the one in big trouble. Not me!"

With that, to my utter amazement, she turned around and stormed out of the office. The administrator stood there with his mouth open. I glanced around the office to see that everyone there, students included, had their mouths open, as well. I couldn't help but smile when I heard one student lean to another and say in a low voice, "She's totally awesome!"

Talk about internalizing a label or two! Here was a case of a student not only using the label as a convenient way to manipulate adults, but the self-fulfilling prophecy had come to its ultimate conclusion. It was now complete justification for her behaviors. She was no longer in charge or responsible. Her condition had become the ultimate deciding factor. In her own mind, she had a legit excuse for anything and everything.

Many educators view these labels as a "necessary evil" — for they are what bring in the buckos from the city, state & national government. These identifications are what makes the holy "matrix" and creates programs, and classrooms, and areas of study, and the necessary degrees and certifications, and its very own lexicon and culture. It becomes this kind of self-sustaining, self-validating creature; a snowball, that once started, simply gets bigger and bigger over time. But there is a different bottom line here, and that is the kids. Our kids. Our students. Our children. Like BBY taught, they are so much more than the labels we stick on them and the neat little constraining-boxes we put them in. The true reality of it all is well beyond our expertise and educated guesses. In other words, BBY taught DBL in LBD in the ESE department at BSU that GOK prevails over OCD & AD/HD & PINS any ol' day! (If I were you, I would definitely read that last line one more time just to make sure you've been paying attention here.)

When all the significant others have had their say, the teachers, the doctors, the therapists, the administrators, the evaluators, the parents and siblings, etc., it still comes down to GOK. What will this child become? What is she or he truly capable of doing? And furthermore, where is the child psychologically, emotionally, and intellectually, right now, at this very moment? GOK. God Only Knows.

Linda's showdown with the AP in the school office was the inspiration for a song I wrote, entitled, "Nobody's Fool." Here are the words, which you can hear, by the way, on my website at www.drlaz.com. Even better, buy the tune for a buck on iTunes, and do us both a favor. This way you'll have it in your own teaching arsenal. It was a lot of fun to produce this tune and, using the Beatles as an example, Mark, the studio engineer from Insane Sounds and I, used all sorts of goodies as background. The Beatles were quite famous for their use of anything and everything to enhance their tunes. John Lennon, for example, blew a straw into a cup of liquid for the special effects behind their hit classic "Yellow Submarine." Since "Nobody's Fool" deals with the notion of using special ed labeling in a rather obnoxious way, I wanted to have some really unrefined and surly audio in the background. See if you can identify the various rackets as you listen to the song. I'll give you two as teasers: At one point you'll hear someone biting into an apple! Another is that sweet, delightful, utterly bone-chilling cacophony of a dentist's drill. Yes, I know these reverberations are a bit abrasive, but who could resist sneaking them into this masterpiece?

Nobody's Fool

V1:

See, my daddy was too strict
My momma, not at all
I had no choice but to rebel
And have myself a ball
Stealing gum when I was little
And your cars when I grew tall
& rippin' off your credit cards
But hey, it ain't my fault

V2:

The shrinks had their hands full
Working hard to classify me
Said I started off with emotional stuff
Compounded by OCD
That's obsessive-compulsive disorder
Way beyond his control
Throw in some ADHD
Man we wuz on a roll

Chorus:

See, my daddy made me do it
My momma, she did to
It's all my environment
I ain't nobody's fool
Wanna thank my new shrink
For teaching me the new Golden Rule
All them others are to blame
I ain't nobody's fool

V3:

My momma didn't nurse me
Not nearly long enough
Or maybe, it was too long
My shrink sure knew his stuff
Grew up culturally disadvantaged
In my middle class suburb
Too much love, or not enough
No wonder I'm disturbed

V4:
I took to the Internet
Broke into the pentagon
No officer, it ain't my doing
Speak to my dad and mom
I smuggled lots of goodies
Across the world's borders
But hey man, don't blame me
It's my dang "OCD ED ADD ADHD PINS ABC XYZ PDQ" disorder

V5:
One day my folks just had enough
Took me to the side
They said son, nuff excuses
Behind them labels you can't hide
They said labeling-is-disabling
With nerves, all frailed
But you'll have time to meditate
Cuz we... ain't postin' bail

What's Good About Labels?

So, after learning all this information about how labeling can indeed be disabling, what, if anything, is good about these label designations? Labels can, I admit, be a source of relief for both the parents and an individual with special needs. I have several friends who knew they had various issues, (and simply didn't "fit in" socially), when they were in high school and college. It wasn't until they were in their 30's that they were diagnosed with a mild form of Asperger's disorder. So, for them it was beneficial in the sense that they now had a definitive handle on what they went through and what, in fact, they were still going through. They've expressed to me how much they wish they had known about it back then. From middle school through high school it was a rough go for them. Those days were filled with complaints from parents and teachers, alike:

*Why can't you just pay more attention?

*Why are you so anti-social?

*Stop moving so much.

*Stop staring into empty space.

*Can't you just try harder?

*What's your problem?

*You look normal but you act weird.

But it was even harder for them when it came to interacting with their peers. Or perhaps I should say, non-interacting with their peers. For them, social interactions ranged from awkward to downright disastrous. The diagnosis and name, (label), for their condition would have brought everyone involved some desperately needed understanding and closure. There would have been no blaming. It would have provided a mechanism to be proactive and move forward towards proper care and treatment. Thus, labeling an individual is a two-edged sword. It requires common sense.

Increase understanding and compassion.

Decrease and eliminate the blame.

Be proactive rather than reactive.

Labeling serves one other very useful and important function. It brings in the buckos. Without the proper screening, diagnosis, and ultimate designation, there would be no funding for programs, which include teachers, supplies, assistant teachers, transportation, specialized equipment, classrooms, etc. When it comes to funding it's a case of labeling-is-abling! Without the necessary labels there'd be no grease for the wheels. As professional care providers and parents we need to take the positive aspects of this labeling process and leave out the negative ramifications. There are times, though, when the labeling process isn't disabling, but rather mislabeling.

Labeling as Mislabeling

I started my professional teaching at Dr. Martin Luther King Jr. School in Buffalo. It was an inner-city setting and most of my 10 special needs students bussed from other geographic areas of the city. I spent many a long hour reviewing their IEP's before that first assignment. I wanted to come in as a good Scout and be fully prepared. I gleaned the most important factors from their IEP's, noting each students' strengths and weaknesses.

Phil was a tough, street-wise 13 year old that, according to his IEP, had "severe auditory memory difficulties." I realized that I couldn't teach him by over-speaking and doing all the usual teacher stuff, and that he would pretty much require an individualized remedial approach. I created all sorts of wonderful lessons that tapped into his visual skills. It was a time-consuming endeavor.

During my second week on the job, while the class was busy doing their early morning bell-work, Phil was humming away some tune by his desk. As I focused in on him, however, I realized that he was actually saying a whole bunch of words. The process seemed to go on endlessly and, at first, I thought he was repeating a phrase or two over and over again. This made sense to me, since many of my students engaged in all sorts of repetitive behaviors.

But then I recognized the tune as one of the new rap songs from the radio. It was a long number indeed, probably well over six minutes.

"I said a hip, a hop," Phil muttered happily under his breath, "a hip hip hop hop, you don't stop to the bang bang boogie boogie, up jumped the boogie, to the rhythm of the boggie to beat... now what you hear is not a test, I'm just a rappin' to the beat."

This went on for a few minutes and finally, I had to confront him. I did it privately of course, not seeking to embarrass him in front of his classmates. But I couldn't let him get away with sneaking a boom box into school when it was totally against school policy. He probably had the earphone cord tucked carefully up his sleeve. Then, he could simply lean on his elbow, right hand propped conveniently by his ear supporting his head as he listened to the radio. I made my way over to his desk and after a thorough FBI examination, was shocked to find no radio whatsoever. These were the pre-iPod days and the boom boxes were about the size of Manhattan — pretty near impossible to hide.

Phil explained that he was simply singing this new rap song to himself.

"Is it a problem?" he asked me.

"How did you learn all that? I mean all those words. The song is like an hour-and-a-half long!"

"Oh c'mon man," he responded somewhat annoyed. "It's new, but it's out there. Know what I'm sayin'? You gotta know this stuff where I live."

"Yeah, but how..."

"I just listened to it a bunch of times and, well, it stays with me, somehow."

I thanked him, told him to carry on with his bell work, and made my way back to my desk. I took out his well-read IEP, grabbed the papers that said, "significant auditory memory dysfunction," and ever-so-deftly, slam dunked it into the circular file, AKA — the garbage can, where it rightfully belonged.

So what went wrong here? How could some evaluator be so off-base? Auditory memory is often a sub-test contained within a full psycho-educational assessment. It usually requires the person to listen to a set of meaningless numbers or words and then repeat them back in order, or sometimes in reverse order. So if I were doing the testing I would say something like: "Here's a set of words, please listen carefully and repeat them back to me in reverse order. Ready? Listen carefully. Here's the list of words: Mother... reply... fix... win... brown... play... copy... today." The individual would then try to say these words in reverse order going: Today... copy... play, etc.

Phil was probably not very motivated for such nonsense. However, take a new rap song with something like 12,000 words put to a beat with some rhymes, and he was a master — likely more accomplished than any Ph.D. evaluator. If there was a contest to see who could memorize a rap song the quickest, I'd put my money on Phil every time. Hands down.

We need to look at IEP's and all the assessments, evaluations, and tests done on our kids as guidelines — not as something written in stone. In this way, we'll get information but, at the same time, we can look beyond the designation stamped on their bodies and wheelchairs. Besides, I've always felt that my students had one fundamental ingredient that was never mentioned in any of my college courses. My students — all of our children — possess something so much deeper and important than any ability to speak, or write a sentence, or calculate the price of a soda, or read a paper, or throw a ball. They all have beautiful, shining, sweet souls. One incident in particular left a tremendous impression on me. I'm grateful that I heard about this event before setting foot in any special needs classroom. It put things into a clearer perspective, and I think contains a deep lesson for anyone involved with special needs.

The Rabbi and the Angel

A famous rabbi — (in Hebrew the word rabbi means teacher) — was once giving a class to several hundred rabbinical students. It was a profound lecture on some esoteric Kabbalistic and Talmudic teachings, and folks came from near and far. Suddenly, in the middle of the class, the rabbi stopped speaking and stood up. If the rabbi stands, well, out of respect, so do the students. Within a second or two the entire room was on their feet. About 20 seconds went by as a rather uncomfortable silence filled the lecture hall. The students were more than puzzled, and many thought that some VIP was about to enter the large room. Rumors quickly circulated through the group. Was the mayor coming inside? The governor? The president? Another equally brilliant Talmudic scholar, perhaps? To their surprise nobody came in. Then, seemingly without reason, the rabbi sat down. This was followed, of course, by all the students sitting down. One student, however, was not content to leave things a mystery. He ran outside to see which important dignitary had passed by and inspired his rabbi to suddenly stand. To his utter shock and amazement, the only person outside was an individual with Downs-syndrome. Soon the entire lecture hall was buzzing more loudly than before. Why did the rabbi stand? Whom did he stand for? Was he simply tired of sitting? Needed to stretch? Just what the heck was going on, anyhow?

The rabbi put out his hand, and quiet returned to the room.

"What's the question?" he asked.

Then, not waiting for an answer, he pointed to the man with Downs-syndrome outside the window, and continued. "When one sees a person of 40-plus years who has never committed one sin in his entire life, how could I not stand? This person is pure and sweet... like an angel."

For more than 3 decades I've been working with individuals who had all sorts of issues and challenges. Some can't walk. Many have trouble maintaining social relationships. Those who can read are sometimes 10 years or more behind grade level for their age. Some can't speak or communicate. Others don't have the ability to go to the bathroom on their own. Some make strange, bizarre sounds. Others make no sounds at all. Some have average intelligence or higher but are, in effect, stuck inside bodies that just don't work too well. But it's what inside that counts. And like that incident with the rabbi, they are all sweet, pure angels. I'm not sure if I was ever up to the challenge, but it's always been an honor to become a part of their lives. Somehow, I never thought I'd be spending a lot of my waking hours working, playing, teaching and singing with angels.

CHAPTER 2

*What are the Expressive Arts &
How Can They Help?*

"Logic will get you from A to B.

Imagination will take you everywhere."

— *Albert Einstein*

The expressive arts are like a hidden gold mine just waiting to be tapped into and discovered. They are especially magic for any individual with special needs. In fact, they're highly effective for any member of the human race. The creative arts have not only been used effectively for individuals in need, but they are a beneficial tool for society at large. Michaelangelo Pistoletto, the winner of the prestigious Wolf Prize In The Arts, states, "artists have a unique and totally free way of understanding and analyzing society." He further comments "art can interact among all the diverse spheres of human activity that form society, and is thereby a generator for responsible transformation of society." (Educating Artists for the Future, Intellect Books, UK. 2008).

In this same thought-provoking and inspiring book, the author, Dr. Mel Alexenberg, shares several strategies that connect areas that, for many of us, seemed rather disconnected to begin with. Dr. Alexenberg, demonstrates, that for an artist to be truly effective in today's complex world, he or she must seek to unify the areas of art, technology, culture, and even science. In this dynamic manner, the expressive arts can both reflect on, speak to, and elevate society at large and the individuals that make up the global village of today.

This "future artist" has been evidenced in dramatic fashion in many countries experiencing the shifts of change in what has been deemed, the "Arab Spring" of 2011. The use of computers, Facebook, digital phone technology, and other social media, has been used quite effectively for sharing photos, and updating current events, including peaceful street demonstrations, while providing a public forum that allowed people to voice their opinions and concerns. New protest songs, "hot of the press" poetry, and other artistic expressions of awakening, were examples of art-in-motion never before witnessed in these oppressive regimes. Thus, in very real and practical terms, the arts can be used as highly effective mediums for transformation. As science and technology become more sophisticated and refined, the possibilities for the arts — and their impact— soars beyond imagination.

This book also deals with transformation in the front lines of education: the individual with special needs. While growth may come in miniscule steps they are nonetheless, just as dramatic and important as those that seem to shape society at large. After all, we sometimes forget that the humongous world around us is made of lots and lots of unique, individual components. Sometimes to change society, we indeed have to start with, as MJ put it, the "man in the mirror." To be sure, changing one person for the better changes the world for the better.

Expressive arts usually involve several areas that include music, dance, drama, writing and visual arts. Each of these generic terms is really an umbrella-like concept that embraces a whole spectrum of activities. For example, music may involve listening to jazz or classical, singing Karaoke style, simply making guttural noises into a microphone, tapping to the beat, or playing on a full drum set. Dance can be as complex as a full ballet or as simple as moving a foot. Visual arts range from drawing a simple picture with crayons to creating elaborate impressions in sand and other mediums. I'm adding several other components to the expressive arts, such as animal & pet therapy, water therapy, use of the great outdoors & environmental interactions, multi-sensory environments (MSE), and even humor therapy, all of which will be discussed later in this book.

I've seen first-hand how these expressive art approaches, often used in combination, tremendously benefit individuals with special needs. The expressive arts involve some sort of movement, response, and give & take, which facilitate change both within the individual, and within the "outside" environment, as well. It's a dynamic process that, in a nutshell, requires and stimulates expression — which is why they are called the expressive arts. Natalie Rogers, in her wonderful book, "The Creative Connection — Expressive Arts as Healing," (Science & Behavior Books, 1993), puts it like this: "We do not become creative by thinking about it. We reawaken our creativity by engaging in the process of creativity."

The beauty of the expressive arts is that they tap into an individual's deeper, creative side by encouraging a variety of expressional formats. It's the process of tapping into this internal connection that makes the expressive arts so powerful and important for our students, and in fact, for all children, and society, in general. **Check out the International Expressive Arts Therapy Association at www.ieata.org.** They sponsor all sorts of educational programs, training, awareness conferences, books, and more. Through the expressive arts, even the most profoundly challenged students continue to surprise me.

Jessica is a 17-year-old young lady with multiple disabilities and challenges. She is deaf, blind, non-verbal, and needs a wheelchair to get around. She is on so many medications that she, in essence, simply sits in her wheelchair all day long barely moving at all. As her special music teacher, I often wondered what, if anything, was getting through to her. Perhaps it was all a waste of time? Recently, she completely surprised me. We placed a small, nylon-string guitar on her wheelchair platform, and she seemed to move her thumb and index finger back and forth across the strings. I immediately got my electric guitar, cranked up the volume on the amp and switched instruments with her. Here too, she continued to ever so slightly manipulate the strings. It was one of those huge/small steps — an opening, perhaps, into helping her make some meaningful contact with the "outside" environment. According to her IEP — Individualized Education Plan — she was "in her own world" and made little, if any, real contact with anything or anyone outside of her difficult inner world. And yet, here she was, suddenly making sounds on a guitar! While this probably occurred when she felt the vibrations of the strings as she passed her thumb and fingers across the fret board, it doesn't diminish the fact that she went from her usual role of being totally passive to that of a more active participant. Something clicked inside her. It was an awakening moment — not only for Jessica but also for all the teachers in my music room.

Our job as teachers, caregivers, and parents of individuals with special needs, is often one of providing opportunities to crack open those dusty doors, to give them the occasion to awaken and thus become more expressive. When individuals with special needs express themselves, they are not only connecting with their inner selves, but just as importantly, they are connecting with the world at large — the outer environment that they so often feel disengaged from.

I teach a graduate level course at Nova Southeastern University in Florida on arts & expressive therapies. I always remind my students that pretty much anything that motivates an individual to take action can be called "expressive arts." It is direct intervention, introduced by a parent, professional therapist, or some significant other that inspires Johnny to move, sing, dance, paint, laugh, make a sound, smile, raise an eyebrow, or rub a guitar string. We need to think outside the box to enhance the likelihood of these "awakening" events. Sometimes we get lucky and our plans and efforts pay off. Other times it's a matter of trial and error, until we figure out something that makes that magic happen. Occasionally, we learn in the most unexpected ways:

The Quest Center in Florida's Broward County public school system — the nation's 6th largest school district — is a unique school that caters to individuals with profound special needs. Before starting the experiential music program on a full-time basis, I taught a self-contained class of eight students with profound special needs. The ages ranged from 13 to 17 years. Most were confined to wheelchairs, only two were slightly verbal; one could make lots of noises and the other liked to repeat things over, and over, (and over), again. Only three of the eight had toileting skills, so this also meant changing diapers on some really big kids. Oh well, another perk of the job! Quite frankly, I wasn't really sure what, if anything, was getting through to my class. I used hand-over-hand techniques to show them letters and numbers. I had hundreds of picture symbols to indicate yes, no, bathroom, stop, go, happy, sad, hungry, thirsty, etc. I was one highly frustrated teacher — anxious to help, but not really too sure whether they were comprehending any of it. The answer came in a most unexpected manner — a large wooden puzzle. Well, let me be more specific. It was a large wooden puzzle that came crashing to the floor when I accidentally knocked it off a high shelf. About five kids in the room burst into spontaneous laughter! Soon the others caught on and the entire class was laughing. I stood there absolutely dumbfounded.

They could process information from the "outside environment" very well. I just hadn't been giving it to them in the form they needed or could respond to. Speaking all the time, showing pictures, reading stories, all the usual "teacher stuff," wasn't getting the job done. Right then and there I decided to become Curly, Larry, & Moe, all rolled up into one, (the famous 3 Stooges). If they liked and responded to slapstick, and those funny loud & sudden noises, well then, I was going to give it to them! As I cleaned the puzzle pieces scattered all over the floor, I suddenly remembered the horsefly from 15 years prior. Despite the passage of time, how had I ever forgotten?

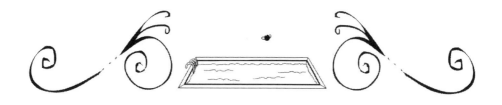

The Horsefly

"Let's go," I urged. "On the count of three we all lift together."

My lifeguards were already used to the procedure, and I couldn't get over how we functioned together like a smooth, synchronized Swiss watch. There was no need to tell them to use their legs and not their back, or to make sure their feet were firmly planted. (The deck was usually a real slippery place).

"Laz," one of the guards said, raising his eyebrows. "Do we really have to?"

I knew exactly what he was thinking.

"Is it worth all this effort?" he continued, verbalizing what most were probably thinking. "I mean, like, what's Simi getting out of all this anyhow?"

It was not only a good question — it was the question. It pervaded all of Simi's activities here at camp. In fact, it's a very common inquiry in general towards individuals with profound special needs. What, if anything, are they processing from the "outside" environment? It's something I hear echoed from both parents and professionals working in the field: "They just seem to be lost in their own world."

"I don't know," I answered. "I really don't, man. Could be something. Maybe nothing. Maybe even lots...lots more than we even imagine. One of those GOK situations, remember?"

"Yeah," they responded. "We were at your training and got the GOK and FID thing down. But still..."

What made Mishkon a unique place was that it was a camp for individuals with profound challenges, like Downs-syndrome, cerebral palsy, autism, and other physical and mental conditions. The campers ranged in age from eight to over sixty years old. Most were non-verbal, and many required wheelchairs for mobility. Mishkon was like the summer camp version of the Quest Center.

As a water-safety and lifeguard instructor, (and certified ESE teacher), I was hired to run the waterfront, which featured a large outdoor pool and lake that offered row boating and canoeing. Under regular circumstances, it's a job that's exciting, fun, outdoor-oriented, and loaded with responsibility. I basically sleep very soundly the day after camp ends — when everyone has gone home, safe & sound.

At Mishkon everything was more intense and much more involved. The attitude was to offer our special campers the usual, fun summer camp experiences that "normal" kids take for granted. This notion included boating and swimming, and each activity was a huge, major production.

First, we had to get the campers safely to the pool or waterfront, out of their wheelchairs, into life jackets or PFD's, (personal floatation devices), then into the water or boats safely. We kept 'em safe and supervised the entire time on the water, and then reversed the entire process to get them back on land and into their wheelchairs. Each component of this process was potentially dangerous and thus, needed to be broken down into minute, yet very important steps. The procedure was made more complicated the heavier the campers were. It was no small feat getting a 250-pound individual with Downs-syndrome out of his wheelchair and onto a boat, or into the pool. Sometimes, it took four or more lifeguards to make it all happen for just one camper. And it was pretty much an impossibility to make any headway if the camper simply didn't want to go into the water or onto a boat. Some of them were so big and so strong that they weren't budging, even with a crane and a division of the US Marines.

I eventually figured out a pretty creative and rather unorthodox way to get our really stubborn campers into the water. It came to me as a flash of wisdom from above. For weeks we were trying to convince one older camper, a guy in his late 50's, to enjoy the water. He had limited verbal abilities and would simply say a long, drawn-out "noooooooooooo," which could go on for several minutes straight, (and shake his head back and forth at the same time). One really hot day it was business as usual, and he wouldn't budge. In fact, if any of my lifeguards got in front of him to show him the lifejacket, he'd start kicking and spitting; one of the many hazards of our job.

"No problem, mates," I said. "But he is going in today!"

My guards looked at me like I had lost my mind. "Too much sun," they figured.

"In fact, not only is he going in the water, but so is his wheelchair!"

It was a stroke of genius. His eyes got real big as we approached the edge. We slowly but surely lowered him into the shallow end of the pool and within moments he was happily splashing away and playing catch with a beach ball. It was the first time we ever allowed a wheelchair to hit the pool, but it sure worked like a charm. They now make specially designed wheelchairs that can be submersed in water without worrying about rust damage. Now the problem was reversed. This particular adult camper didn't want to leave the water!

But I have to admit that, at Camp Mishkon, getting Simi into some cold water in a large outdoor pool didn't seem to make all that much sense. It wasn't that Simi was too heavy for us. Quite the opposite. Although 19 years old at the time, he was on the small, frail side. His arms and legs were even smaller, and they seemed to stick out awkwardly from his body. He was basically non-verbal, sometimes making these strange, guttural sounds. Quite frankly, I wasn't sure what, if anything, (you'll pardon the expression), was sinking-in with Simi whenever I did manage to get him in the water. I'd have to hold him in front of me, almost like cradling a baby, then I'd try to move he stiff appendages, to get some blood flowing.

So there we were, me holding Simi in our outdoor pool, standing in about four feet of rather cold water. Within a minute or two he started shivering. I couldn't help but question; why-oh-why we were subjecting Simi to this. It seemed that the only thing he was getting from this wonderful experience was a cold, and a cold wouldn't do his tiny, frail body any good at all.

But I was about to get the GOK lesson of my life. As we stood in this position, I kept trying to keep things on the positive side.

"Good, Simi." I said. "Oh, you be doing a great job there, buddy. Yeah, let's move this arm. Good. Now, this one."

Poor Simi was shaking badly and I knew we'd have to get him out in a few seconds. It all seemed like cruel and unusual punishment. That little voice of doubt was getting bolder inside me. Who even knew if Simi was processing any of this at all? Was any of this experience beneficial in any way whatsoever, for him? Was it worth all the effort?

Then, Divine Providence sent a little messenger to me. A very small messenger, but one that packs a powerful wallop in some very strong little jaws. A horsefly, to be exact. I don't know if you've ever had the experience of encountering one of these little suckers, but watch out, especially if your back is nice and exposed. These little guys draw blood.

Unbeknownst to me, this little guy landed somewhere near the middle of my back and sunk in some teeth.

"Ahhhhhhhhhhhhhhhh," I shouted out loud, swinging one arm around and smacking myself in the back, all the while trying not to lose Simi below the surface, while performing my desperate, clumsy dance of survival.

My left arm still held securely onto Simi, floating and shivering in the water. I gave myself several smacks, desperately trying to get the killer bug off me. It was all so frustrating, because my immediate reaction was to dive underwater and escape my tormenter, which wouldn't have worked all that well for Simi.

To my utter amazement, Simi himself had something to say about the situation. He suddenly started laughing out loud with these deep, loud guffaws.

"Ha-ha-ha-ha-ha," he roared, his eyes totally lighting up.

I was in shock. Not from the horsefly, mind you, but from Simi. I think the horsefly may have laid into my flesh a few more times, but those further bites didn't faze me one iota. I was only vaguely aware of that nasty critter. Instead, I stared gratefully at Simi, my mouth open, and a few tears of joy streaming down my face. No, he wasn't some sort of mere blob unable to process anything from the "outside." He was not only highly aware of his environment, but he had a great sense of humor, to boot. Like my class at the Quest Center, he absolutely loved slapstick. From that point on, I did my best to keep Simi a happy camper. I'd walk into walls in the dining room, or pretend to slip and fall, just to hear Simi roar with delight. And always, without fail, whenever he came to the pool, I'd yell out from the top of the tall lifeguard stand; "Hey Camp Mishkon! Is everyone happy?" Those with the verbal skills shouted back a loud yes, which of course, I wasn't satisfied with, and asked the question several more times. Then, I would cannonball off the lifeguard stand into the deep end, to their roaring approval.

Now, I'm the kinda guy who'll rescue a fly trapped in water in my sink. But I also take pride in my ability to smack a horsefly into orbit. Not with a wide canoe paddle, mind you, but with a really thin lifeguard rescue pole. Now that's skill. Horseflies? C'mon. Open season. But that one that bit me while I was holding Simi in the Mishkon swimming pool? It got away, and I'm happy it did. I figure it was the least I could do. In the meantime, as I developed my slapstick routines for Simi and, in fact, the entire camp, I could only hope I wouldn't need too many horsefly reminders in the future. Yes, these individuals can learn. They can process and respond and even laugh appropriately. To become awakeners we have to stay awake. I have to thank Simi and my Quest students for the wakeup calls. Let's further discuss this important tool in a parent or teacher's arsenal. It's called humor.

Use humor! Time to smile & laugh.

As they say, "lighten up." Remember, if momma ain't happy —nobody is! Humor therapy puts everyone, including the teacher or parent, in a good mood. Laughter & good vibes are contagious. We all need to smile & laugh more often. The renowned philosopher and writer Nietzsche wrote, "we should call every truth false, which was not accompanied by at least one laugh."

From the day I dropped the box in my room, humor therapy has been part of my teaching/awakening arsenal. I walk into walls and doors or wear funny hats and outfits. I go through a long process of pretending to sneeze rather loudly, which leads to a dramatic climax that includes throwing things into the air to highlight the effect. My students now anticipate the grand outcome. Their eyes start to twinkle and light up, and they begin laughing and smiling, right as I start the whole elaborate sneezing process. Any time I start my "ahhhhh — ahhhhhhh — ahhhhhh" routine, and they perk right up. They know that something fun and wild and crazy, is about to happen, and they are suddenly tuned in, receptive, and excited. It took my wheelchair-bound, non-verbal students to teach me the importance of making learning fun. It's a simple way to maximize your chances for success.

It's interesting to note that the great Talmudic scholar, Rava, would open with a joke before lecturing to his rabbinical students on complicated manners in civil and criminal law. He found that this little technique put his students at ease and made them more receptive. In this manner too, I think, he established a connection with his students. I think humor helps keep us young. A friend once told me that a smile is a crooked little line that can straighten out so much! Mighty profound words in that saying. There's so much in the media that's downright depressing. They seem to thrive on that ancient method of, "the fear factor." And so, besides regular worries about our kids and students, we now have to sleep with such notions as terrorism, nuclear arms in the hands of not-such-peaceful characters, the planet getting too cold...or too hot, (depending on which scientist you listen to), species becoming extinct, and the list goes on and on. It's no wonder modern society has become a drug culture. There's basically a drug for anything and everything out there to help counter the media use of this fear culture upon us. It's also no wonder that millions of folks suffer from sleeping disorders. Who the heck can sleep when there's so much worrying to do?

Take & make time to laugh.

My wife and I came up with a remedy that works better than any sleep medication. You may, however, get addicted, so no promises from my end. We decided that as part of our overall therapy plan, to try our best to be in good moods. How do we accomplish this after a long day, and before hitting the sack? Very simple. We put on one episode of Seinfeld! Soon we're both laughing away and suddenly the world seems like not such a bad place, after all. In this matter, of course, it's an individual choice. Whatever floats your boat. You may opt for some of the classic reruns like Princess Bride, Robin Hood, or Men In Tights. And let's not forget the great bean-eating scene from Blazing Saddles, which, I admit, is something that seems to be very gender-oriented humor. Men find the scene hilarious. Women are basically grossed-out by our usual crude, obnoxious behavior.

The main point, however, is to be proactive and find something you enjoy that brings a smile or two — and preferably a lot more — to your face. I'm not suggesting we hide our faces in the sand regarding the problems of life and the difficulties facing planet earth. We simply face these issues from a much stronger and healthier position if we ourselves are in a positive state of being. Being bitter or depressed and sleep deprived will accomplish nothing, and will in fact, make matters worse. Whether you're living or working with individuals with special needs, you've got to be on your #1 game. This means being your healthiest in mind, body and spirit.

Getting Adults To Laugh

While this might be something we take for granted, it's often not so easy to pre-plan laughter activities for adults. Going from the state of being a child to one of adulthood, is not merely that of reaching a certain age or fulfilling specific requirements, and it doesn't happen automatically when one turns 13 or 18 or 21, or even 120. I've met many individuals who are "older" within society's framework, such as in their 70's or 80's, but whose attitude and outlook toward life, and just as importantly, toward themselves, has them thinking, acting, and even feeling like they're in the 20's and 30's.

Once, while golfing at a local public course, an older gentleman asked me if he could join in. Turned out he was a young 92 years old, and he did his best to hit the links several times a week. He also, to my amazement, sent every shot about 125 yards straight as an arrow down the fairway. He saw me get frustrated after a lousy shot and remarked, "Hey, don't sweat it! Why get all hot and bothered? Never take your game or yourself too seriously. Besides, you're outdoors. The sun is shining. You're moving your body. It's another beautiful day in Paradise!" I was stunned at his healthy, positive, upbeat attitude, (which I was hoping would somehow rub off on me — at least a bit). After all, it wasn't like I was playing in the PGA Tour, taking a shot worth a million bucks. I always try to put his advice into practice, especially when it comes to my golf game, but I think he's right on target when it comes to life in general.

Unfortunately, I've encountered many individuals that society would refer to as "young," who walk around depressed, rarely smiling, cynical, and seemingly without meaning or purpose. They have no zest for life, and see their lives as empty. This is clearly not the purpose of getting older — to go from the state of innocence and laughter to one of withdrawal, depression, and sarcasm. But I think that many of us as we age, simply don't take the time to enjoy life, to keep smiling, and yes, to laugh. It seems to me that the ability to laugh might be the one critical phenomenon that distinguishes the human race. I can't think of any other creature on the planet that can engage in knee-slapping, roll-on-the-floor laughter, whether the object of laughter is ourselves or something else.

One animal species is given the name of Laughing Hyena, because of its' strange vocalizations. But these sounds are a far cry from laughter. If you start hearing those critters "laughing" while you're walking in the woods, it's high time to find a safe spot, because it is indeed, no laughing matter, (you'll pardon the expression). A pack of hyenas can be a vicious bunch, fully capable of chasing a lion from a fresh kill.

Kabbalah writings often refer to the human species as "medaber," which means, "the speaker," in Hebrew. In other words, it is our ability with language that has elevated our species. But I would add that "medaber" — the speaker — also includes our ability to engage in pure, (notice the following word), unadulterated, (not tainted by the concept of adult), laughing! Strange, how even in our language, the word unadulterated has come to mean, "not perverted by cynicism, sarcasm and negativity." Thus, even in our lexicon, being an "adult" somehow means not laughing as much. Tis a sad state of affairs and something that as teachers and parents we should try our best to amend. For a bit of inspiration to awaken some brain cells that have overslept way too long, check out the Logical Song by the group Supertramp. I once worked together with a school psychologist who wore a pin that said it all: It's Never Too Late To Have A Happy Childhood!

I remember those crazy late 60's when lots of us "baby boomers" were suddenly pushed out of the womb of high school and parental protection to living on our own. It was a weird mixture of excitement and dread, as the world around us seemed to descend into war, hatred, and lunacy. The time of innocence seemed to be lost forever. New leaders arose from the underground calling for us to "drop out, turn on, and tune in." Dylan sang that, "the times are a-changin," as we struggled to understand just what these dramatic developments entailed. It was a era that insisted, "out with the old and in with the new." These philosophies translated as a sloshy mixture of fresh optimistic ideas mixed with a frightening look at the crazy world around us. We ditched the ties, put on bellbottom jeans and grew long hair. Forget about trying to make a living. Many of us simply wanted to know how to live and what we were living for.

There were folks back then that called for, as the Stone's said, "violent revolution." However, I rarely saw those folks smile or laugh, and I felt that they would just replace one form of negativity with another. The Stones could make great rock 'n roll, no doubt. But the Beatles message spoke louder and clearer to me, back then: "If you want money for people with minds that hate. All I can tell you is brother, you'll have to wait." The Fab Four had a great capacity for humor. They joked with the press and their fans, and seemed to enjoy life. Besides their versatile music, I think their sense of fun and spontaneity was part of their big attraction for many fans. The medicine for a dark, negative world wasn't more of the same, but rather a fresh outlook, one that meant putting tomfoolery back on the planet, and smiles onto people's faces.

Like the saying goes, "laughter is indeed the best medicine." The movie, "Patch Adams" was about the real life hero, Dr. Hunter "Patch" Adams, who's both a medical doctor and a humor therapist. You'd be wiser and happier if you checked out his website at www.patchadams.org for some ideas, and some laughs. He writes on his website that "the most revolutionary act one can commit in our world, is to be happy." Stop for just 15 seconds and think about that bomb of a line. Radio show and TV host Dennis Prager writes in his ever-timely book, "Happiness Is A Serious Problem," (Regan Books, 1995), that this notion of being happy is actually a moral obligation, since how we come across has a direct effect on others. In chapter one of his book he states "we owe it to our husband or wife, our fellow workers, our children, our friends, indeed to everyone who comes into our lives, to be as happy as we can be." I would add the words, "our students" to this quote, but I'm sure it's well implied. Check out his website at www.dennisprager.com which is loaded with all sorts of helpful tips and strategies on essentially leading a more fulfilling, and happier life. Another site to visit to get some inspiration for healthy laughing is Michael Coleman's www.LaughingMatters.org. He runs all sorts of wonderful workshops about how to incorporate laughter as the medicine we truly need in today's world.

In order to counter the fear-factor mentality, it's not enough to create a more productive world that functions like a high-precision, well-oiled machine. We've got to make the world a happier place. This starts with the microcosm, which in turn, affects the macrocosm. Use humor techniques to reach your child, students, or colleagues. I suggest you first start humming George Harrison's wonderful tune, Here Comes The Sun: "Little darling, the smiles returning to the faces... little darling, seems like years since it's been here."

The Ha-Ha Technique!

In all likelihood, us responsible, hard-working worry-bodies known as adults, will have a tougher time stirring up laughs. Here's one technique that I first encountered at a camp I worked for in the late 60's. It's called the Ha-Ha Maneuver and it's actually quite simple to do. Each person participating in the Ha-Ha must lay down on his or her back. Let's say we have eight people in this group that are in desperate need of some joyful laughter. Person number two lays down perpendicular to the first participant, resting his head on #1's belly. Person #3 puts his or her head on #2's belly, and so on, and so forth, until all the participants look like some large human domino set, spread out on the floor. Here's how Ha-Ha works. Person #1 says out loud one, "Ha!" When person #1 is done, person #2 says, "Ha! Ha!" Person #3 then says out loud three ha-has: "Ha! Ha! Ha!" If you make it past person #8, then the first person has to say out loud, nine flippin' Ha-Has! Usually, the group won't even make it to number's five or six because everyone starts laughing. What adds to the fun of it all is that as somebody laughs, his or her belly shakes a bit and thus, the head on top of this belly bobbles to the laugh. It's all kinds of crazy fun, and pretty much guaranteed to elicit some laughter. The only drawback is that you may have a hard time stopping the laughter, and coming back to the real, "unreal" world.

Another interesting phenomenon that many people have engaged in is called Humor Yoga. It combines various yoga-type exercises with laughing and "lightness" strategies. Several people and organizations sponsor these classes, so check online and see if there are any near your location. If not, you can probably take some online sessions, or simply watch various clips on YouTube for ideas. The point here is to be proactive about increasing in your sense of joy and happiness. Then you'll definitely want to share the good vibes with others.

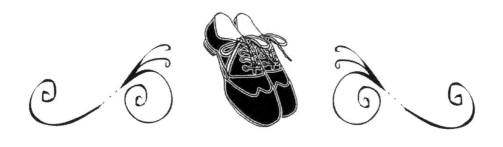

We Like To Move It, Move It

One of my first teaching assignments was with tough, inner-city adolescents. It was a self-contained class of young men with emotional, psychological, and learning difficulties. They often brought weapons to school as a kind of "show & tell" thing — not to intimidate me — but to share something that represented power and prestige on the streets. They were a rough bunch, and I knew things would only get worse after they took that 45 minutes bus ride to school each morning. On the bus, they would indulge in "breakfast" goodies, which usually consisted of ten pieces of licorice, two doughnuts, one can of soda, (or, as we call it in Buffalo, soda pop), and maybe even a Twinkie, or three. Clearly, after imbibing all these treats, they were no longer in the mood for sitting still at their desks and doing multiplication problems. I decided that each and every morning we'd go behind the school and run. Of course, I couldn't just sit on the sidelines and watch them. They'd need a role model, and so, run I did. We'd often run for 20 straight minutes. Only then would I even think about making our way back to the confines of the four-walled classroom. If the weather wasn't cooperating, and in Buffalo that's a highly likely event, we'd go to the gym or even exercise in our room. But the rule was that there was no formal learning until we moved the bodies.

Whether it's indoors, due to weather, or in the great outdoors, get 'em moving! Stretching and morning warm-up exercises get the blood flowing and help everyone get more in tune, (and in tone). It's a great way to enhance all sorts of skills, such as following directions, active listening, directionality, opposites, etc. See if you can identify all the skills involved in this "simple" dialogue I have with classes each morning.

"Okay class," I begin, after they're seated and have picked up the drumsticks by their seats. "Good morning. Great to see you all. Let's everyone put our drum sticks down and stand up."

Even if kids aren't exactly aware of some of these terms, they see others doing it and follow along. They're picking up on concepts like down, ("drum sticks down"), and stand, (as opposed to sit), and up, (as opposed to down).

"Let's all stand straight. Now reach up and touch the sky! C'mon, reach high…so high. Awesome. We can almost touch the ceiling. Let's stretch to one side. Good. Now the other side. That's it. Great. Now let your arms hang down low. So low. All the way to your toes."

They're picking up on important concepts like straight, reach, up, one side, other side, high & low, as well as body parts, such as arms and toes. And let's not forget the critical skill of following directions in sequence. Besides being medicine for the body, these short stretching and exercise experiences reinforce a whole variety of important skills for kids. They also help build a sense of group cohesiveness. We all need to move. This is particularly true for individuals with special needs. All too often, our classes and school systems try to force these kids to sit still for unhealthy periods of time. Movement is a tremendous technique that can be utilized in beneficial therapeutic situations.

Movement Therapy

In supporting literature, it is most often referred to as Dance/Movement Therapy, (DMT). Many people are intimidated by the notion of dance. They'll respond with something like; "oh, that's not for me… I'm not a good dancer." I remind them that it's really just moving, and that it can be done in all sorts of ways, from sitting in a wheelchair, to elaborate choreographed movements accompanied by a musical composition. DMT views the person as a whole entity, with a powerful connection between the mind, heart and body. Thus, in our effort to improve the mind and one's outlook, one must reach the heart and body.

There are all sorts of books and materials on dance & movement therapy. There's also a DMT Association, and their motto says it all: "Healing through Movement."

Life is movement. Inside our bodies things are moving, pulsating, pumping, opening, closing, and contracting. Cells are in motion, chemicals are being secreted and put to work, membranes are giving and receiving, and neurons are firing away at a rate that would make the most modern MacBook look like a tortoise on barbiturates. Life, in all its glory, while busy doing its thing inside us — is movement — to the max. Movement is both good, and necessary. When little Johnny is moving his legs and feet under the desk, he's simply trying to keep the blood flowing, and his brain on a more alert status. All too often, the teacher's common response is to stop Johnny in his tracks. "Hey! Stop with the feet, will ya? You need to sit still." But Johnny is not doing this to annoy the teacher or to be the class clown. He's simply not ready to sit completely still like a robot. This teacher would do everyone a big favor by engaging Johnny in some gross-motor activities. Check out the American Dance/Movement Therapy Association, (www.adta.org) for more information, including books, DVD's, upcoming conferences, and more. ADTA also helps interested individuals get certified as dance/movement therapists.

Dance and movement is a major part of my Quest music program and the expressive-arts therapy class I teach at Nova University. I utilize many different activities with my graduate students, many of whom are professional dancers and have their own studios. Clearly, I'm no match to them when it comes to dancing. They are pros and I feel like a total klutz trying to mimic their dazzling maneuvers. So what can I, a special education teacher who utilizes the expressive arts with my students and clients, possibly offer these dancing and movement pros? Ah, good question indeed. I simply show them the ways that the expressive arts can and should be incorporated into any educational or therapeutic program. The expressive arts works wonders for anyone, from young students to the elderly, from an individual facing profound challenges, to the person classified as "gifted."

While the primary focus in my own personal work concerns experiential music and drama, movement is where it all begins. Movement stirs us in the most profound manner. It touches our core as human beings. This is probably due to several factors. First, as mentioned, our entire beings are in a state of constant movement — at least on the inside, beyond the exterior, wondrous membrane known as the skin. But even our skin, which seems to only move when we will it to, is alive and acting out all sorts of incredible, movement-oriented phenomenon. It not only gives shape, structure, and support to the entire body, it is busy like crazy with a variety of important functions. Here are but a few of the things our skin does:

*Helps maintain proper healthy-body temperature by constantly sending signals to the brain's hypothalamus, which then sends messages back to the blood vessels and sweat glands in the skin. [If it's deemed too hot, the skin starts the sweating process. If it's too cold, the blood vessels in the skin constrict and the tiny hairs stand up.]

*Gives us a remarkable waterproof coat against the elements.

*Keeps out unwanted visitors such as tiny, funky microorganisms that would create havoc inside us.

Thus, even our skin, which seems to just "sit there" without stirring, is actually alive, kicking, and full of animation, albeit on a scale that we ignore, simply because we can't see or perceive this constant activity. Life is sound, energy, change, and motion, and whether we are aware of it or not, a remarkable, constant process is occurring all around us...in the wide world of nature, within ourselves, and even on the exterior surfaces of our bodies! To demand a cessation of mobility, to require our kids to become inert, is in my opinion, the very opposite of life. We all know what state the body is in when it's totally quiet and motionless, inside and out. That phenomenon indicates we belong six feet under. Quite frankly, I'm in no rush to get there. Why impose this harsh, constricting, lifeless state on our kids?

I'm not suggesting that we allow our kids to constantly bounce off the walls, but we can allow them some exertion in our classrooms. Let them learn, then get up and stretch when they feel the need to. Let them tap their fingers, or bounce their legs up and down, even while they're sitting at their desks or by a table, as long as it's not disturbing others. A bit of a confession here, folks. Back in the late 60's, when yoga and meditation became quite popular on college campuses, I gave it a real try. Yoga I enjoyed because it was stretching, gentle bending, twisting, and deep breathing; it wasn't just about sitting in some awkward, weird position, legs folded, hands on top of my head, elbows uncomfortably pointed out, trying to be silent. No, the latter was meditation. Our meditation instructor told us to "be utterly quiet and find the stillness within." All I could feel was my back aching, my legs getting cramped, my stomach gurgling, and my brain demanding some action, some release from it all.

Meditation, as least in that form, was definitely not for me. I had to be still enough in my college classrooms back then, why should I have to pay to be still in some extra-curricular activity? And if I had to be "still," I much preferred to go into the woods and lay on a sleeping bag, or even a nice, soft pile of leaves. There I could put my head back, look up at the clouds or stars and listen to the sounds of nature, which was full of life, sounds, smells, and by the way, movement.

It's interesting that in many religions prayer is regarded as a form of meditation. In the Jewish faith prayer is meant to be something spoken from the heart. But the format for this prayer, or "davening," as it's called, is actually accompanied by body movement. The person usually holds a prayer book in hand, or sometimes just closes his or her eyes, and quietly says some words from the heart while the body is in movement. Rocking back and forth has a distinct role in the act of praying. It's as if encouraging this act enables the body and brain to function better together, freeing up the mind and soul, as it were, to flow without having to worry about keeping the body "still." In other words, it's this repetitive, almost trance-inducing movement — not cessation of movement — that actually assists the meditation process! In any case, I kept up with yoga and dropped the meditation class in favor of some tennis and guitar lessons.

My students seem to go from one extreme to the other. During the day, I work with individuals with profound special needs. Evenings find me at Nova University, working with bright, focused, success-oriented graduate students. Nonetheless, the techniques discussed in this book work magic for both groups! Expressive arts techniques, movement strategies, and body/mind/spirit meditations, (and prayer), are all based on the foundation of reaching the individual at his or her own level. They utilize a student and person-centered approach, one that touches the individual and helps them move to an active, pro-active, and healthier position.

As adults, most of us don't move around enough. Many of us go from our pencil-pushing jobs where we sit working at computers, to sitting in cars for the commute home. Once there, we lounge around the house watching TV, sit at the dinner table, and sit even during our nightly movie and more TV time. It's this constant sitting mode that encourages body fat and causes the waistline to grow. I utilize a wide variety of techniques with my students to encourage movement. I've found that this progression works nicely, and pretty soon even the most reluctant and self-conscious is up, grooving to the music. This progression begins with individual movements, progresses to paired interactive movements, and is culminated in group movements. Each phase has its own benefits. I call this dynamic progression, "The Magical Moving Movement Maneuvers." When indoors, I always dim the lights in the room. It helps everyone get more comfortable, and makes them less self-conscious about engaging in body movement in front of others.

The Magical Mystical Moving Movement Maneuvers

1. Individual stretching and warm-up.

For this warm-up activity I favor the classics, and I'm not talking about great 60's rock. That, I save for later. We're talking the real classics, such as "Vivaldi's Four Seasons" or the awesomely soothing "Pachelbel's Canon in D Major," (what many simply refer to as the "wedding song.") Pretty much any Mozart will do the trick here. We stretch and groove for a good five to ten minutes. You can have different people lead this activity, or lead it yourself. People can do their own thing to the music or try to mirror the leader's movements. At this point, each person is moving as an individual, and there is no direct contact with a partner or the group.

2. Individuals lead the group.

Once warmed up, we're ready for something a bit faster. But here too, you can have students pick their own special songs to move to. Students can take turns leading this next activity or continue with follow the leader, if they so prefer. Their selections are interesting, and always convey a sense of individuality. They pick a whole variety of genres, such as romantic ballads, heavy metal, jazz, big band, straight up rock, reggae, and the still ever popular, MJ — Michael Jackson.

3. Partner/Mirroring.

Now they're ready to work and interact with a colleague. For this next activity in the progression, students work with a partner. Here too, music helps set the tone, so be creative and try out different musical forms. Each team of two can determine whether they want to take turns leading while the other follows, or simply freestyle it together. Usually, the team will begin to gel as the song progresses. I've found that in all movement-oriented activities, it can be very helpful to dim the lights. This helps participants feel less self-conscious as they move to the musical selection. It also helps create a theatre-like atmosphere. For many of the sessions, I completely cut the lights and turn on soft lighting, such as one that simulates a wave-like action with slow color changes. Lighting effects can be purchased from most music stores in their DJ section, and they help set the tone for some really creative and therapeutic sessions.

My Expressive Arts Therapies Course in action at NOVA University.Students take turns directing the action in "Follow the Leader."

Challenging group movement activity..."Keep-in-Touch" requires the group to move as a unit - always staying in physical contact. Individuals take turns leading this dynamic, flowing group to a musical selection of his or her choice.

4. Keep In Touch.

Now they're ready for a group maneuver. One interesting activity is to orchestrate the next dance/movement maneuver to occur while all the participants keep in physical

52

contact with one another. It can be as simple as holding hands and placing fingertips together, or performing the "wave" while holding hands, etc. My graduate students have executed some incredibly creative maneuvers with twists, turns, spins, bends, etc., while maintaining physical contact. This one gets very interesting when the "leaders" choose their own musical selection, but sometimes participants decide to move and groove without any music playing whatsoever!

5. Open group maneuvers.

Open up the room and tell the participants that they can move about anywhere in the room they want. One of my students put on a great modern dance piece from West Side Story and had the group following along, snapping their fingers to the beat, weaving in and out of the rows of desks and even crawling underneath tables.

6. Cool it.

After 30 minutes-plus of these fun and wonderful activities, we're ready for a pillow and blanket. So, make sure to end with some quiet, relaxing, stretching-activities as you enter this important cool-down phase. Allow for open discussion, at this point. There are a variety of questions and issues that can be discussed.

- *How did you feel during that last piece?*
- *Did you like that music selection?*
- *Did anything surprise you or get you thinking about something or someone in particular?*
- *Did you like the lighting?*
- *Any suggestions or other thoughts?*

Movement and dance-oriented activities work wonders. Make sure they're part of your overall educational and therapeutic program. The expressive arts therapies work their magic because they touch the child first, as an individual, then help them feel more connected within, and finally, help them feel more connected with others. It's quite difficult to connect in meaningful ways with others if the individual feels disconnected from the inside. The expressive arts translate into a student-centered approach.

Student-centered Process

The interesting thing about Individualized Education Plans, (IEP's — the "holy grail" of special ed.), is that many of my Quest students were not supposed to be able to engage in the process of "anticipating outcomes." They supposedly lacked this cognitive skill, because they were on too low of a functioning level. My shenanigans and their reactions have proved this notion was not always correct. They clearly responded to humor and noises, and when I begin the "sneeze process," they start to perk up, anticipating the grand climax. We need to make the expressive arts a major component in their overall therapy, or remedial plan. The expressive arts work because they are student-centered. They give the individual child a meaningful way to become more engaged. Besides that, they are just downright fun. If we look back to our own education, it's usually the fun, hands-on lessons we remember the most. When the lessons are fun and infused with life, magic clicks inside us. We open up and become receptive to new concepts, ideas, and any physical objects we're interacting with. For individuals with any type of special needs, learning has to become student-centered or it misses the mark. Most of what we refer to as "traditional" education is the opposite. It's something that I think could be called Teacher-Centered. The teacher speaks a lot, the students engage in note taking and memorizing. In this archaic system of learning, movement is allowed — but only by the teacher. He or she gets to move around the classroom while the entire class must sit as still as stuffed animals on a shelf. There's very little room for critical-thinking skill development, because the focus is on listening and memorizing. For many students, this kind of approach becomes a lesson in patience, and is motivated only by watching the clock tick by, ever-so-depressingly-slow.

This lack of movement allowed for the students often translates into a disaster waiting to happen. Forcing kids to sit still is unproductive and unhealthy. Let's be reasonable here, folks, Remember what it's like to fly for us big responsible grownups full of smarts and self-control! After just a few minutes buckled into our seats we begin to fidget, shake our feet, tap our fingers, and try without too much success to stretch our legs under the seat in front of us, which is unfortunately packed to the gills with our backpack and jacket. We begin wishing we could stretch out and fly like birds, or at least hang ten on a magic carpet. For our kids in our typical classrooms, they are basically sitting in airline seats all day long. And we wonder why some — the more "normal" ones I think, begin to act out. Learning without movement is ridiculous at best and oppressive at worst. Kids need to move. As professional educators and as educated parents, we need to provide them with the opportunities to channel this energy in healthy and productive ways.

A Fall 2011 NEA (National Education Association) Today magazine hits it right on the head — or should I say on the feet? — in a short but enlightening article called "Kids Who Can't Sit Still." This article by Rebecca Bright, focused on educators who have devised all sorts of clever ways that allow kids to move, even while sitting or standing by their desks for learning. One teacher worked with an ergonomic furniture company and together they developed desks that can be adjusted to various heights. This gives the students options to sit and even stand while still "at" their desks. These same desks have specially built in swinging footrests, which allow little Johnny or Julia to move them cute little (or big) "feeties" while focusing on the academic stuff. Other teachers saved some buckos and simply built their own movable footrests from old tires and tubes. Another teacher came up with a "read & ride" project that has students engaging in stationary bike riding while participating in reading activities. All these hip educators have seen positive results and know the importance of being proactive when it comes to movement and learning.

The very act of learning is a tricky concept. It's often referred to as the MTM — The Most Teachable Moment. The idea here is that all the cards have to be lined up, for real learning and growth to occur. The teacher has to be able to present it in an appropriate way. The student has to be ready to receive it. The materials and methods have to be set. Everything must click at once, at this magical moment. Student-centered learning enhances every factor in this formula. But most importantly perhaps, is the fact the expressive arts touches some "sweet spot" inside the child that, in turn, causes a reaction and response from the self-outwards. Student-centered learning is experiential learning, in every sense of the term. The events and lessons we experience are the ones that affect us the most, and in fact, stay with us forever. They are also the events that we can build upon to foster healing, recovery, learning, growth and happiness.

Lessons from the bottom of the Niagara River:

Learning Comes Alive Through Real-Life Experiences

This is often referred to as experiential learning.

There's wisdom in that often used expression: "Keep it real."

It's often the unexpected events that help us open our eyes and see the possibilities. This particular event happened, of all places, under the sea. Well, to be more specific, under the river. The Niagara River, to be exact. This episode made me break a rather solemn promise I made upon my own high school graduation. As my friends and I chucked our large, incredibly boring history books into the garbage can, I took the following oath out loud:

"I promise never ever again to open up a stupid, boring, fact-filled, dead-end history book. Goodbye, and good riddance! You might bore someone else to death, but you will not do that to me ever again! And thank you, God, for getting me out alive from the prison called high school. Yahoooooooooo!"

About 12 years later, as a certified scuba diver, circumstances provided me an opportunity to try my luck at a rather famous spot near my hometown of Buffalo, NY. The area is known as the Coin Pile, because old coins, and lots and lots of old and new junk get carried along the bottom by that strong Niagara River current. Eventually, down-river, it spills over the awesomely powerful Niagara Falls. Well, let me clarify that. It would spill over the falls, except that Buffalo built a break-wall to protect the city's harbor. This area around the break-wall is the famous Coin Pile.

At first, all I could hear was this incredibly weird giggle. It presented as a kind of gurgle and was accompanied by lots of bubbles. Hearing my partner's laughter automatically caused me to break up laughing, which was like feeding fuel to a fire. He started laughing even harder, which of course, increased my own. But it was a bit on the dangerous side, as one wasn't really supposed to crack up uncontrollably while wearing full scuba gear. The potential to aspirate lots of cold, dirty water grew tenfold when laughing with a regulator in one's mouth.

The water depth wasn't too deep, maybe we around 15 — 18 feet beneath the surface. It all seemed on the silly side. Here we were, two supposedly-grown men, each married with kids, sitting on the bottom of the river, digging away with our little shovels. I felt like a little kid in a sandbox, except that the visibility was horrible and it was really cold — even in our thick wetsuits. So, the laughter was good medicine, I suppose, to get our bodies moving and warmed up a bit. I couldn't see my dive buddy very clearly, even though he was a mere 10 feet away from me. We had a rope connecting the two of us, in case we lost visual contact. A slight tug of the rope meant that my partner wanted my attention. I would then look up through my dive mask, and hopefully see what he was pointing to.

I suddenly felt this urgent, huge tug on the rope and was praying it wasn't some crazy great white shark that had somehow gotten lost from the Atlantic Ocean, and ended up cruising the dark waters of the Niagara. Hey, your mind plays some crazy tricks when you are sitting on the bottom of a huge, dark, cold lake, squinting to see your fingers in front of your face.

My dive buddy pointed to a large, somewhat round-shaped object, encrusted with lots of crazy-looking underwater critters. It seemed a bit smaller than a bowling ball and was, in fact, very heavy when I tried lifting it.

We eventually got both it and ourselves to the surface, where the dive-master on board the boat remarked reverently, "Wow, I think you guys just found a real cannon ball!" I was very surprised by his next action. He quickly got a bucket, filled it with river water and gently put the heavy, ball-like object inside. If it had been me, I would have been trying to dry the thing and scrape off all the weird growth that covered it. But the dive-master remarked that it was good fortune indeed, that this cannon ball had found a home in cold, fresh water and not warm, salt water. "Once out of the water," he added, "it can quickly oxidize and start rusting and breaking down." Live & learn, eh? Or is that dive & learn?

A trip to the Buffalo Historical Society the following day confirmed his suspicions. My buddy had indeed found an authentic cannon ball sitting at the bottom of the Niagara River!

Right then and there, I knew I simply had to break my high school graduation promise. I opened up every book I could find on the history of the Niagara River. I wanted to know everything I could about this little cannon ball. Who owned it? Did someone actually shoot this thing? Who was he shooting at? Why? Who lived here? Who fought here? All at once I had a million questions and few answers. After all, I hadn't really paid too much attention during those long, tedious, fact-remembering, (and forgetting), high school history lectures. In fact, that was the crux of the problem. I got through the history honors exam just fine, but basically forgot all those thousands of facts a mere week or two later. (Perhaps it was only days). It was quite remarkable how little I actually knew about the history of my own city and area. Despite taking "honors" history, the classes were utterly boring, 60-minute sessions of brutal note-taking that seemed like an eternity.

Rather than becoming just a lesson in memorizing, history can and should be taught in a student-centered way. So can just about any subject, for that matter. This is the only method that makes learning come alive, which is particularly important for individuals with special needs. Words on a page, no matter how insightful or amazing, are still two-dimensional. They might inspire you for a while, but unless something is done to make the process come to life, it's a lesson that will soon be forgotten. Student-centered learning is experiential. It makes the material, the concepts, and ideas take on form, and helps them come to life. Student-centered learning is hands-on, and comes mainly from the students rather than the teacher, who functions more as a guide to the process. Learning becomes real, within and outside of the child, as he or she becomes fully engaged in this amazing act of discovery and expression.

Am I suggesting that you take your kids and students scuba diving? In essence, yes. If you have the time and funding to do so, what could be better for kicking off a unit of history! But on the practical side, we simply need to make the learning come alive. Now, as you might imagine, I can't get enough of history. I find it completely fascinating. We might not be able to change history, but if we teach this awesome subject in a motivational manner, history can change us.

Experiential learning is student-centered learning

& involves direct, hands-on activities.

Make each activity as experiential as possible.

More on this a bit later, but first we need to discuss Sponge Theory. Sometimes, to really understand what something is, you've got to know what it isn't. Much of education today is based on what I call the Sponge Theory. This archaic notion views the child as a mere receptacle. The teacher is the almighty giver of knowledge and the student/child functions as the sponge, absorbing as much as is physically and mentally possible. This process usually involves the teacher talking, writing on the board a lot, and demonstrating little, if anything, while junior takes lots and lots of notes. (Chances are fairly decent that all these volumes of notes will meet the "circular file" — aka, the garbage can, soon after the class ends). In this learning method, the child is essentially a passive blob, the sponge, while the teacher/parent tries to cram as much into this sponge as possible. How does one tell if "learning" has taken place in this system? For that answer we examine the next phase of this system — the "spit back" phase. Like squeezing a sponge to see what's inside, the child has to "spit back" the information on some test. Depending upon how much he or she was able to memorize and spit back, determines the percentage of learning, and the child's grade.

There are several faulty key elements in this sponge style of learning. First, it is very boring and does little to inspire anyone — child, student, or adult for that matter. Second, the very nature of this method alienates the student from the subject. And third, it does little to insure true learning has taken place. Without an intrinsic connection to the lesson or subject, the child feels removed and distant. Thus, we can graduate hundreds of thousands of students in history, for example, but precious few want to major in the field as a potential profession. For those who do pursue history as a career or hobby, it means they've either had a great teacher along the way, or the subject was taught in a more experiential fashion. (Or they too, discovered a cannon ball while scuba diving).

The Lubavitcher Rebbe once expressed that there are several essential components of education. In order of importance they are, "the warm atmosphere — the enthusiasm for learning. The connection between teacher and student. And the information and skills. Unfortunately, many schools today have turned into information factories, leaving out the very foundation — the love and motivation for learning." In this factory system, we end graduating kids who have accumulated vast amounts of knowledge and facts, but they no longer have the interest to pursue these subjects! We need to ask ourselves a hard question: After all the blood, sweat and tears, all the facts presented, all the books and articles read, all the tests passed, what have we ultimately accomplished if we have, in effect, turned off this student to the very subject we crammed down his or her little throat? For learning to be meaningful for our children and students, it must have some life, some vitality to it. Student-centered learning is pretty much the opposite of the sponge/factory theory. It places the child at the very center of this magical process. It makes the learning exciting, creative and involves expression from the individual. It's active rather than passive.

Outside the Box: AKA-The Classroom!

For some reason, unbeknownst to me at the time, my parents signed me up in a local Scout troop. I wanted none of that nonsense, but when I found out that a couple of my close friends were also signed up, I decided to give it a try. I'm pretty sure it was a way for our folks to keep us rambunctious boys out of trouble for a bit, but it was one of the best decisions of my life. I looked forward to our meetings all week long. My list of important things learned via scouting would resemble that famous work by Robert Fulghum: "All I Really Need To Know I Learned in Kindergarten." (My list would substitute the word Scouting for the word Kindergarten). Scouting was as student/child-centered as it gets, and it was downright fun and challenging at the same time. Through this magic formula, I learned a whole lot.

All I Really Need To Know I Learned From Scouting

- *How to share.*
- *To try my best, and that this mattered more than winning.*
- *Not to fret if I came in second or lost, but to congratulate the winner and move on.*
- *That I was part of a team, and that we needed each other to succeed.*
- *To delay gratification, and that the merit badges come only after lots of work!*
- *That life is full of wonder, and is out there waiting for us to explore and appreciate.*
- *The importance of exercise.*
- *How to use a compass, and not get lost in the woods.*
- *How to light a matchless fire using only flint & steel.*
- *To be concerned and involved with the community.*
- *Not to blame others for my own faults.*
- *To take time to pause and be grateful for all of our blessings.*
- *To try my best to follow Scout laws, and be trustworthy, loyal, helpful, friendly, courteous, kind, obedient, cheerful, thrifty, brave, clean, and reverent.*
- *To be more self-sufficient.*
- *That learning, real learning, was exciting, fun-filled, and worth the effort.*

My list could go on and on but, here's the clincher: Me, Mister Non-Reader, was suddenly reading and studying several hours each day about animals, plants, trees, first-aid, astronomy, survival skills, sports, and more. Trust me on this one — if I could do it, anyone could! The amazing part was that none of it ever felt forced, unlike when I was studying for a test at school. It was all an absolute joy to me. Why? I think because I was experiencing this learning in a direct, child-centered, experiential fashion. It was pretty much the opposite of what most of my "education" was like in school. There, it was all memorization, and an exercise in patience, while I watched the clock slowly tick by the minutes.

But this world of scouting was different. It was experiential, child-centered and it was, in a word, real. It wasn't just reading about first-aid for a test. We were doing first-aid drills. We were putting on fake bandages and splints, and learning how to give proper chest compressions for CPR. It wasn't just reading about how to survive in the wilderness, we went outdoors to locate, identify and eat edible wild plants. In other words, we were living all of this knowledge, experiencing it in a very practical, motivational, and down-to-earth way. Once this motivation kicked in, I simply could not get my hands on enough books. My folks even signed me up for a book-of-the-month club, and each month I eagerly awaited my new book. I would run upstairs to my room, clutching it like some great treasure. Then I would close the door and gaze at the cover. The next phase was looking through the entire book. First at the pictures inside, although sometimes there weren't very many at all. Then, I would lie back on my bed and dive right in.

Learning through experiencing reinforces that connection between the individual self and the outside world. By its very nature, experiential learning, since it connects to the individual, automatically enhances expression and meaningful learning.

While running a special education program for the Manhattan Day School (MDS), I had a student named Solly. He was essentially a non-reader. He was 13 years old, and was reading on a 1st grade level. Solly was the kid who would pretend to read a menu at a restaurant, and when it came to ordering from the waitress, would simply say, "Yeah, I'll take the same as him." Along with his parents, we tried every trick in the book, from color-coding, a motivational reward-system, biofeedback, cranial massages, acupuncture, and even colored glasses.

Nothing seemed to click until he took a first-aid course with me. Back in those days, the American Red Cross Community first aid course consisted of 10 separate books. No joke. The students had to learn all 10 books and take a test on each one. To my utter amazement, he was one of two students in my class who passed the course. The other student was a son of a doctor and nurse, so no great surprise there. But Solly? I couldn't fathom how he accomplished this great feat. Reading 10 books and passing each test, which of course, I gave orally. He knew the material cold.

"How did you do it?" I asked incredulously.

"Easy," he responded. "My sister read the books to me out loud at night, and I learned it!"

I knew he was one of the oldest kids in his family.

"Your younger sister?"

"Uh-huh. That's all I have, are younger ones."

So here was Solly, who didn't mind swallowing his pride to have a younger sibling read to him each night for a good three weeks in order to pass those 10 tests. He earned that Red Cross first aid card, along with a patch that he soon began wearing on one of his jackets.

The formula might read something like:

Student centered learning =

intrinsic motivation =

growth & development.

Motivation is a powerful gateway to real learning. Once this door is opened there's no telling what your children and students will do. But one thing is certain — you're in for some pleasant surprises.

There was one other component that made scouting such a hit. In three words: The great outdoors. Outdoors opens the mind as well as the lungs! It's true thinking outside the box. The box I'm referring to here is none other than the confining four walls of the classroom. (Or the living room or bedroom — and in all likelihood, the "holy sanctuary" known as the TV room, in your own homes). The camping trips were the highlight of our small troops' activities, and at 15 years old, I journeyed to Philmont Scout Ranch in New Mexico, for a 10-day hiking/camping trip, completely removed from civilization. Our small Buffalo troop brought along dehydrated food, since it was so much lighter to carry in backpacks. We ate wild, edible plants. We purified our drinking water. We encountered several black bears, a rattlesnake, and even a mountain lion. But we were safe, because we had learned how to be safe in these situations. Me and my other scouting buddies soon turned 16, and to this day, I regret becoming too cool for "babyish" things like scouting.

As an adult, however, I did return to scouting and my outdoor roots. I became a Scout Master, directing scout troops from Buffalo, to NYC, to Florida, where I run Troop 613, a unique scouting group that caters to youth who keep kosher. I know first-hand, what Scouting and the great outdoors does for kids. It worked wonders for me, and running a troop is my way of sharing this magic with others.

It's even more crucial in today's society, where kids simply don't play outdoors like they used to. Today's entertainment features our kids, from the very young, to the not-so-young, staring at computer screens, and PlayStations, and iPod touch screens, and X-boxes, and Wii' machines, and their Droid cellphones. It's no wonder that our society has a problem with overweight and depressed kids. Combine this lack of healthy outdoor exercise and movement with fast food and junk-food diets, and it's no wonder we're seeing a dramatic increase in all sorts of children's illnesses — which automatically translates into a surge of kids on meds.

In the eye-opening book, "The China Study," by Dr. Campbell, (First BenBella Books, 2006), the author makes a compelling case that a change in the typical American diet can lead to tremendous benefits, especially for our children. He writes, "we are leading our youth down a path of disease earlier and earlier in their lives." Citing many studies and research programs, Campbell feels that the main cause of this dilemma is poor nutrition, coupled with general ignorance, and misinformation about what constitutes a healthy diet. According to the National Center for Health Statistics, (US Dept. of Health & Human Services News Release, Oct. 2003), nearly a third of the population is considered overweight, or darn close to it. Campbell puts it on the line — or, is that waistline? — and writes that, "it all comes down to three things: breakfast, lunch & dinner."

Facing financial difficulties, many schools have cut back on the arts & physical education. After sitting for a very long day at school, kids come home to more of the same. Oh, they get plenty of exercise all right. Their eye/hand coordination improves tremendously as long as it involves subtle maneuvers like texting on a cell phone, playing on an x-box, Gameboy, or a 3-inch PlayStation screen. And then, of course, there's the 72-inch high-definition TV that each kid must have in his or her own room. So forget about imparting social skills, or quality "family time," (while families watch something together and hold a group discussion, afterwards). Instead, it's Little Johnny watching and doing his own thing behind closed doors in the privacy of his own room.

Richard Louv, in his awesome book, "Last Child in the Woods," (Algonquin Paperbacks, 2008), speaks about a new disorder that many of our children are confronted with. He calls it the NDD; that's Nature Deficit Disorder! He writes about how today's society actually teaches children to avoid direct contact, and real-life experiences with nature. "Reducing the NDD," Louv writes, "is critical because our mental, physical, and spiritual health depends on it. The health of the earth is at stake as well." We need to reconnect, and to accomplish this, we have to disconnect from other arenas.

Put Some Limits on Uncle Seymour

I should have been alarmed much sooner, but I just didn't see it coming, at all. Uncle Seymour moved into our home when I was a young child. At first, he was a lot of fun. He stayed with us when my parents went out for dinner. He babysat us when my folks went on long vacations. He was mighty cool, and opened our eyes to all sorts of things, and probably a whole lot we shouldn't have known about. But who could resist Uncle Seymour's charm and persuasion? Pretty soon, he simply took over, telling us what to wear, what to buy, even when to leave the room. Uncle Seymour had not only taken over our home, but more dangerously, had subverted our thoughts and feelings. Sometimes, we'd be in the kitchen eating a nice meal, and Seymour would be babbling away from the next room. No one, not even my mom or dad, dared tell Seymour "no," or "not now," or, "save it for later."

Seymour, you see, was the nickname we gave to the large wonder- box in the family den. The TV, in all its glory! We called it Seymour because we always wanted to "See More." In those days, while growing up in my small city of Buffalo, NY, families had one TV. There were three basic channels. Still, we played a lot outdoors — whether it was hide 'n seek, kick the can, touch football on the street, or just biking around the neighborhood.

Admittedly, it was easier back then not to get addicted to the "boob tube." They were huge, weighed a ton-and-a-half, and were not very sophisticated. It wasn't all that uncommon to see more static on the screen, than picture. In those more-innocent times, our surroundings were more conducive to staying fit and trim, since we were actually in an environment, (outside), that encouraged running, jumping, skipping, throwing, dodging, skating, bending, reaching, and lots and lots of movement. Back then, since it was a luxury to even own one of these giant televisions, we watched various shows together. Today, there's little "family time," where the entire crew gets together to watch a favorite show, other than perhaps a Sunday football game. Even then, kids often choose the company of friends during these occasions, or, as mentioned earlier, simply watch in isolation, on laptops or personal TV sets. It's no secret that the kids today are much more tech-savvy than their older, old-school, old-fashioned parents. While this might be a good thing, it is seldom balanced with physical activity and varied social interaction. There's an awesome quote from the comic writer, Demetri Martin in his uproarious, "This Is A Book," (Grand Central Publishing, 2011), that says it all, folks. Ponder this one while channel surfing: "As televisions become flatter — people become rounder."

My suggestion here is to get rid of as many TV's as possible in the home, and if you must own one, keep it in the family room. While you're at it, limit the amount of time children are allowed to use a computer, watch TV, and use their gaming systems. If you want your child to read a book then you, as a parent or significant adult, need to read as well. You need to model this valuable behavior. If you want your kids to go outside and play ball, then you very well may have to go out and play ball with them, which, of course, isn't a bad idea, anyhow. If you want your kids to stay healthy and on the trimmer side, then you may have to show them what exercise is all about. It doesn't have to be an expensive gym membership. It can be as wonderfully simple as bike riding, or skating together, or walking to the local store, rather than taking the car. The point is, to really think outside the box, one has to actually be outside the box. It's a bit of a contradiction to think outside the box while still being confined inside one. For many individuals with special needs, just the act of going outside is a liberating experience. Don't just think outside the box — get outside the box!

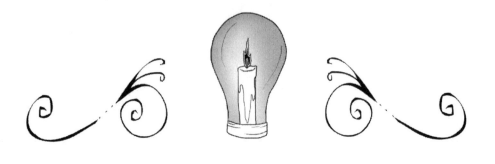

Kudos to Katrina & Wilma

We can be a stubborn and tough species to motivate beyond our comfort zone. Unfortunately, for many of us, (our kids included), this comfort zone translates as the not-so-great indoors. The home and school becomes one giant, confining box, allowing for little, (if any), physical movement. But there are times that acts of good ol' Divine Providence give us no choice but to step beyond the threshold, into the wondrous outdoors.

My family and I have lived through several rough hurricane seasons in South Florida. A few years back we experienced hurricanes that ran through the entire alphabet, from A to Z, and back to letter A again. In other words, there were more than 26 dangerous storms, that in one way or another, affected hundreds of thousands of people, time and time again. But it was hurricanes Katrina and Wilma that gave us the double-whammy, and by knocking out our electricity, made us see the light.

We had no electrical power for 17 long days. For those of you who read this as a mere number with little significance, I challenge you to go without these incredible comforts, comforts we simply take for granted, for a mere 72 hours. That's only three days. That means no lights, no fans, no working refrigerators, no electric ovens, no television or radio, unless it's battery operated. All cell phones that require an electrical charge, will all-too-soon stop functioning. For most folks, it will also mean no hot water, since pilot lights usually work on electricity. If, by some major miracle, you make it through those 72 hours, then realize that an two additional full weeks are required to match our record.

For us as the days extended, people began gobbling up those horrendously loud generators so they could at least plug in some essentials, such as a light or two, maybe a few fans, and definitely the fridge, so the food wouldn't spoil. City and government trucks drove through many of the worst affected areas, giving out blocks of ice, and even dry ice. After Katrina and Wilma hit town, my comfy, rather quiet residential neighborhood of North Miami Beach was drastically altered, and more closely resembled a war zone. Huge branches, often entire trees, were uprooted and scattered across once-busy intersections and streets. Traffic crept along in bizarre fashion, since there were no working traffic lights. Two branches fell from one of our large oak trees, just missing the house and the cars in the driveway. Still, they landed with such weight and power that they made large craters in the driveway. In fact, these branches were so huge that looking from the street, they totally blocked the view of our home.

In addition to the lack of basic comforts and necessities, there were lots of underlying fears and anxieties such as: "When would relief come? Would it come at all? What if another storm hits before we can clean up and get ready? How will we eat? What will we eat? When can we use warm water again for bathing and washing clothes? How will we drive our cars if there's no gas left at the stations?" Despite all this and more...in fact, in the very midst of all this agitation and discomfort, something absolutely extraordinary occurred:

At first I couldn't quite put my finger on it. And then, it hit me. Hurricanes Katrina and Wilma had brought me back to my childhood years, growing up in Buffalo. It brought all of us back to those sweeter, more-innocent times. For now, due to high temperatures, sticky humidity, and no functioning AC within miles, people were outside! There were kids of all sizes, shapes, and colors, playing, running, and throwing balls, with adults of all sizes, shapes, and colors. Folks were barbequing, and hosting all sorts of spontaneous parties for the express purpose of sharing meals. In a four block radius I counted 3 ongoing games of Hide-N-Go-Seek, and more than 8 games of Hop Scotch! Hula-hoops came out of the closet, and I even witnessed some yo-yo competitions near our canal! Yes, you read that correctly. Hula-hoops and yo-yos! The hurricanes had forced us out of our homes and into the great outdoors. More importantly, it forced us to reach beyond ourselves and help one another.

After 17 days of being blissfully transported back to my childhood, I have to admit I cheered, as did the entire community, when the electricity came back on. It meant that once again we could stock our fridges with all sorts of goodies. It meant that we could use our toaster ovens, and computers, and cell phones, and faxes, and Gameboys, and iPods, and Wii 98's; and that our fans, and even that blessing known as AC, would be back in our lives. It meant that all the zillions of gadgets that in some strange way define and control us, would be back in full glory. But I must confess, there was something absolutely wonderful and even liberating during those 17 days without all the electronic leashes surrounding us, occupying our thoughts and emotions, and demanding our unequivocal attention.

Katrina and Wilma gave many of us a glimpse of not only what was, but more importantly, of what could be. We can and need to break away from all the electronic gizmos that, while promising more fun, happiness, and liberation, really give us less and less quality time. It always boggles my mind when I go jogging or skim-boarding at the beach, and see some individual so tied to his laptop, cell phone, iPod, or iTouch that rather than hitting-the-surf, or closing his eyes and relaxing to the sound of nature, he responds to each in turn, as if he were the dog in Pavlov's experiment. Soon, the hours slip by while several manatees swim within view, a few giant rays display their wares, and his son, who is waiting to play Frisbee, returns to the hotel room to watch TV or play video games.

Those doozy tropical storms that walloped us, showed us that we can not only survive without these taken-for-granted comforts for a spell, but that we can really enjoy each other's company in the great outdoors.

Get outside & leave the electronic leashes behind.

Doesn't matter which activity you choose, whether a jog around the block, a game of hop scotch, throwing a ball together, or that all-time favorite, oldie-but-goody, Kick The Can. Leave your electronic life behind for a few precious minutes. If you feel that you need your cell phone for safety reasons, then at least put it on vibrate. I'm hoping we don't need another visit from Katrina or Wilma to show us the way. While you're enjoying the fresh air, you might try having a barbeque and inviting your neighbors. Pretty soon you'll be having block parties together. Remember, it takes a village to raise a child. Your kid will learn some valuable lessons from these awesome neighborhood interactions. In fact, the only way any child can learn positive social skills is by experiencing their community with other caring people. Playing outdoors is an awesome way to build these important aptitudes. A child in this environment learns to wait to be heard, and to be patient with others. They learn to talk nicely to people — and learn that no one wants to play with them if they don't play nice. They learn to be part of a team, and that it's fun to interact with others. They learn that it really doesn't matter who wins or loses — that the game itself is totally cool.

When my kids were young teenagers, I used to make it a habit to play some street ball with them on the Sabbath, which for us begins on Friday night at sundown, and ends Saturday evening when the stars come out. So sometimes, the Sabbath day, that all day Saturday thing, can get mighty long, especially if it doesn't get dark 'till 8 or 9 at night. After the special afternoon meal, complete with songs and discussions, we'd often go outside for some two-hand touch football or basketball. I put a hoop up by our driveway. These outdoor games got bigger as time went on, and often guys from other streets would come by, hoping to get into the game. The street was kind of narrow, so we never really had more than a five-on-five game. One time, another father complained that we shouldn't be playing ball on the Sabbath, and that it was better to follow his example. I knew that he was one to take long afternoon naps, particularly on the Sabbath. So I remarked that if I followed his example, I would have a great siesta and, like him, have no flippin' idea where my kids were, what they were doing, and whom they were hanging out with. At first he was speechless, but a few weeks later he came out to try his hand at quarterbacking.

More Movement

Add physical movement activities & the great outdoors to the realm of expressive arts. Kids need to get out and explore. The great outdoors is the number one multi-sensory environment, filled with sights, sounds, smells, and all sorts of tactile information. It's a MSE... that's Multi-Sensory Extravaganza!

Make free time outside a priority, (with supervision if necessary). Let them smell the fresh air, feel the breezes, hear birds chirping, and the sounds of other kids playing. Then you can add your own joyous sounds to this outdoor symphony. Once free from the confining walls of a room, they too will begin to express themselves in this open, expansive, outdoor environment. Some kids like rolling in the grass. For those with physical challenges, take them out of their wheelchairs and lay them on a blanket on the ground. This way, they too can feel and experience the outdoors, unencumbered by the restraints of wheelchairs and safety straps.

There are many worthwhile activities you can engage in that utilize the outdoors as a catalyst for your child or student's expressive arts. Here's a brief selection of some favorites that my own kids and students have enjoyed. These activities encompass several main areas of the expressive arts, including, visual stimulation, movement, music, drama, and writing.

1) Tree rubbings

Take any large sheet of paper, such as drawing paper, place it against the bark of a tree and rub the surface of the paper with crayons or colored chalk. You can have your child feel the bark from different trees, and compare them. Some may be smooth... others, rough to the touch. Some may be soft, and others hard. Tactile activities such as these are great for individuals with vision difficulties. Some folks use this same technique to do gravestone rubbings — especially at older cemeteries. Build on the concept by turning it into a reality-based social studies lesson. Who's buried here? Were they the first folks to settle in this area? What countries did they come from?

2) Body traces in the sand.

If on the ground, small stones can be placed along the body's outline. Kids and adults alike seem to like the experience of having their bodies traced. It gives a perspective of yourself that you seldom get to see.

3) If at the beach...

Ah, the advantages of living in Miami. Here, you've got one incredible outdoor MSE for the child with special needs. This is one that caters to the senses, with the sounds and smells of the ocean waves, and the feel of the water and breezes. Have your child or student build a sand structure or castle. Teach them to write their names, or any other words, by using sand. This way they can also feel the letters and words. The more senses they utilize to reinforce a concept the more quickly it will be learned.

4) About the great outdoors...

It is probably the best place to engage in some physical activity. You don't have the usual constraints of a roof and walls surrounding the person. There's a built-in sense of freedom and exhilaration. I personally would much rather run, rollerblade, swim, or play catch outdoors, than inside in a gym. Many kids seem to come to life outside. Take advantage of this and have them participate in some movement-therapy activities with you. This will, of course, depend on the individual child's strengths and weaknesses. For some, it might mean lifting one arm or leg at a time. You may have to help the individual, by slowly stretching the limb involved.

5) For kids with a bit or a lot of extra hyperactivity in their genes...

The outdoors is a great place to let them run it off. Being inside is often a tough number for persons with ADD or ADHD. It seems like they always have to work hard to fit in — like square pegs in a round hole. No matter how many meds adults prescribe, they still have a rough time sitting on their rear-ends all day, indoors. Who can blame them? The more you get these individuals outside the better for everyone — including yourself. Take turns playing follow the leader. Demonstrate new dance moves or martial arts maneuvers. Take them into the water and let them splash and play around. Needless to say, supervision is a must when in, or even around water. You'll have fun, but you can't take your eyes off of them for a moment.

6) Name The Sounds

This is a fun game for kids of all ages, including the young-at-heart. You simply lay back in the great outdoors, close your eyes, and remain silent for several minutes. In this exercise, you try to identify all the different sounds you hear. It can be anything from the wind rustling in the trees, to birds, or planes overhead, or car horns, etc. Parents & teachers can use a timer to indicate when silence time is over. But the important thing with this exercise, is to allow several minutes of non-talking so people can adjust to all the intonations that are really going on out there. Our brains frequently turn-off these noises so they don't become annoying or bothersome to us. You'll be amazed at how many sounds really are happening all around us.

7) Visual Arts

There's no end to what can be done outside using the visual arts as an expressive tool. Allow your kids the freedom to draw what they see or feel, using a variety of mediums, such as crayons, pastels, watercolors, etc. Clay is a wonderful medium for individuals to use to express themselves outdoors. Here too, it could be making a model of what they see and experience, or simply expressing their feelings in the clay creation. Students with minimal hand control can participate to the best of their abilities. Helpers can offer hand-over-hand assistance. Students with more profound physical challenges can use adaptive switches to paint and draw.

I subscribe to many outdoor-oriented magazines, because I find that they help me keep me motivated to engage in these activities. So, besides the more commonly found National Geographic, I'm also an avid reader of, (ain't this a surprise), "Outside Magazine". It contains good articles and amazing nature pics that will knock your socks off. Check out their site at: www.outsideonline.com. I also get a couple of golf and ski magazines, and even one on kayaking & canoeing. And while we're at it, let's not forget my very own subscription of "Mother Earth News". Hey, each to their own, right? Articles that deal with becoming more self-sufficient inspire me. It's jam-packed with all sorts of goodies from building your own log cabin, to doing your own home repairs, to getting healthier veggies from your very own organic garden. Visit their website at www.motherearthnews.com and you'll soon be digging away in your own backyard.

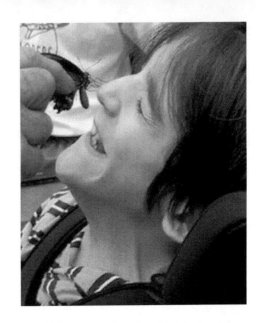

My Expressive Arts Therapies course in action at NOVA University. Students take turns directing the action in Follow The Leader. Mikey getting up close and personal with one of the stars of our new butterfly garden.

Gardening, by the way, is an absolutely incredible way to involve kids in healthy and productive activities. Do your students and your kids a big favor and visit this awesome site to learn how to start your own butterfly and vegetable garden: www.kidsgardening.org. Their mission statement says it all: "To promote home, school, and community gardening as a means to renew and sustain the essential connections between people, plants, and the environment." Gardening accomplishes many important things for our kids. First, it gets them outside more often, which translates into more movement and exercise. It's a tremendous motivator, because they get to see the plants and flowers grow before their very eyes. They also learn practical skills, regarding which plants attract certain butterflies, or how to properly care for their plants —including which types of fertilizer to give them, and the right amount of watering.

Gardening can have a calming effect on our kids, and it's a welcome change of pace from sitting in front of the boob tube or doing all the social media things on their cell phones. Kids confined to wheelchairs can also be given these opportunities. Teachers can use hand-over-hand to help them dig into the ground, till the soil, plant the seeds, water the flowers, touch the caterpillars, let the butterflies rest on their noses, etc. Gardening is great stuff, and should be part of any special education program. As a result of receiving several grants I helped write for my school, we now have an awesome butterfly garden. We turned a large empty, dusty field into a delight for the senses. It now boasts six royal Poinciana trees, one gumbo-limbo, and hundreds of passionflowers, butterfly bush plants, and other indigenous species. The trees were planted several years ago and they've grown from four feet tall to well over 25 feet with ever-expanding shade canopies. The field is often teeming with all sorts of butterflies, and lots of dragonflies swooping about. It's something that both our students and faculty enjoy on a daily basis. The next phase, made possible through one of our newer grants, will involve planting more butterfly-friendly plants along the Quest Center's wheelchair pathway.

T-Man and I check out the Quest Center's once barren field; now a beautiful butterfly garden, courtesy of several grants and lots of hard work.

The above-mentioned magazines keep me motivated and inspire me to improve my skills and, of course, on rare moments, purchase new and better gear. But all of this translates to a bottom line of doing what it takes to get you into the great outdoors. Gardening takes the outdoor experience to a higher level for kids. Don't just look or play. Start digging and watch the fruits of your labor!

Scouting and outdoor-oriented activities automatically mean that the old system of teacher-centered learning with motionless students is, you'll pardon the expression, history! It translates directly into highly motivational — and fun — student-centered activities. This puts the onus of learning where it belongs — on the child's shoulders. "You want to learn how to navigate using the stars," my patrol leader once asked me, "so you'll never get lost?" I simply nodded my head. "Great." he said. "Then meet me back here tonight when the stars come out and you'll learn." If I wanted to excel in some particular area of interest, whether it was canoeing, life-guarding, or ecology, then I had to not only read up on the subject, but learn first-hand, and eventually demonstrate skills pertaining to the subject area. Gardening is an easy and fun way to insure that student-centered learning occurs both at school and at home.

Projects!

Children of all sizes, shapes, colors, ages, and abilities, will learn much more quickly and efficiently if they're doing a project to reflect their work. This is a very simple and useful tool. Projects are hands-on, and there's no limit to one's creativity. A project is an extension of the self, and a valuable means of expression. Students of all backgrounds will learn the material faster, and in a more meaningful manner, when it's done in project format. These projects may be as simple as a drawing on a piece of paper, to an elaborate video production that's shared with the rest of the class or family. Projects are also extremely motivational for any child who feels turned off, or threatened by the system, at large.

Adam was one of my students at the Manhattan Day School. He was 15 at the time, and was diagnosed as having ADHD in addition to learning disabilities. I had Adam for two years in a row, teaching him math, science, and history. We were learning about the Native Americans, and I gave them a choice of which tribe to present. Adam picked the Nez Perce Indians, and on his own, came up with one of the most creative projects I've ever seen from one of my students. He dressed up everyone in his family as Nez Perce Indians and had his dad film and interview Adam, who was acting out the part of the tribe's leader, Chief Joseph. The interviewer was also pretending he was from that time period, and he asked Joseph lots of deep, candid questions. What are your plans with the Nez Perce? Why won't you sign this treaty? Didn't your own father sign a treaty years ago? Will you take your followers to the reservation? Why? Why not? The project was not only entertaining, but was loaded to the gills with historical facts and situations regarding the Nez Perce.

There's no way that Adam would have produced such an incredible piece of expressive art or, in fact, would have learned so much about the Nez Perce, if we had been utilizing the usual "sponge" method in a regular class. He, like myself, would probably have closed the book on history upon graduation. Projects help make learning come alive. The student becomes the focus of the learning, and for many children, it's a totally refreshing experience. Projects are, perhaps, the most useful educational tool for promoting positive social skills. Students can work on their projects with another student, or even with a small group of students. The same idea applies to the home front. If there's a chore, task, or project that needs completed, put one or more siblings together and reward them as a team.

For six years I had the wonderful opportunity of directing the special education program at MDS. We had four self-contained classes ranging from 2nd grade through 8th and most importantly, the school had an administrator, Rabbi David Kaminetsky, better known as RDK, who was miles ahead of the pack. I remember when I first interviewed for the job. Coming to NYC from my much smaller and quieter town of Buffalo, I really wasn't too interested in the position. Me? In the wilds of Manhattan? I felt a lot like a fish out of water. Nonetheless, I put together a list of my top priorities — goodies that I knew worked best for kids with special needs. "I want to implement these," I said, handing him the list, "if I accept the position." I knew this list wouldn't fly with the regular, run-of-the-mill principal, so I wouldn't require any excuse to turn down the offer. This doozy of a list read something like:

- *Peer tutoring and interactive learning.*
- *Hands-on science center that includes not your typical creatures like goldfish and gerbils, but snakes, tarantulas, and a live beehives on the school roof.*
- *Camping trips with my students to begin and end the school year.*
- *A behavior modification point system that featured winner's trips to the movies and local professional sports games like the Knicks, Rangers, Giants, etc. (Of course the trips would be scheduled when my Buffalo Bills & Sabres were challenging)!*
- *Scuba diving &/or snorkeling trips during the year.*
- *Having my students participate and help run the Special Olympics.*
- *Expressive arts, including hands-on music, as an integral part of the overall curriculum.*
- *Extra sports activities for the special ed students. (And I confess, myself, of course).*
- *Cutting edge technology for the students — use of computers, communication devices, etc.*

RDK smiled as he read my list. I thought for sure I could remain in good ol' Buffalo. But then he dropped the bomb:

"I'm a camper," he said looking into my eyes. "I run a summer camp, and I think these ideas are amazing. You can do 'em all!"

By the end of that interview, I not only had accepted the position to run the MDS special ed department, but I was also hired to help run his special ed and nature program at Camp Heller, in the beautiful Catskill Mountains in NY State. Like that, he became my boss, 12 months a year.

"Camp," RDK he continued, "does tremendous things for a child. I only wish our schools were more like summer camp. We'd all be a lot better off."

Through daily and direct encounters, kids of all sizes,
shapes, colors, and ages soon lose their fear of animals.
Instead they learn to enjoy, respect and feed them!

I couldn't agree more with RDK's statement. In fact, if we reversed things and made school last two months and camp the other ten, it might lead to dramatic improvements for our youth and society, in general. Well, let me qualify that statement a bit. Camp should really only be eight months. School would remain at two. The other two months? Simple. That's family time to hit the road together. You know, get out there and enjoy each other's company. Fish, swim, hike, bike, and travel together. And take lots of pictures.

I exaggerate on the above time framework — school two months — to make the point that schools could help nurture happier, healthier, more productive and creative students, by nurturing the whole child. This formula is what works so well for summer camps, and why our kids, (and adults), love going to these facilities. It's no small wonder that so many students who take meds for ADD and ADHD during the school year — when they're often forced and coerced to sit still and try to focus for hours on

80

end — leave the meds at home when it comes to summertime and summer camps. Many of these school-medicated kids do totally fine at their summer camps.

I've worked at summer camps for nearly as long as I've been teaching. So, we're talking 30 plus years in a row of adult summer camp experience. Let's do the math here. Thirty years at an average of two months per year, equals 60 months, or five full years of camping, since becoming a camp employee. These five years don't include my camp experience as a camper. I went to camps pretty much my whole life as a kid growing up in Buffalo, NY. The progression went from day camp, to overnight camp, to Scout camp, to Philmont Scout Ranch in NM, to finally working at various summer camps. Somehow our special needs kids just don't seem so "special" — so different — when it comes to summer camps. They have more opportunities to move — to run and play and express their creativity, to participate in a variety of fun group activities... than during the entire ten months of the sitting/school year.

For the past 15 years straight, I've received personal merit and pleasure while working at an incredible summer camp in the middle of beautiful NY State. I've seen first-hand, what Camp Mesorah has done for both the campers and staff members. Sometimes change occurs while kids participate in their drama productions, where by the way, I often get to rig a fancy rope setup to get kids literally flying in the air, such as in Peter Pan. Other times, it's when adolescents pass their first aid and swim courses. Perhaps they click in while making their own pottery or jewelry. Or maybe they awaken while picking fresh organic veggies from the camp garden. I have a hunch that all the hands-on work and responsibilities required to take care of the Mesorah farm animals has positively affected more than one child. Then too, it may just be all the inspiring, awesome, and often wild, singing and dancing on the Shabbat, (the Sabbath). But let's not forget the awesome presence of nature that, at long last in their lives, is everywhere to be found.

Mel & Jordy reconnect with nature at Camp Mesorah. These "city kids" became my trusty sidekicks for the summer farm.

One easy and fun-filled way to help introduce animals to city kids is by using the

"Once There Was A..." series. These unique books also come with very cute songs, all developed by the wonderful children's entertainer and educator Lisa Coleman. She's spent years working on a farm, where she also taught horseback riding to students. Her books and songs are about her real-life encounters with some of her favorite animals. Check out her site at www.lisacolemanmusic.com.

In truth, it's all the above and so much more. Camp teaches so much, and it's all done in a fun, meaningful, and experiential way. You're living and breathing the whole gestalt, and there's no need for memorization and tests and grades. At camp, you're flying and succeeding in a much higher zone. Kids get turned on to so many wonderful things at camp. The key here is that they become motivated and inspired, and once these factors kick in, there's no limit to what a child can accomplish. It's no wonder campers and staff alike shed many a tear when camp ends. There's this sense of the impending blahs — the return to the real, unreal world, devoid of movement, of life — plugged into the zillion different gadgets, going from "ah-life" to the "i-Life" — or is that the "ugh-life," of seeing nature from a distance... if you're lucky.

I've found during my close to four decades of working with youth, that once exposed to the great outdoors, kids gravitate towards nature. They'll even stop squishing spiders once they learn that our 8-legged buddies eat our real enemy — the mosquito! Same thing holds true for bats. Once they get some real knowledge and outdoor experience tucked under their belts, they soon realize that bats are nothing to be afraid of, especially since just one little bat can consume hundreds of "skeeters" a night. Kids learn mighty quickly that the open, awesome, wide world of nature is something magnificent, healing, and inspiring that needs our loving care. Rather than being protected from nature, these city kids soon drop their scary movie stereotypes about the woods and the dark — and they assume the responsible roles of protecting nature. They learn to, you'll pardon the expression, nurture nature.

One of my inner-city students was once called a nerd by his fellow classmates for protecting some ants from being stepped on. He answered back with one of the best lines I've ever heard from a 15 year-old young man with special needs, "So what?" he responded to their negative remarks. "That makes me a nerd nurturing nature." And then he quickly added, "Naturally!"

There's no doubt that animals need people to help protect them. But it's a two-way street. People, especially kids, need animals too. Animals, and in particular dogs, give unconditional love. It's interesting to note that the Hebrew word for dog is "kelev." The same three letters can also be read in Hebrew as "k'lev" — which means "like the heart."

Throughout history, dogs have indeed been "man's best friend." Dogs accept us for who we are. They don't care what sort of car we drive, how much or how little we make, and they don't care if someone is given a label of ADHD or PINS or ED or Gifted. They are happy to see us when we come home from school or work, no matter what kind of mood we're in or the lousy grade on our spelling quiz. They love to go for walks and runs with us. They love to be around us, and in my opinion, they give us far more than we give them.

This is especially true when it comes to kids taking care of animals in distress. There are many farms and wildlife sanctuaries throughout the states that offer unique, hands-on programs where you get to roll up your sleeves and do all sorts of farming and animal-care activities. Check out www.farmsanctuary.org, which has several facilities where you can get down, dirty, back to some of nature's roots, and help out our animal friends at the same time. By the way, you can probably leave your Ritalin, anti-depressants, and sleeping pills at home. You'll be too busy and too tired at the end of the day to need anything extra in your system.

The use of animals in therapeutic settings for both kids and adults in need has been well documented. Some groups use specially trained dogs, or even cats. Other programs feature individuals working closely with horses. For some, it involves interacting with marine mammals. This unique branch of therapy is often referred to in the media as Animal Assisted Therapy or Pet Therapy. There are several university and off-campus programs that lead to certification in this promising field. Current research indicates that there are all sorts of wonderful benefits from interacting with animals. These include lowering blood pressure, reducing anxiety, increasing a sense of relaxation, and possibly prolonging one's life span.

A recent article from the Washington Post, (Nov. 28, 2011), Riding program offers therapy, life-changing experiences by Steven Muck, describes an amazing program that involves more than 20 high school students with autism and other profound challenges, riding specially-trained horses. These students head up to the Rainbow Therapeutic Riding Center on a once-a-week basis, where they learn all sorts of important skills, such as grooming, feeding, communication, and of course, riding. The program has led to not only an increase in strength and physical skills for the participants, but also has helped build their confidence and self-esteem. Check out their fascinating program at www.rainbowriding.org. While you're at it, take a look at the Professional Association of Therapeutic Horsemanship International, better known as PATH Int: www.pathintl.org. Their website is jam-packed with information about this highly specialized form of therapy. You can find centers that offer these programs and provide other resources. Who knows? You may get so inspired that you take the "path" and become a certified equine therapist.

Camps keep these built-in therapy programs running full steam. From water therapy, to all the expressive arts, to animal & pet therapy, it's all happening 24/7. Now, do the math here. Imagine if we had to pay hourly rates for these incredible services; summer camps would cost well over $50,000 per kid. Even the more expensive camps that cost between $5,000 and $7500 a summer seem a real bargain when seen in that light. How amazing that good ol' Divine Providence brought me into contact with this incredible principal and camp director, RDK.

Visitors arriving from places like busy Hollywood, Florida, attend summer camps that expand their horizons.

Ben gravitated towards the nature & pioneering activities like an eagle to a forest. Taking care of farm animals teaches a child responsibilities, and to love and care for nature.

True to his word, a few months down the road, MDS, (located on the ever busy and crowded upper West Side of Manhattan), had a new director for the special education program. It also had a live beehive on its roof!

TEACH ME IF YOU CAN!
CHAPTER 3

The Magic of Music

"I was born with music inside me.

Like my ribs, my heart. Like my blood.

It was a necessity for me — like food or water."

— *Ray Charles*

"Music is a higher revelation than all wisdom

and philosophy."

— *Beethoven*

What is Music & what does it do?

There's been a lot written about music and its effects on people. Some have even studied the impact of music on animals and plants. One thing is very evident when it comes to music: it is a powerful medium, capable of stimulating and evoking all kinds of feelings, thoughts, emotions, and even actions. Let's take love, for example. Most of us, if we put our minds to it, could probably come up with 100 plus songs about this wonderful human emotion. Ballads, operas, classical pieces and even soft-rock have been used to both express and inspire love. They say that Johnny Mathis was responsible for more babies being born during the late 50's and early 60's than any other performer. His soft, yet deep crooning voice was more powerful than any fertility drug of the time. It's no wonder that John was such a popular name back then. Music has been used to psyche up warriors for battle since biblical times, whether it was horn blasts intended to frighten an enemy or some war-weary GI listening to a crazy death metal tune on his iPod. Music is also a very individualistic experience. What is considered music to one person may be rejected as obnoxious "noise" to another. When the Beatles first hit the U.S. on the Ed Sullivan Show, I can still hear my friends' parents saying, somewhat alarmed, "You call that music?" Funny thing is, that I sometimes now say that very same thing to some of my students. In any case, music is something that seems to penetrate into the very essence of our beings. It is also something that stays with us over the years. For an in-depth analysis as to what constitutes this phenomenon we call "music," see Daniel Levitin's incredible book called "This Is Your Brain On Music," (2007). Levitin approaches this subject from both the emotional and intellectual perspectives. He was heavily involved in the music industry as a recording artist, sound engineer, and producer. He got to hang out with all sorts of very talented and famous musicians. Levitin then went on to become a respected neuroscientist, who has spent much of his combined career studying the profound effects music has on us all.

We forget details from our past, perhaps even as recently as yesterday, but somehow, those tunes from way back when never leave us, and can resurface at the strangest times. This sometimes comes in real handy — especially when it comes to a hot and heavy radio contest of "Name That Tune."

Lessons from a Beatles Contest

"**W**hoa," my friend Dave Coleman shouted. "Not so loud!"

"Relax DC," I responded, cranking up the radio even louder. "I gotta hear this."

I had a whole bunch of nicknames for him, including the Dster, DC, (his initials, of course), and Washington, based on the same initials D.C. And sometimes, Capitol or George, based on Washington, based on his initials. The possibilities were endless.

"This is important, DC," I protested. "I can't miss one note!" My hand stayed on the volume button.

"At this decibel level," he continued, "you won't hear anything!"

"Hey," I protested. "You put together some awesome videos and documentaries. But I got the music down, bro!"

He just laughed, but he knew this was serious business. It was not just any ol' contest. This one involved the Fab Four — the Beatles, my absolute favorite group of all time. The winner would receive a new Beatles book, an Abbey Road T-shirt, and two DVD's, including some of George Harrison's live performances. But it was more than just the prizes looming before my eyes, well, make that before my ears. It was my pride. DC knew about my ability to hear a mere few notes of a song and properly identify the name and artist. In fact, it boggled my own mind, as well. Somehow, in some deep mysterious way, songs, tunes, TV jingles, anything having to do with music, penetrated my cerebral cortex and stayed there for years and years. It usually took just a few notes, sometimes even just that first chord, to reawaken a whole series of responses from my brain that ranged from "Oh, I know that tune!" to "I remember who I was with when we heard this song!" to, "I know exactly what I was wearing when I was listening to this!" to, something even more profound: "I remember the sensation, the feeling I had back then...in fact, I feel now, the very same deep emotion!"

This is true for songs from my earliest childhood memories, spanning 30 or 40 years ago. And so, I myself am living proof of the amazing power of music. My friends insist that my musical-recall ability is better than most. Perhaps this is because I was not just a listener, but also an active participant. Like many kids back in the day, my parents offered me piano lessons when I was still in elementary school. Well, let's be more specific. They strongly encouraged me to take these lessons. And typically, like most students back then, both my teacher and I decided to give it a rest — she quit on me after I quit on her, of course — and now I sure wish I had stuck with it. But back then, I was feeling a different urge in my bones, in my soul. I wanted to play drums. I wanted to play like Krupa, who was from my parent's era, but he sure could dazzle them skins. Finally for my Bar Mitzvah, as I turned 13, my folks gave into my pleas and signed me up for drum lessons. It was the most wonderful birthday of my life up to that point in time. But my folks were very smart, and they weren't going to rush into yet another set of wasted music lessons. My track record with piano wasn't too shiny.

"You want drums," my dad told me, "then prove yourself. Every month you stick with your lessons, and we see you making progress, we'll get you another piece. Whether you have a full set or just one pair of sticks and a drum pad is up to you!"

"But Dad," I protested. "There's like 20 pieces to a full kit. It'll take me years to get a set!"

"You better work on them math skills too," he responded with a smile. "It's only a year and eight months away."

"Oh that's great news," I muttered, hoping he was only kidding with me.

Those lessons were my ticket to ride. I proudly carried my pad & sticks on my walk to Mr. Rowland's home, taking the shortcut under the Shoshone Park train trestle, in our north Buffalo neighborhood. Mr. Rowland was the head percussionist of the Buffalo Philharmonic back then, and he was absolutely incredible. He taught me the basic rudiments and somehow got me to read four lines of drum music at once. It was all quite complicated, challenging, and complete fun. I was practicing without any coercion whatsoever. In fact, not even the promise of new drums mattered. I seemed to be playing just for the sake of playing. Making music had this intrinsic reward to it. It was as if I was making this connection to something higher and beyond myself, and yet, at the very same time, to some deep, essential part of me. In six months I earned my drum set, and I'm playing to this very day — and I still marvel at my folk's wisdom.

Shine those rays. Every kid plays!

An instrument, that is.

More importantly than buying your kid an iPod or iPhone, or even a Guitar Hero setup, is getting them a musical instrument. Free radio, Pandora, and those applications that play your personal listening preferences, are mighty cool indeed. Even the sound on the latest cell phones is stereophonic and awesome. But you'll be doing your students and kids a much bigger favor by getting them an instrument or two, (or more), to play on. Playing the drums was my magic. I not only increased my musical skills, but improved my academic subjects in school, as well. Learning drums and working toward the drum set with the hopes of playing in my very own band, was extremely motivational. It taught me patience, goal setting, responsibility, the value of hard work, the importance of doing something I personally loved, and opened my eyes and mind to another world. I could not only listen to music... I could make it! Everyone, no matter what challenges they face, can be involved in the act of making music. David Sousa, in his important book, "How The Brain Learns," (2001), writes that the activities involved in making and creating music "provide many more cerebral advantages" than simply passively listening. It's this notion of going from a state of passivity to one of more-active participation.

There was something else I got from both piano and drum lessons, and that was the notion of listening to music in a more critical fashion. Not that I sat back, cold and calculative, and dissected each piece, but I would listen in this kind of open manner, allowing the music to hit me and fill me up. At the same time, I would listen for the separate instruments, and hear what the drummer was doing, hear the hi-hat, and make mental note of the bass drum timing, etc. Most drummers played their set just for background beat. It was the backbone, the skeleton of the song. The driving force. But a few drummers played the skins in a more creative way. It was more than providing the beat. These drummers played their sets like a melodic instrument. They made the drums sing. Ringo was a master in the 60's, and in my opinion still remains one of the most underrated drummers on the planet. Listening to music back then, I would also focus in on the bass guitar line, the lead line, hear the marvel of voices in harmony, and yet, it was always the song in its entirety, its "gestalt," that struck something inside me. If the song was good, if the artist was authentic, I could somehow not just hear it... but feel it, inside.

So, perhaps my ability to remember a song from eons ago by a mere few notes, is that my music lessons placed me in a position of not just listening to music, but of making and creating music. I had become a creative partner in the music process and that somehow translated into about 16 billion tunes sleeping inside my head, just waiting for their chance to come out from under the covers.

"Can you imagine," Dster said, interrupting my thoughts, "if you knew Talmud, or any other area of knowledge, like math, the way you remember music? You'd make Einstein look like he was in Pre-K!"

"If only I had a buck for every time I heard that line, my brother. I'd also be a very rich man."

It was true, and it did boggle my mind. Why didn't I remember my Talmudic lessons, or all the info I read in a zillion different books, the same way I could recall notes and words of songs from years and years ago? Even songs that I haven't heard in more than two, or three or four decades! Somehow, my regular subjects were the exact opposite. I spent hours and hours memorizing science concepts, math formulas, world leaders, and political movements in social studies, and all these mental facts and exercises strangely disappeared out the window — in some cases, just days after the big exams. For some reason, unlike music, all these zillions of "important" facts never made the jump from short-term memory to long-term memory. Music, you'll pardon the expression, strikes a chord deep inside one's very being. It does an amazing job of tickling those long-term memory cells. To this day, I believe the only reason I remember that Columbus came to America in 1492 was that it was put to a short poem: "In 1492, Columbus sailed the ocean blue." Poetry is certainly more melodic than all those dry, dead words on the dry, dead pages of our textbooks. Poetry, like music perhaps, makes the concepts come to life.

I'm convinced that this is one of the reasons I was successful in my studies at Rabbinical College after I finished my undergrad work at University of Buffalo. At the Rabbinical College of America in Morristown, NJ, I often hit the books for six, eight, even ten plus hours a day. And here's the kicker — I loved it! For my undergraduate work at the University of Buffalo, I kind of breezed through things, maybe studying six to eight hours a week. I think I even studied more in high school. Granted, one reason was that this was the late 60's, you know, the Woodstock generation with our mantra of "turn on, tune in, and drop out!" There definitely was a lack of motivation to participate in the traditional approach to education. But it was deeper than that. It wasn't just that I found some new sense of dedication at rabbinical school; it was the actual method of learning that took place. It was an unusual combination of peer learning and verbalizing material. It wasn't just saying the words out loud. There was this kind of singsong melody that was part & parcel of the learning itself. It was this wonderful, and quite unique combination of factors that made the learning process exciting, active, student-centered and very motivational.

Verbalize the learning. Move those lips.

Verbalizing the learning brings it closer to the magic realm of music. At the very least, it's a step closer to poetry.

Yes, you heard it right. In fact, if you really heard this correctly, you are saying this very sentence out loud. Not in decibel levels that will get you arrested for disturbing the peace, or a one-way ticket to the psych ward, but just loud enough for your ears to pick up those important syllables and concepts, and pass them along to your magnificent human brain.

This approach to learning is often the opposite of what is practiced in nearly every classroom on the planet. Teachers are taught, and then reinforce this notion, that reading out loud — even moving one's lips while reading - is slow, ineffective reading. I even had a teacher in elementary school that, during individual reading time, went around the room gently closing my lips with her thumb and fingers. "There now," she would say, "much better. Much, much better."

I'm not suggesting utilizing the verbalization technique for reading your favorite novel as you lay in bed at night. But for the acquisition of new concepts and learning, you can't beat the verbalization system. My educated guess is that saying the words out loud activates other areas of the brain, creating more neural connections and pathways. It's a more active process than simply looking at the words and thinking about them. It's putting some action into what is otherwise a very passive experience. In a fascinating discussion on prayer, it's interesting to note that, according to the Talmud, audible movement of the lips — even whispers, is called "ma'aseh," which in Hebrew means action. Here the Talmud speaks about the difference between prayer and meditation. Meditation is often done quietly and involves this phenomenon of deep thinking. Prayer, on the other hand, requires some verbalization, at least in whisper form, loud enough for the ears to hear something. By insisting on absolute quiet when reading or learning, you actually minimize the cerebral opportunities for memory, which is only the beginning stage of the learning process.

Verbalizing also has a connection to music, or more specifically to poetry and rap. Why do our kids and students seem to know every new tune out there, and yet have such trouble with seemingly easy math or science concepts? One of the reasons is that we have created an all-too-quiet, unreal school world, by not allowing our kids to speak out loud, to express themselves, to actively share, swap, discuss, and even sing new ideas and thoughts. There's no doubt in my mind, that if we put more of our conceptual learning into song format our students would learn by leaps & bounds. I'm not just talking about something as basic as the times tables in math. Let's take something as complex and as intimidating as the infamous Periodic Table! No way, you say? Not a chance, you respond, remembering how you nearly flunked out of high school due to that difficult chemistry course. After all, we're talking over 100 elements with doozy names such as Molybdenum, Technetium, and let's not forget Reontgenium, of course. It's hard enough to pronounce those names properly let alone memorize all the elements of the Periodic Table, unless of course, you're a scientist who lives and breathes the stuff. And yet, I once had a student who bet me $20 that he could rattle off the entire Periodic Table to me without the assistance of a computer or glancing at the back of his tie every three seconds. Since I was on a teacher's salary, I immediately took that bet, figuring it was good for some gas in my car and maybe even a slice of pizza, as well. "In fact," he told me, "you can blindfold me while I recite them to ya!" Here was a bet I simply couldn't lose. First, he was all of 12 years old. Secondly, he wasn't a biologist or scientist. Thirdly, he had some attention/hyperactivity issues going on, so there was no way I was losing this bet. I thought about doubling the amount but my conscience got the better of me. How could I take $40 from the kid when his parents were already paying for his extra tutoring session with me?

To my utter amazement and shock, however, three minutes later I was 20 bucks in the hole. I lost that bet hands down. How did this 12-year-old non-scientist accomplish such an awesome feat? In one word: music! More specifically it was Tom Lehrer's wild and crazy "Element Song," that did the trick. Set to a rapid-fire beat, this tune does indeed go through all the elements. Isn't it interesting, that nearly every student who's ever taken chemistry could seldom name all the elements despite hours and hours of focused learning on the subject? We're talking millions of chemistry students throughout the world, and I would wager that only a few are able to name all of the elements. Here was this 12-year- old student of mine, with some special needs mind you, and he knew the elements cold! Kudos to him and to Mr. Lehrer for inventing such a wacky and wonderful tune. My student told me later that it only took him a few hours of listening and repeating the lines of the Element Song, to completely memorize it. Someone definitely needs to write a tune about Einstein's theory of relativity.

Sing it out! Put those learning concepts to song.

Any concept or skill you want your kids or students to learn can be put to music. This is true even for social etiquette, such as sharing, playing nicely, taking turns, etc. Get creative with it, and don't worry about the technology. You don't need a professional recording studio. And old-school style tape recorder will do the trick. The main point here is to put these concepts to music. Don't worry about plagiarizing, unless of course, you do plan on publishing your songs. If, however, you're just using them with your own kids and students, then it's best to put these words and learning concepts to familiar tunes. Let's take something as well known as Old McDonald. Say, for example, you want to teach the necessary social skill of waiting in line. Here's one for ya just off the top of my head: "This is how we wait in line, ee-i ee-i-oh. I listen to my teacher all the time, ee-i ee-i-oh."

Despite all the colorful posters on the walls, our classrooms bear a striking resemblance to the quiet, sterile environment of the dentist's office. We've got to realize that quiet doesn't always equate to learning. Conversely, a raised noise level in a class doesn't always mean chaos. It may, in fact, indicate that more active learning and valuable discussion is taking place.

One other point to mention here is the notion of peer learning. Most of the actual learning at a Rabbinical College is with your peer, or "chaver," in Hebrew - which means friend or colleague. A bit of a tongue twister. I guess you could call it "paired/peer" learning, in its highest form. The rabbi, or teacher, functions more as a guide to the learning process. This means that you're no longer at the bottom of the totem pole. It's not you, the lower receiving-student, always listening to the higher giving-teacher. It's now you and your peer, your educational match. Thus, the onus for learning — and teaching - now falls on your shoulders… and your partner's. In this system, learning itself is more about self-growth and discovery. Put in the other magical component of verbalization - saying the material out loud, (which adds the musical touch to the whole process), and you can't lose! This kind of learning is active participation, and highly motivational, almost the opposite of the traditional college, library-style learning, which is done all hush-hush, on the solo side. I don't know about you, but given a choice between active participation and passive observance, I'd stick with the former and drop the latter like a stack of outdated, boring 8th-grade social studies books. For more on this topic, please see the chapter on peer learning, later in the book. For now, there's a very important contest demanding our attention.

"Shhhhhh," I urged DC. "It's now!" I pulled the car over to the side of the road. Now was the time to concentrate, free from any distractions.

"Ohhhhhhh," Washington whispered. "No one like de Lazmon! Try to get two Beatles shirts, ya hear?"

I cranked up the radio, while we both put the radio station's phone number into our cell phones. We were all set to go.

"You best share the goodies with me, bro," Dster said.

I gave him the thumbs up sign.

"Getting the tune right should be easy," I replied. "Getting through to the station? That's the tough part."

"Ok folks," the DJ announced. "Here are your three notes. That's all ya get. Good luck and we'll take the 9th caller. First one to correctly identify the exact name of the song and the group, wins that awesome Beatles package. Good luck!"

I was pretty confident that I'd name the tune aok. There aren't too many folks on the planet that can match me note for note, providing I know the tune, of course. Zahava, the keyboard player in my band, has me hands down when it comes to naming songs. If it takes me three notes, she'll do it in two. Her repertoire is probably in the hundreds of thousands. She's one of those few people that has perfect pitch, and knows what key a song is in after hearing it for a few moments. The crazy thing is that she can't read a note of music. It's all in her head. But, I digress. The real problem here was getting through to the station. That would take a whole lot of good luck indeed. Then, of course, you had to be number nine at the same time. That would take nothing short of divine intervention from above. But I would do my part, and leave the rest to providence.

The notes came on in rapid-fire, lasting a mere second or less, but that was more than enough. The music triggered some amazingly rapid-fire action in my brain cells, and the song in its full glory came to life inside me.

"Got it, bro!" I said excitedly. "Piece of cake, amigo!"

DC let out a yell, patted my shoulders, as our thumbs immediately pushed the magic call button on our cell phones. Things went as usual, with both of us getting the busy signal. We kept redialing for the next five minutes straight. Here we were, a couple of "grown" men, sitting in a parked car at the side of the road, frantically redialing time after time, trying to win a Beatles t-shirt! Okay, so it's true. Men are just boys at heart, with a bit more facial hair. I did feel kind of silly, but we were not giving up.

In a stroke of good fortune, the DJ came on to announce that the 9th caller was wrong, and so was the 10th and 11th, and a whole lot of others. I usually never got through, but now, with all the others wrong, my chances improved dramatically. We kept on trying, going through that maddening process of hitting the call button, waiting for the call to get through, hearing that annoying "busy" sound, pushing the "end call" button and repeating the entire process over, and over, and over.

Five minutes went by, in what seemed more like five hours.

"Ughhhhhhh," DC grunted. "This is…"

"Wait!" I shouted. "It's ringing. It's actually ringing!"

"Hi. You're caller 68!" The DJ announced in my left ear.

Caller 68? I thought to myself. How could so many be so wrong?

"Really?"

"Really."

"Are you gonna be the one to get the song right?" the DJ asked. "I'm really hoping someone will."

"I think I got it," I responded, pumping my arm silently in the air.

"Name the band, and exact title of the song, and that great Beatle's package is yours!"

"Okay, here's goes." I had to motion for DC to stop pinching my arm. "The band is Mitch Ryder & The Detroit Wheels."

"Ok," he said, not too enthusiastically. "Let's see if you can get the correct title. Remember, it's gotta be the exact title."

"The tune is Devil With A Blue Dress On — Good Golly Miss Molly."

"Yeah," the DJ shouted with joy. "You got it! Well folks. We got us a winner! Ya know, lots of people said it was Devil With A Blue Dress. And lots said it was Good Golly Miss

Molly. But you're the first to give the exact full title, which is both!"

DC and I were hugging and high-fiving in the car.

"Hold on my friend," the DJ announced on air. "Gotta get your name and info. This amazing Beatles package is yours. But who are you? You must be the head of a music company?"

"I'm a special education teacher," I said. "But I have a rock band and it's more like songs just stay in my head."

"And in our souls." he added. "Your students are lucky to have a rock 'n roller for a teacher. Guess that great music will stay with us forever."

Any DJ since has never spoken truer words. I could only hope he was right on the first part as well. I've always been one to incorporate music as an integral part of my overall teaching strategy. It can be used as background music while the students are engaged in some activity, even bell-work, or some type of assignment.

For this type of activity, I suggest something mellow in the background, but I have inner-city students who listen to reggae, hip-hop and even rap, while completing various academic-oriented tasks. Many educators frown upon such activities, claiming that this sort of music is a distraction, and keeps kids from focusing. One has to use good judgment, because every situation and every child is unique. Some individuals work really well with music going, while others have a rough time. In this day and age, where nearly everyone has an iPod or MP3 player, there's no need for a speaker blasting a single tune into your classroom. Each kid can have the music his or her own way and style. And some kids work even better with the music going — even rap and hip-hop. I think it helps them relax, acting perhaps, as a bridge between the between the "unreal" classroom and the real-life of the streets outdoors.

Music research has come a long way. Today, music's effects on the human brain are studied using all sorts of imagery technology. It has been found to actively stimulate many parts of the brain all at once. In the past, it was believed that music stimulated one particular area of the brain and was responded to by some sort of "music center," similar perhaps, to the "vision center" or "speech center." But in fact, music goes past these more clearly defined physical areas, and hits many different parts of the brain en masse, and in all sorts of colorful ways. Dr. Gottfried Schlaug is a professor of neurology at Beth Israel Deaconess Medical Center and Harvard Medical School. He runs a unique program at Beth Israel called, The Music, Neuroimaging & Stroke Recovery Laboratories. In 2009, Dr. Schlaug presented at the Neuro-Education Initiative at The John Hopkins University, in a national summit sponsored by the Dana Foundation. In the follow-up booklet from this special conference entitled, "Neuroeducation: Learning, Arts, & The Brain," (2009), Dr. Schlaug writes that creating music is a "multisensory experience, but it also involves attention networks, and the motivation and reward system." I would challenge everybody to come up with another activity that engages as much real estate in the brain as music-making does."

We know that a song can trigger deep-rooted feelings and sentiments ranging from love, to longing, to depression, sadness, and even anger and hostility. It can elicit memories from years before, often ones that we haven't given a conscious thought to in ages. It can also aid in relaxation and therapeutic situations. But the amazing act of creating and making music seems to far & away surpass the mere act and benefits of simply listening to a tune.

For nearly seven years, my alternative boys high school program, (previously mentioned), attracted teens that simply didn't fit the mold at their regular high schools. They dubbed themselves the "misfits," and it became obvious to me that they needed a few "extras" to make their in-school time meaningful. My small extras, which ended up being major factors in the success of the program, included the following:

- *Peer tutoring - where the students did most of the class work with one another*

- *Daily physical education and sports activities*

- *A focus on GEDs and getting their diploma as soon as possible*

- *No tests whatsoever, as grades were based on effort rather than end-product*

- *Vocational training*

- *Lifeguard training*

- *Hands-on music activities*

Students were allowed to listen to the music of their choice, as long as they did so using personal earphones. Many of my students would come to hear my band play in the evenings. Some developed a real sense for running the sound system. For some of them, this hands-on apprentice-type learning, led to sound technician careers in the music industry. For our musical group activities, we sometimes listened to tunes the entire group agreed upon. And then there were the drums.

Let the drums begin! Using Drum Circles & Percussion Activities

Drumming, in my opinion, is the basis of all music. It is, in fact, the first musical experience a growing fetus has inside the womb — hearing and feeling of both its' mother's heartbeat, and then its own. Let's be more specific about drumming. It's the beat that carries the tune, whether it's a complicated symphony, or an impromptu drum circle. You've got to have the beat, and hear the beat, to make it work. For personal therapy, say when working with one individual at a time, the beat isn't the crucial focus. It doesn't matter whether he or she can stay with a beat, keep in time, or whether the person speeds up, slows down, stops to take breaks, or beats till the drum heads break — which thankfully doesn't happen too often. For individual sessions, the main thing is that the individual is expressing him or herself. Drumming can be extremely healthy and beneficial. I've used this technique many times with clients classified as ADD or ADHD. It helps these individuals focus, and gives them a productive way of channeling their high level of energy. What may start off as loud noise often ends up being slower, more controlled, and more melodic.

Before engaging in group drumming and percussion activities, I tell the participants that it's important to listen to what others are doing. I remind them that I tell my band members the very same thing. "You've got to hear what the others are doing to stay in the rhythm and to know where the song is." So, a good musician and performer is also a good and effective listener. In many different ethnic groups, drumming is considered sacred. People sometimes receive visions, often through dreams, and they embark on a spiritual quest to find their own unique drum, with its own special voice. It's an earthy type of experience, one that connects us perhaps, to something deeper than ourselves.

There are many ways that drumming activities can be incorporated as part of an expressive arts program.

• Everyone plays on a hand drum, such as a djembe, at the same time. Usually, in these type of drum circle activities, one person will start the beat and others join in as they begin to feel the rhythm. A modification is to add another instrument's sound as you go around the circle. In this way, the sound becomes fuller as you complete the circle.

Jo-Jo feeling utter joy on the "skins."

• The above activity can be modified if there's a shortage of drums. Even one drum can hold the beat and then the others can join in using various percussion instruments. Percussion instruments can easily be made using all sorts of commonly found items from home or school. Cans, plastic bottles, even small boxes can be filled with raw beans or peas. Just use your imagination. Almost anything can be used to make noise. Make sure it's a safe item. Some of my most memorable music events featured impromptu drumming and percussion. At one outdoor art show, people in the audience simply began using empty soda cans. Some folks struck them together; others scraped them along the sidewalks. Soon people began tapping sticks, and even hitting garbage cans to produce percussion-type sounds. We literally had hundreds of people in this spontaneous drum/percussion "circle."

• Put on some music and have the individual or group play along with the song. This is often a useful technique for people who might be too shy or too reluctant to "stand out." Playing to background music helps blend the sounds.

• For individuals with profound special needs and physical challenges, you can use hand-over-hand techniques to assist them with various movements. There are also a variety of switches that can be hooked to adaptive drums. For example, a child who can operate a knee or head switch would hit his or her switch. This, in turn, would activate the percussion device, such as a drum effect. In this way, everyone can, and should, participate in these awesome drum circles, whether it's drumming alone or everyone playing along to music.

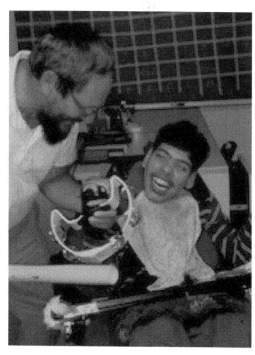

With some hand-over-hand assistance, Moshe feels the groove and the joy.

Andrea was one of my former students at the Quest Center. She was 16 years old, blind, non-verbal, wheelchair bound, and had multiple challenges, including a debilitating physical condition. Quite frankly, I wasn't sure what, if anything, would reach her or help her in any way, during our hands-on music sessions. My assistant would play a tune on the keyboards while I roamed around the classroom, using hand-over-hand techniques so that the students could participate. Andrea rarely moved or made any sounds, except an occasional cry or whine. It was frustrating, as I had tried so many different songs and techniques to try to reach her, yet nothing seemed to click.

One time while holding a tambourine in my right hand, I grasped her hand with my open left hand and brought it up to clap my right wrist. In this way, I reasoned, she would hear and feel the tambourine moving up and down, making its ringing sound to the beat of the music. The song being played was "Let's Go!" I then whispered the beat in her ear, "1-2...1-2-3... 1-2-3-4, Let's Go!" She suddenly burst out laughing, grinning ear to ear. This soon became her theme song. I would see her in the hallways and whisper those magic words in her ear and nearly every time, would get this fabulous happy response. We caught her on camera, laughing and smiling, and her mom remarked that she rarely saw Andrea with such a happy expression.

Her mom has an 8x10 enlargement of her daughter's beautiful smile, hanging in her home. Andrea unfortunately passed on as a result of complications from her difficult condition, but she taught us all so much in her short time here. One thing I learned from her is to never give up. You never know what might click and make that magic of music take effect. For Andrea it was a tambourine and a very simple song, mostly all rhythm. And yet, for some reason, it worked for her.

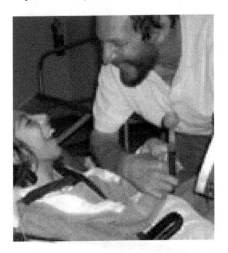

Andrea breaks out in a laugh to her song –
Let's Go!

Tony, aka the T-Man, is a young man in his early 20's. Although his body is very thin and frail, his spirit is huge. Tony, like many of my students, requires a wheelchair for mobility. He must be lifted in and out of his chair for toileting, and to simply lie down and stretch out. He's essentially non-verbal, although he too can make various vocalizations and groaning-type sounds. For months I tried every trick in the book to reach Tony. Then, quite by accident, it all clicked in. I started singing the song "Day-Oh," that great island song by Harry Belafonte. As soon as I hit the chorus of "day, iz-a-day, iz-a-day, iz-a-day-ay-ay-oh," Tony lit up like 4th of July fireworks. He started rocking back and forth in his wheelchair, a huge ear-to-ear grin. He loved the silly stuff. Not so much the slapstick or the loud noises, but just plain ol' silly nonsense-words. I soon added to Tony's repertoire, songs like "Supercalifragilisticexpialidocious," and "The Bird Is The Word". "Day-Oh" has, however, remained his true theme song.

Fortunately, I had stumbled across a working key for Tony. The T-Man has been a huge part of our travelling performing group. Even though he graduated from the Quest Center a year ago, his amazing parents make sure Tony helps us out at every gig. But, I'm getting ahead of myself. More on this incredible group of performers later in the book. Scout's honor.

Anything and everything can be used as a percussion instrument!

No need to buy expensive equipment here. Ask any percussionist or drummer and you'll soon realize that the entire world and everything in it is one awesome play toy after another, whether they're hitting the Brooklyn Bridge to produce some interesting sound, or simply banging away on the dining room table. Pretty much anything can produce some sound when it's struck or banged or rubbed or hit. Now, I wouldn't suggest using peanut butter or ice cream for this, but you definitely can put to good use those empty containers. You can even fill 'em right up with some extra beans, or seeds or small pebbles, and voila! — you've got yourself some nifty little sound-makers. Now it's true that some of the local music stores will have stronger and longer-lasting percussion instruments to scratch, shake, move and bang on. But it's also true that they'll cost a whole lot more than the stuff you were going put into the recycling or garbage containers. In fact, you can make some wonderful percussion sounds with homemade goodies, not to mention the regular stuff you have lying around the house collecting dust. Why not put 'em to work in your music program!

One summer at Camp Mishkon, we had the pleasure of having the great guitarist Piamenta for a concert — the media often refers to him as the "Jewish Hendrix". His band showed up minus the drummer, who got lost somewhere in the Catskill Mountains in NY State. He may still be wandering around the "borsht belt" to this very day. The concert was pre GPS and pre cell phone days, so poor Piamenta was facing a concert for the entire camp of 250 plus, minus his drummer — the driving beat of the band! I couldn't even help him out because my drums were back home in good ol'

Brooklyn. As Piamenta paced back & forth across the stage wondering how he was going to pull this off, George, one of older campers with Downs-syndrome, provided the answer. As us supposedly wise grownups debated the options, George sat on the stage and with stick in hand, started banging away on the floor. The idea went off in our heads like a light bulb. "Go to the kitchen," Piamenta said, "and bring every kind of pot and pan you can find! The bigger the better! And don't forget those large spoons!"

It was, in Piamenta's own words to me after the show, "the best concert of my entire life!" Coming from a guy who's probably done over 10,000 shows, those are mighty strong words to ponder.

Our campers, ranging in age from eight to 60 plus years, all with profound special needs, sat on the stage and in their wheelchairs, hitting and banging away to the beat. No "real" drums necessary here, folks. We did indeed raid the camp kitchen, and used pots, frying pans, and large wooden spoons as drumsticks and beaters. Sometimes, when concerts become totally contrived affairs, when even the jokes and the so-called spontaneous stuff is all-too-well rehearsed, they lose life and zest. But the Piamenta concert that night at Camp Mishkon, was a joyous musical-theatrical adventure no one there will ever forget. Our campers and staff became part of the magic, as they joined Piamenta in what was probably his biggest backup band ever.

Singing & Vocalizations

Get out the microphone & crank up the volume!

Music and a microphone... powerful medicine.

L et them sing, vocalize, hum, even breathe into the mike. Time to bring out their "inner ham."

Singing and verbalizing to music is another effective and easy way to reach and help those with special needs. I encourage any sort of verbal output. The main thing, is that the individual is producing some sound to the music. For some it might be a very repetitious, guttural type sound. Others will enunciate a consonant or two. And for some, it might be just a sigh or humming-type of noise. Nonetheless, these sounds should not be minimized, for the individual is "singing" to the best of his or her ability at that particular moment in time. Here, the simple trick for enhancing the event is a microphone. Anything that gives vocalization some amplification often works magic for the "singer." For some students it may, in fact, be the very first time they get to hear their voice amplified. Students are usually fascinated with the way they sound, and they may repeat their vocalizations, however strange-sounding to those with more verbal abilities. Talking and singing is usually something we take for granted. Like the profound chorus from Joni Mitchell's song Big Yellow Taxi: "Don't it always seem to go, ya don't know what you've got till it's gone."

Many individuals with profound special needs aren't very verbal, but they can vocalize all sorts of sounds. An inexpensive microphone should be part of any parent or teacher's arsenal. There are all sorts of low priced Karaoke systems. There are even microphones that run on a battery and have a built-in, tiny amp on the end. While these sorts of mikes wouldn't cut it for a music band, they often work just fine at home or in the special needs classroom. The results of using the mike to amplify vocal output often produces some very surprising results.

Use hand-over-hand for students who are blind or visually impaired. Once they learn the skills for using the microphone, they'll do fine on their own.

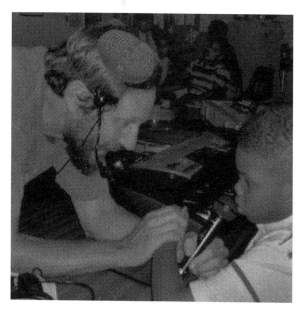

Dani, a 19-year-old male, was one of my students with multiple challenges, including Downs-syndrome. He exhibited self-stimulation behaviors all day long. These included waving something back and forth in his hand, rocking back and forth on his feet, and repeating over and over the utterances "Ooo-bah, ooo-bah, ooo-bah." He'd even carry on with these particular behaviors while using the bathroom. Perhaps for a bit of selfish reasons, I decided I had to cure him of these behaviors, especially the "ooo-bah" vocalizations. Quite frankly, they were driving me and my assistants off the wall. It's one thing to hear for a few minutes. Maybe even an hour. But all day long? I knew I had to do something about the situation when I started dreaming at night of huge scary monsters that made this monotonous ooo-bah sound. I tried all sorts of techniques. I'd interrupt his repetitious behaviors by bouncing a ball to him. That would work for a while, but I simply could not play catch with him all day. I tried using tangible and delicious edible rewards. That also worked. For a minute or two. And then it was back to the rocking & shaking movements, accompanied by the ooo-bahs. The ooo-bahs were quickly turning into oy-veys.

The breakthrough came during music class, which at the time, I was holding in the school's cafeteria. While a song was playing through the sound system, I walked around the room, my magic mike in hand. For students unable to hold the mike I placed it in front of their mouths until they made some vocal sounds. Often their eyes would get real big when they realized that they were making such loud sounds. Then, there looming before me, was Dani, doing his ooo-bah routine, rocking away as usual, seemingly oblivious to the music. I held the mike in front of him, but he paid no attention, whatsoever. I moved his hand to help hold the mike, and he quickly yanked it away. I placed the mike about an inch from the front of his mouth and actually had to move the mike back and forth to his rocking motions, so the mike wouldn't hit into his face. Suddenly, there were these tremendously loud and deep "ooo-bah" sounds penetrating and echoing all over the large empty space of the cafeteria. It was as if some strange creature had landed from outer space and was speaking to us in his alien language.

Dani looked at me, and his eyes opened wide as he realized that it was his voice filling the air with these booming "ooo-bah" utterances. To my amazement, he stopped rocking back and forth, stopped shaking the piece of paper in his hand, and stopped his vocalizations altogether. It was suddenly very quiet. I patted him on the back and said "way to go Dani, that was you singing!"

As soon as I moved the mike away from his face, he started up with his regular routine, ooo-bahs included. I then placed the mike by his mouth and he stopped, once again. This procedure went on for several minutes until he became totally quiet. After a good 10 minutes of this procedure, he actually tried some other vocal sounds besides the usual ooo-bahs. The most interesting thing happened the very next time Dani came to music. All I had to do was show him the microphone, and he stopped the self-stimulating behaviors. According to his diagnosis, Dani is supposedly on too low of a functioning level to engage in self-evaluation and predicting outcomes. Dani, however, proved his IEP wrong when it came to using the mike and "singing."

Using the microphone enabled Dani to hear what he sounded like. Most people thoroughly enjoy this experience, and will often do their best to "ham it up." They'll sing louder, try different pitches and tones, and many will try their best to emulate favorite singers. Dani, however, needed this experience on the mike to accurately hear himself out loud and make some necessary responses to change. It took a while for Dani to find sounds that he enjoyed, which included breathing into the mike as well as other humming type sounds. Working with Dani showed me that even our supposed "low- functioning" kids can become more aware of their surroundings and themselves, when given the opportunity. A simple microphone needs to be included in every caregiver's package of goodies. It's a technique not to be missed.

- Allow each child, no matter what the extent of his or her challenges, to use a microphone. Sometimes just hearing themselves breathe out loud will evoke a reaction.

- It takes some guesswork, but have each person sing along to a song. Try to find what genre of music, or particular song they like singing to. Even if they simply vocalize and make bizarre sounds to the music, allow them to experience this sensation.

- Some individuals will respond to music videos of the singers and songs they like. Put these on first, and evaluate your student or child's reactions. If it seems like a positive experience, then the next step is to play the music video while he or she holds the microphone. For those who lack the physical ability to hold the mike, it can be attached to a small stand and placed in front of the person's mouth. Head mikes, the kind that secretaries sometimes wear, are available at local music stores at a pretty reasonable price. These mikes are hands-free and are simply worn on the head like a set of headphones. Many students will try to mimic the singing and movements of the performers in the music videos. Remember, it's process, not product! Allow them freedom of expression both in terms of singing, and movement. Each student should feel that he or she is totally free to sing and move, no matter how awkward or strange it might look to an outsider. One of my students, Sierra, used to love to mimic Beyoncé. She held the mike, made some noises into it and occasionally, even pronounced a full word in the right place during the song. But it was her movements that won us all over, and the entire staff would cheer whenever she performed the song. Despite going through heart and back surgeries several times, and reduced to walking bent over, she did her absolute best on that stage. In our eyes, she was far greater than Beyoncé could ever imagine. There was rarely a dry eye during Sierra's glorious performances.

Sounds of Silence & Black-Light

There are many researchers and therapists today who use various sounds as part of the healing and recovery process. These are typically soothing types of sounds, such as pre-recorded sounds of actual ocean waves, the rainforest, birds chirping, a gentle rainfall, etc. Others use sounds of various instruments such as flutes, didgeridoos, sitars, and other meditative music often referred to as "new age." The basic gist of this approach is to relax and sooth the listener, and even to induce a meditative sense of consciousness. Like that saying made popular in the 60's - be here, now. The point is, that sounds, like music, may be very useful in easing tension and stress, and helping release more endorphins into the body. These little chemical powerhouses help trigger the "feel good" response, and an overall sense of wellbeing. I use sound therapy to help set the tone while my students enter my classroom. I want them to be hit with what I call the "wow" effect. My music room is in reality, a multi-sensory environment (MSE). As they enter, the room is totally dark except for a special screensaver that is projected onto the back wall and part of the ceiling, overhead. I choose interesting screensavers with beautiful images. One of their favorites is the undersea adventure. It's all done from a scuba diver's perspective, and one feels as if they are underwater with the diver, observing all the wonderful creatures and sea life. The computer is hooked up to speakers that play soothing, under-water bubbling-type sounds. I can let this run on its own, while I play live music to fit the amazing images moving about the room. Typically, I will play tunes such as "Under The Sea," and "Octopus's Garden" to jive with the visuals. The students play along on their percussion instruments or adaptive drums, others using keyboards, some playing on xylophones. The music, background sounds, and visuals all seem to fit together. Through this type of sensory integration, we maximize the learning and growth opportunities. It's not a double-whammy or even a triple-whammy. It's a quadruple-whammy! They hear, see, feel and move under the sea, and in the octopus's garden.

Best of both worlds. What could be better than playing drums under Black Light!

Tony, (front left), uses his head switch to operate the adaptive drum in bottom right corner, while other students play various percussion instruments. To my left is Larry Bisceglia, a fellow colleague in the field, and a true expert on special needs & assistive technology.

Parents and teachers can easily turn one room, or area of a room, into a MSE. This area should be dark, except for the special lighting effects in place. Here, black light is a big plus, for it automatically forces the individual to focus on what you have highlighted. Thus it could be a name, number, or a picture that you have prepared beforehand with glow-in-the-dark paint or on fluorescent paper. These items will totally "stand out" in black light. Place as many switches as possible in this area for the child to manipulate. These switches should be hooked up to activate visual and sensory- stimulating items, such as spinning color balls, lava lamps, moon flowers, bubble machines, small fans, etc. Many of these items can be purchased inexpensively at your local drug store, CVS, Walgreen's, Wal-Mart, etc. Care should be taken to properly tape or screw down the switches, and the cords should be tied neatly under the table out of reach of both feet and hands.

It's important to remember that sound is the very basis of music. Each instrument, each note in fact, is producing its own sound wave. Some we find pleasing. Others, such as very high pitches, sirens, jack hammers, etc., are rather annoying and stress inducing. People who live in major cities are often bombarded with sounds, both during the day and at night...all the more reason to set up your own quiet MSE for your child. You may find that it's so conducive for learning and relaxing, that you spend more time together in this area. Another point to remember, is that everything on the planet produces its own wavelength and vibrations. Thus, everything is somehow producing its own resonance- although most of these waves are beyond or below our hearing spectrum. Take that little piece of quartz, for example. You may have a large-sized crystal on your shelf at home. Quartz is used in all sorts of watches and time keeping devices due to its near-constant vibrations. The point here, is that we are actually living in a world in which everything is buzzing, humming, and resonating with life. This may help explain why sound/music therapy is so effective. We certainly need to be more selective with the sounds we subject ourselves and our kids to. A useful exercise is to jot down all the various noises and sounds you hear in a typical day. Keep a small notepad and pen handy as you go throughout your day and evening. You will probably be amazed at all that background noise — most of which we simply tune out and pay no attention to. But it's occurring, nonetheless. Whether we're aware of it all or not, our brains are forced to deal with this noise pollution in some manner or another.

Many researchers in the field of exceptional education, think that there are some kids who simply cannot turn off these obnoxious sounds as easily and as efficiently as others. You might walk into a room and be totally fine, ready to read, work, talk to others, and eat a meal. But someone with special needs may be hearing that overhead fluorescent light humming away at a loud, obnoxious decibel level. He or she might be hearing the water pipes shaking and making strange noises, or the car horns from two streets away. We need to be more sensitive to this world of sound and help manage the environment to make it more pleasant for our kids.

While Simon & Garfunkle sang about the "Sounds of Silence," there really is no such thing. There may be silence in a total vacuum, but not on our living planet, Mother Earth. It is full of intonations, and everything has its own cadence and subtle pulse. I guess we should be grateful that we cannot perceive all of these sounds, because I think it would drive us mad in no time. But we can make an effort to minimize annoying tones, and maximize the pleasant, positive ones for our child's health and wellbeing.

Smell The Roses!

This game is best played in the great outdoors, in locations as far away as possible from the hustle & bustle of busy streets. Deep inside a large park, will probably work fine. The goal here is to simply stop movement, lay back or sit down somewhere in a nature-type setting, and listen to all the sounds. Try to be quiet for a certain time period. This can be modified to accommodate individual needs. You might be able to stay quiet for 30 minutes or more, whereas a student or child might be able to remain silent for only a few minutes, or even less. You can bring large pictures of various birds and insects and then, when you hear these sounds, show the pictures to your child. The next time the sound occurs, try to have the student or child point to, or identify the picture that indicates the correct source. Students with higher cognitive abilities can fill out checklists as part of this wonderful outdoor learning game. You'll be amazed how quickly they'll know the difference between the sounds of cardinals and blue jays. If you get lucky, depending on where you live of course, you might even hear and see owls. Use this same experiential approach for identifying various plants and flowers, through their sense of smell. Pretty soon they'll be able to identify a flower or plant by keeping their eyes closed, and just using their noses! This is a fun way to get kids to slow down, smell the roses, and listen to the wondrous, and busy sounds of nature.

Group Singing & Signing

Singing, vocalizations, and music, are the combinations for some powerful medicine, but the next level, group singing, packs an even greater wallop. There's a certain dynamic flow and energy that occurs when more than one person is singing. It's a way for person to feel not only connected to the music, or to him or herself in a deeper way, but it's also a means to build strong, positive social bonds. These bonds would not exist without the music, and singing is the cement that holds it all together. I've seen this play out time and time again with my special needs students. A common remark I hear about these kids, is that they often "seem to be in their own private world," unable to make meaningful connections to anything or anyone on the "outside." We cannot pretend to know what goes on in their own worlds, inside their heads, bodies and souls. But we can and must do whatever it takes to help them build bridges to this outside world.

What about non-verbal students? Is there a way that he or she can participate more fully and reap the benefits of music? Besides listening and playing along on various instruments, I've found that many students who are either non-verbal or who simply don't use words proficiently, can learn to sing along using sign language. There are many decent computer programs on sign language. American Sign Language, (ASL), is a very popular one, and is recognized by most signers throughout America and, in fact, in many places around the world. Many students with Downs-syndrome enjoy using ASL and to my surprise, they never forget a sign. I work together with speech & language therapists to make sure that I am signing correctly, and with just a bit of effort and time, you too, will be signing away. Your special needs kids will, of course, pick it up much more quickly. Unlike myself, they never ever forget a sign - even if it's a song we haven't done in several years! While I have to dig out the old song sheets and give myself a refresher course regarding the appropriate signs, they are usually right on the money. In other words, sign language can be a very useful tool, not only for communication, but also as a means for non-verbal individuals to "sing along" and express themselves to music. Sign language is a type of movement-therapy that jives nicely with expressive music. It also allows kids with limited verbal abilities to get out there and be part of a performing group.

One particular time, we were performing at a senior center in the community. Our group was first known as the "Sing & Sign" Choir. Lately, they've been calling us, Dr. Laz & The Sensations, which I guess is more to my liking, because it highlights the fact that the special needs student performers are truly sensational! It's something remarkable to watch while some of them use ASL with live music. Others operate the adaptive drums, percussion instruments, and visual effects — including a bubble machine - from switches attached to their wheelchairs. Danielle, a 21-year-old young lady with severe cerebral palsy, operates the slideshows that go with each song. She has the cognitive ability to know when to hit her switch and move along to the next visual. Let's take one of our group's favorites, Wonderful World. When I sing, "I see trees of green," Danielle knows that the slide on the large screen should be one of green trees. The next line I sing is "red roses too." Here, she has to push her knee or head switch, which communicates wirelessly to the computer and moves on to the next slide of beautiful red roses. It's actually a rather hard song, with lots of chord changes, and during this particular performance I totally blanked out on the second verse, completely forgetting the words. But, as they say, the show must go on, so I did the first thing that came to mind - made up some words! To this day I have no blooming idea what I said, only that it probably would not have won me a Grammy. But there we were, in front of about 100 senior citizens. The funny thing was, that they were totally ok with the song. The only person who realized something wasn't too kosher, was Danielle. She gave me that "huh?" look and started to crack up, which, in turn of course, made me crack up. The four students with Downs-syndrome kept right on signing, thus totally saving the song. The seniors kept right on grooving to the beat. And Danielle kept on laughing. Right then and there, I vowed to always bring my music sheets to a gig.

Students with milder forms of special needs, such as ADD/ADHD, behavioral challenges, learning disabilities, etc., should be allowed and encouraged to participate in musical groups and singing choirs. No child should ever be told that his or her voice isn't good enough. So, they can't sing on perfect pitch. So what? They may not get to sing a solo, but their voices will blend in with the others and no one will be able to tell that anyone is off pitch. Teachers can make or break a child. The impact, for better or worse, that teachers have on an individual child cannot be underestimated.

When my wife Gittel was in elementary school, all of 7 years old, she tried out for the school choir. After hearing her voice, the "educator" asked her not to sing but just to pretend, by moving her lips. Gittel was devastated and to this day, won't even sing to herself in the shower. Now perhaps her voice back then wasn't anywhere near a

Barbara Streisand, or an Ella Fitzgerald, or an Aretha Franklin, but it also wasn't loud or screechy. It could have blended just fine with all those other kids' voices. And who knows what might have been? Perhaps being a part of that choir experience in 3rd grade might have inspired her to take some voice lessons. Maybe, just maybe, she would have ended up singing and performing today. Instead, this supposed teacher utterly squashed her enthusiasm, embarrassed her, and made her totally self-conscious about her voice. As a musician and performer, I can assure you that her singing is actually pretty darn good. Rather than opening a door of opportunity, her teacher closed it and threw away the key.

Our students need all the help they can get, and allowing them to be part of a larger singing and performing group serves many wonderful purposes. First, it's a tremendous boost to self-esteem, which is usually on the low side when it comes to special education kids. Secondly, these group activities help improve group skills. It's that simple. It's often been said that there's really only one way to learn expressive arts — and that's to be expressive! The same can be said for social skills. They can only be acquired by putting individuals in positive social situations where they can model appropriate behaviors. Put simply, to learn social skills one has to be social.

Two performers share a sweet moment during one of our shows.

During these awesome group music/choir activities they learn many positive attributes, including:

- *Patience*
- *To wait for cues*
- *To memorize words and model actions*
- *To not always be first, and that's it's ok to be in the background*
- *To delay gratification - that one doesn't have to be the superstar or center of attention to have fun*
- *To acknowledge another, to say, (or use a communication*

device to express), a yes, no or thank you
- *To share*
- *To feel part of a team, a group*
- *To enjoy each other's company*

There is also a kind of emotional, spiritual high when singing or performing together with others. There's this magical quality that occurs that is simply not available for a solo performer, as good as his or her voice might be. Somehow, singing with others, especially if harmonies are going on, creates a sense of wonder. It's like a full orchestra symphony, compared to a piano solo. The solo might be great, even enthralling, but the symphony will knock you off your feet. It's like the difference between Barry Manilow and the Beatles, or James Brown versus the Temptations. Barry has a smooth voice, capable of reaching the deep lows to the high notes - way up on the musical scale. But the Beatles' three & four part harmonies transport you to a different place. The "Father of Soul" could always rock a crowd, but the Temptations not only get you up on our feet - they melt you away. Our kids need the exposure of performing with others, whether it's through music, drama, or any of the expressive arts.

I was fortunate that I got to experience the wonders of singing with some rather large groups. I'm not referring to Barbershop quartettes or Doo-Wop street corner groups, (which I have had the pleasure of sharing some vocalizations with). And I'm not even talking about humming along to your favorite group while you wave your lighter high in the air at a Woodstock reunion, (which I've also had the pleasure of playing for). I'm speaking about singing along, in unison, with over 15,000 people on pretty much a once-a-week basis. These extraordinary events occurred whenever the Rebbe, the chief rabbi and spiritual leader of the Chabad movement, would hold special get-togethers for his Hassidim and followers. They often occurred on the Sabbath, when no microphone usage was permitted, but with literally thousands of folks singing or humming along. A microphone was the last thing on anyone's mind. These special events, known as Farbrengens, (which in Yiddish simply means gatherings), featured the Rebbe sharing various insights into community and religious matters. The Rebbe used these gatherings to inspire people to grow and improve themselves. Like Michael Jackson's awesome song, the Rebbe would often tell his followers to change the world for the better by starting with the "man in the mirror." "Even our imperfections," the Rebbe would add, "shouldn't stop us from increasing in acts of goodness and kindness."

In between the Rebbe's discourses, the Hassidim and guests, would sing various melodies, some fast and catchy tunes, others slow with almost haunting melodies. Most of the songs were, in fact, melodies without words and they would often go on for ten minutes or longer. The truth of the matter is, that these extraordinary gatherings were meant to be experienced, and thus, no words can truly capture or describe them accurately. But suffice it to say that you always left there somehow, a changed person. I would encourage you to search the Internet for some video footage of these unique gatherings. You can Google search under the terms: Lubavitcher Rebbe, Farbrengens, Chabad Rebbe, etc. It's something to be seen and heard, to really appreciate. Although I'm sure there were many people there who couldn't carry a C major to the store if it was packed in a box, the beauty was that nonetheless, they were there singing their hearts out with thousands of others, during this powerful, moving event. Each person's voice, no matter how on or off-key, was necessary to make it all happen.

During one of those gatherings several years ago, I got to witness something quite remarkable. Menachem Begin was Prime Minister of Israel and he had come to NYC to visit the Rebbe and ask for some advice and blessings. Needless to say, he sat up front at the main table, close by the Rebbe. Somehow, a room that had the capacity for 10,000 was holding nearly double that amount. After one of the Rebbe's discourses, the singing began, but this time it seemed to be even more important than usual. It was a slow and incredibly emotional melody, almost a pleading that would reach crescendos that took your breath away. People rocked or swayed back and forth, as they seemed to lose themselves in the haunting, powerful refrain. I looked around to see that not only did the Rebbe have his eyes closed, but so did PM Begin the other 19,998 people - all but two at that moment, the Prime Minister's personal bodyguard, and me. Despite the power of the melody, and the moment, the bodyguard stood there motionless, with only his head moving slowly back and forth while he scanned the crowd. He stood in the middle of the huge crowd, jam-packed in a hall like sardines in a can, everyone moving and groovin' to a tune that could melt a mountain and he simply did his job, seemingly unaffected by it all. I was more than impressed.

The equation of music might be something like: Music = Magic = Mystery = Medicine = Motivation. Music inspires change within the individual, and elicits responses from all facets of one's being, from the biological to the emotional, to the psychological and more. In fact, expressive therapies, including music, movement, visual arts & humor, are something that should be part & parcel of any hospital or doctor's recovery plan. Dr. Oliver Sacks, in his best-selling book "Musicophilia," writes about his very own recovery from a leg injury he sustained in a climbing accident. After being in a cast for an extended time period, he found it difficult to walk again. He somehow had forgotten the skill of putting one foot in front of another. He used music to aid in this process that so many of us simply take for granted. Somehow it was Mendelsohn's "Violin Concerto in E Minor," playing in his head, that got his legs in proper sync.

Nearly everyone is familiar with the incredible story of Gabrielle Gifford. Just to refresh your memory cells here, she's the congresswoman who was shot in the head outside a Tucson, Arizona supermarket by a deranged young man. ABC television recently ran a special edition of 20/20 about this remarkable woman called, "Gabby and Mark — Courage & Hope." With Diane Sawyer as the host, this story is incredibly uplifting, as Gabby continues to work so hard at recovery. As I watched this revealing interview and special feature, I was struck by the power of music, and the important role it has played in Gabby's remarkable progress. In fact, music continues to play a strong role in helping Gabby regain her use of language, memory, and even her capacity for movement.

I have experienced the healing power of music on several occasions. The first time I almost closed the door of opportunity. I let my ego get in the way. My band was hired to play for a holiday show in South Florida, and let's just say that crowd control wasn't a major issue. (Music also highlights the importance of quality over quantity. It was a lesson I needed to learn). I should have been tuned into this notion of expecting the unexpected. I should have been open to making the musical connections happen. When it comes to people and education, quality always wins out over quantity. But it was time for yet another wakeup call.

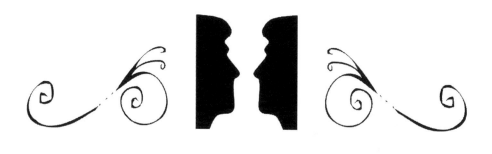

Quality Over Quantity

"**L**et's just call it a day," I said. "It was a nice try, but, as they say, no dice."

What do you mean?" he responded.

"I just feel bad for ya. That's all."

It was, to put it mildly, kind of depressing. I knew it was my ego acting up, but I simply couldn't help it. C'mon. Me, my whole group, a four-piece band, playing for 18 people?

Forget loading of all the music gear into my van. The drum set. The sound system. Those outrageously huge, heavy speakers. This was a gig I could have done completely acoustic. Who needed all these "extra" musicians? Never mind schlepping out to Weston, Florida, a good 45-minute ride from my abode. There were two factors operating here. One was that I truly felt bad for the rabbi that it was such a low turnout for this Chanukah party. Second, I felt bad for, well, myself. Didn't I deserve a much larger crowd? You know, a few thousand at least? Some cops on hand for crowd control? This was the Dr. Laz & the CURE band here, amigos. The first Jewish rapper and reggae star, going back, way back, before Matisyahu was in diapers.

I just couldn't get excited about unloading, setting everything up and playing.

"You can throw on some CDs," I continued. "I feel bad taking your money for something like this."

"No," he insisted, shaking his head. "You play. Do your thing. It's not about quantity. It's quality."

Two more folks came in, so we were now up to a whopping 20. This was beginning to feel more like a family birthday party, and not a major holiday show.

I knew he was right, of course, but I was having a rough time getting psyched for the gig. My band members could see it written all over me.

"Abba," my drummer son Yossi said, "you always tell us that."

"What's that?"

"The same thing that the rabbi told you. That it's quality, not quantity, that matters."

"My words coming back to haunt me, eh?"

"Yeah. Remember story #46?"

"What's that one?"

"Binghamton."

"Ah yes, good ol' 46," I answered, gently pinching his cheeks. "That one indeed. And when you're right — you're right. Okay, let's set it all up and hope for the best."

Binghamton was indeed the classic case of quality over quantity. It was a special weekend event for the Chabad Student Center at University of Binghamton. Yours truly was the guest speaker, which meant I had to give a talk/presentation on Friday night and Saturday, and then play a gig on Saturday evening. All went smoothly until Saturday morning. You see, I was invited to give the rabbi's Saturday morning class for the students. Of course, I told the rabbi, as the featured guest speaker it would be an honor.

Friday evening's meal was amazing, as more than 125 college students attended. We sang special Sabbath melodies, had some awesome homemade challah breads, and made a whole lot of toasts. Mostly as a result of the latter, I kind of overslept that Saturday morning class. I awoke, in fact, to the rabbi's loud, animated voice coming from down the hallway, fairly close to my bedroom. Yikes, I said out loud, jumping out of bed. The situation rapidly deteriorated as I quickly realized that my clothes were, in fact, in the bathroom. This meant that I had to cross the hallway in my PJ's, Davey Crockett ones, of course — they were a present, okay?

But this was no easy feat, since the hallway was in full view of those listening attentively to the rabbi's teachings. I debated my options. Wait till the class was over, and then get dressed. This was quickly nixed, because that would make me look even worse, getting there so late. So I decided to be brave and make a mad dash for the bathroom, get dressed Superman style, and then stroll in as unobtrusively as possible. I also decided that I would fly past the hallway and not even turn my head towards the rabbi's enthusiastic voice, and the many students that were, for lack of a better expression, on time.

I leaped past the open hallway, jumped into the bathroom, donned my lovely Sabbath clothes, did a quick gargle, brush of the hair, and strolled as cool as a cucumber into the large room at the end of the short hall. The whole time, (it took me perhaps, four and a half minutes), the rabbi's voice continued to reverberate with emotion. It wasn't loud, but you could tell that he was very into it and that whatever he was saying meant a lot to him. No way was there just 15 students, or 20. For such an enthusiastic delivery there had to be 50. Maybe even a hundred. But upon entering the room I was stopped cold in my tracks. I was motionless, and my mouth dropped open in utter shock. The rabbi was learning with one student! One! I was, putting it mildly, totally amazed. If that would've been me, I probably would have told that one student to come back later, and caught some more shut-eye.

The rabbi later told me that he'd never be in this business to begin with, if he made quantity an issue. "I started with one or two students for Friday night dinner. We're now well over a hundred! The Saturday morning class is a little harder, but we carry on no matter who, or how many show up."

Indeed.

I tried to keep this story in mind as the band, yes, my four-piece band, set up for this small, very intimate holiday party. With all our sound equipment and amps, we had enough power to play Madison Square Garden, but here we were in this tiny storefront inside a typical, Florida strip mall.

During one of my rap tunes, I went out into the small crowd. Most were sitting in chairs that ran along the wall. The rabbi and his wife were busy passing out dreidles, potato pancakes with applesauce, and other festive treats.

I'd say the first part of the sentence, and they'd have to respond with the appropriate word. I went over the words for a few minutes then the band kicked it in with the drums and bass.

"Working together is the way to..."

I gently put the wireless mike in front of their mouths, one by one, going down the row.

"Be," came the right response.

"That's how we survive through..."

The next person in line shouted into the mike "history!"

"So do the mitzvos cuz it's lots of..."

"Fun!" the next person sang out.

"The peace will reign and the world'll be..."

"One!" an older gentleman said in a rather low tone, into the mike. His eyes lit up as he responded and continued to kind of hold the mike close to his mouth. So I figured he wanted to rap some more with me, so we repeated the entire chorus several times, with him coming in on cue each time.

We finished my rap on racial harmony and several more tunes. It was a good 45 minutes before we took a break. A middle-age woman and a younger gal came up to me as I was shutting off the sound system. I noticed that they both were crying and my first thought was, ooops, sorry it was so bad, or that it was way too loud.

"I have to tell you something," the older lady said.

"Sure," I said, expecting the worst.

"You know the man who you did the rap song with?"

"Which one?"

"The one who rapped the entire chorus with you?" the younger one said.

"Yeah, sure. What's up?"

"I'm his wife, and this is my daughter," she said. "I want you to know something. He had a stroke about six months ago. The doctor told him months ago that he can and should start speaking again. But he hasn't. At least, not until tonight."

"This is the first time we've heard his voice in months," the daughter said with tears streaming down her cheeks.

122

I was speechless, especially when I realized how close I had come to walking out on the gig. Look at the incredible opportunity I would have missed if I had given in to my stubborn ego. Thank God both the rabbi and my son had not let quantity win over quality.

"Take this," I said, giving them one of my CD's. "Let him listen to the music and try doing my rap with him. He's got that song down!"

Music is the language of the soul, but I think its effects on the body are equally profound.

One time I brought my special needs choir to a senior home for a performance. My students were singing and communicating using American Sign Language, (ASL), while I backed them up with live music. We usually end with an upbeat number like, "This Little Heart Of Mine," or "I Can See Clearly Now." At this point, my students go into the audience and pick a dance partner. Sometimes, it's one of my wheelchair-bound students holding hands and "dancing" with a senior who's also in a wheelchair. We all try to get the crowd rockin' at this juncture in the show, and these last tunes have been known to go on for close to 10 minutes. I had the wireless head mike on, so I was able to roam the crowd as Zahava, my assistant on the keyboards, kept the tune going strong.

As I passed this one elderly woman, she actually reached out her hands to me, indicating that she too wanted to dance. Not one to refuse such an invitation, I quickly bent down and removed her wheelchair tray. She was somewhat on the heavy side, but with some assistance from one of our parent volunteers she slowly stood on her feet by her chair, as I held her by supporting her arms and upper body. She was definitely groovin' to the music as she rocked a bit up and down in harmony to the beat. We both wore smiles from ear to ear. But then I noticed some of the home workers looking intently at us. Some were actually crying. One of the caretakers had her hand over her mouth, as if in shock. Had I done something wrong? My brain went into overdrive. Oh great, I thought to myself, she probably had hip replacement surgery a few days ago and here I am getting her up from her wheelchair, and forcing her to stand way too early!

When the song was over, I carefully lowered my dance partner into the safety of her wheelchair. I was afraid to look at the home staff that was standing by the wall, but I couldn't escape my fate. Two of them were briskly walking over to me. Perhaps my school board medical insurance would cover any damages I had just done?

"Unbelievable," one of the senior home staff said, grabbing my upper arm. "Completely unbelievable."

"Oh, I uh... well..." I stammered. "I'm really..."

"Yes," the second woman said ignoring my attempt at self-defense. "We've never seen this."

"I didn't mean any…"

"We've both been here over two years," the first chimed in. "We've never seen her out of her wheelchair. Except for bedtime, of course. But even then, we only take her out of the chair, and straight into her bed."

"It's true," said her colleague. "This is the first time I've seen her standing. Ever!"

They both shook my hand and, to my utter surprise, said, "it's like a miracle!"

Before we left the senior home to head back to our school, I met with the home's director. She too was in awe over what had occurred.

"The miracle," I told her, "is that music can create real magic for people…no matter how old or how challenged. You've should do daily music and dance therapy for her, and for all your clients. You'll be amazed at what they can do."

I also made sure that they booked us for a future gig. The point here, is that we need to keep trying until we find something, some song or words or sound, that opens up a door inside our children, students, or even elderly adults who haven't stood in several years.

You never know what might click and make that magic of music take effect. For Andrea it was a tambourine and a very simple song. And yet, for some reason, it worked for her. For Danielle, it was using assistive technology that enabled her to be part of the band. For Dani, it was using a microphone that helped him evaluate and change his own behavior. For that man at the holiday show and the woman who danced with me at that senior center, it was feeling the rhythm and beat of a song, and suddenly getting that urge, that need to stop being a passive observer; that the time was now to be expressive and creative, and become an active participant.

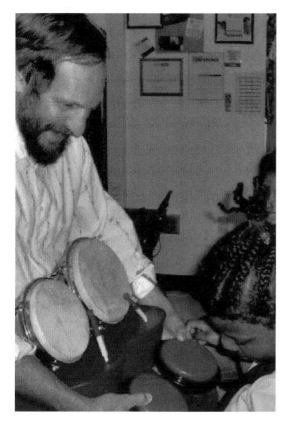

Adaptive drums & assistive technology. Switches enable students with challenges to become more-active participants in the magic of making music.

In an interesting article entitled, "Music Gets Backing For Addressing Autism," from the Miami Herald, (Jean Hwang, March 24, 2009), music therapist Majin Kim is quoted as saying that, "music may be effective because it compliments the cognitive abilities of people with autism, which includes a strong inclination for creating patterns." In other words, the inherent structure and patterns within music may indeed be a unique medium that captures the attention of individuals with autism. What is clear is that, at this point in time, we are only beginning to understand the inner workings of the brain when it is exposed to music, both in terms of passive listening, and actively making music. It is also quite evident that music can and should be, a powerful tool in any parent, teacher, or care provider's kit.

We need to keep trying until we find something, some song or words or sound, or even a genre of music that opens a door inside a child or student, and inside ourselves. The doors of discovery, growth, and creativity are waiting to be opened. Music, and in particular making music, is the great key.

CHAPTER 4

Students As Teachers

"Few things help an individual more than to place responsibility upon him, and to let him know that you trust him."

— *Booker T. Washington*

"If you want children to keep their feet on the ground, put some responsibility on their shoulders."

— *Abigail Van Buren*

"I don't think I can do this," Leland protested. "Look at 'em, man."

"Yeah. So?"

"Well, they're you know..."

"They're what?"

"I don't know. All smart, and looking so, I don't know, professional and everything!"

"You're just as smart as them," I said, trying to keep his spirits up. "No, in fact, ya know what? You're smarter!"

He just shook his head back and forth, not really believing what I was saying.

"Look," I continued. "They're all nice and good, and yes, they are high achievers. But they know nothing from real world stuff. You got both... book smarts and real-world smarts!"

Life is often filled with the little surprises, the curve balls that truly keep us on our toes. Steve Lipman, a lifelong buddy and writer for a bunch of different newspapers, wrote a nice long article on a peer & cross-age tutoring program that I started at Dr.

Martin Luther King, Jr. Community School. It featured utilizing special needs students as peer-teachers in this Buffalo, NY public school. We're not talking straight-A honors students from private, Ivy League schools. And we're not talking students from a Rabbinical College, where I experienced first-hand the wonders of this peer, interactive-learning style. It worked wonders for me. I figured it might just do the trick for my tough, inner-city students — adolescent males with learning, emotional and behavioral challenges. Throw in some crazy hormonal issues, and to put it mildly, there was never a dull moment in my class.

Steve's article on my program, entitled "Talmudic Ideas Used in the Ghetto," complete with some pictures, hit the front page of section B of the NY Times. Suddenly, folks from around the country and world, were contacting me for more info on this educational goldmine. A few people even sent donations. But I was particularly surprised when I got a request to present at a statewide conference on educational programs that work. They wanted as much info as possible on my tutoring program, which was indeed working its magic at Dr. MLK School. I agreed, on the condition that my student tutors attend and present with me. The two tutoring programs being featured were an exclusive prep school and mine. To make matters worse for Leland, we were presenting second. He had to follow those superstar, straight-A, top-notch students, who were, of course, all dressed to the nines.

Leland raised his eyebrows and gave me that look that conveyed as much doubt as fear.

"Don't worry," I said, patting him on the shoulders. "Just be yourself. And I'm sitting here, right next to ya, ok?"

"Might be better if you were in front," he responded with a smile.

"Block the tomatoes and eggs, huh?"

We both cracked up, but I knew that Leland would really touch these educators at this conference on student tutoring programs. Leland would have to follow a presentation by a local private school, where their selection of tutors was based on scholastic performance and character assessments. Their school used only the crème de la crème for tutors. I was using my tough, inner-city, special needs students, who also frequented the principal's office — but for very different reasons.

I simply couldn't resist the test. This magic formula worked so well for me back at the Rabbinical College in Morristown, NJ, (which we promptly dubbed the Mo-Town Yeshiva), I was anxious to give it the hardcore test in a public school setting. During my undergraduate days at University of Buffalo, I probably hit the books for an average of eight hours a week. On a good week, mind you. I hit that number on a daily basis at the Mo-Town Yeshiva. On the one hand, it was true that being more mature, I was more focused. But here's the clincher. I put in eight plus hours a day and totally loved it. I remember sometimes waking up in the middle of the night smiling. There was no forced effort. No fear of tests pushing me on. No dread of criticism from supervising adults. I simply could not get enough of the learning. I attributed much of this dynamic change and growth to the learning style itself.

The Rabbinical College utilizes what is called the "chavruso" method of learning, and it's the very backbone of authentic Jewish education. It's also been around a long, long time. To my surprise, according to the Talmud, this was the same learning style and format that Moses engaged in on Mt. Sinai. I somehow have always maintained this childish notion that Moses goes up the mountain and the good Lord just kind of blasts him with these rays. "Stand still," he might have rebuked this awesome Biblical leader. "I'm about to zap you with some instant, spiritual knowledge. At the end of your 40-day visit, head on back and share it all with the masses. Okay, now put your arms out, close your eyes, cuz here it comes!" Instead, the Talmud tells us that Moses had to work hard at this learning, to put himself into it, to experience the frustrations and triumphs of personal growth and true learning. His learning with the "Boss," was done in this give & take, active participatory fashion. No spoon-feeding. No blasting gamma rays. Just student-centered, peer learning at its best.

"Chavruso," in Hebrew, comes from the word Chaver, which means friend. It also comes from the Hebrew word "chebar" which means bond or attachment. Thus, the learning process takes place with your chaver, your partner, with whom you form this cohesive partnership.

This awesome style of learning is an active, motivational process that puts the onus of learning smack dab where it belongs - on your shoulders. It's as student-centered as it gets. The teacher functions mainly as a guide. You get stuck on a certain section, lost on a particular meaning or definition of terms, you do your best to figure it out with your partner. When that doesn't work out, then you turn to other friends who might just have some ideas. At this point, if you're still stuck and unable to move on, then you turn to the teacher for some help. There's no spoon-feeding allowed in a student tutoring/learning system. Rather, the essence of learning takes place between you and your learning partner as you delve deeper into the text and material. It's an active, participatory, discovery process. It's the exact opposite of the teacher-speaks/student-listens system, which often translates into teacher-bores/student-sleeps format. No one falls asleep when engaged in peer or cross-age tutoring, unless of course, the individual didn't get any sleep the night before. This paired, interactive learning format is another powerful tool in the student-centered approach.

First, let's define some important terms. Peer tutoring usually refers to two or more students of similar age working together on some academic area, subject, or project. Cross-age tutoring involves an older student working with a younger student, or group of students. This second approach is usually more effective for individuals with special needs, since it places the child in the better-defined role of being the teacher.

Leland had some serious learning issues, but they had moved out of the picture since he began working with students much younger than himself. Leland was 14 at that time, and reading somewhere near a 3rd-grade level. But this wasn't an issue, since he was tutoring kids in first grade. It was the first time in his life that he was asked to teach, to give to another. It was a breakthrough, life-altering experience for Leland. More than any remedial reading or math program, or psychological counseling session, this was the medicine he needed.

The first group completed their presentation and it was, I admit, a solid job. Everyone at the private school had obviously embraced the student-tutoring project. They showed slides that depicted the tutors in action, working diligently with other students. The tutors explained that they were required to have nearly perfect records, in order to become responsible and effective teachers for their peers. Leland squirmed in his seat when one PowerPoint presentation dealt with the impressive credentials of the tutors, listing various school and civic awards extended to them during middle school and high school.

"Dang Laz," he leaned over and whispered in my ear. "I could list the number of schools I got kicked out of, and it still wouldn't be as long as their awards!"

"They ain't nothing," I jived back. "Candy coated. Soft ice cream, brother. We got the real stuff."

It was our inner city, rap/reggae joke between us. Whenever something seemed too out of touch with the real world, too complacent, too goody-goody, my students would respond with statements like "you soft!" or "you soft ice-cream, bro!" A more recent reggae tune featured a line that simply said "no ice-cream sound." It all translates into the same general meaning; no wimpy stuff allowed. Keep it real. Keep it strong.

We chuckled again and I was hoping that my humor tactics would help him relax a bit.

The conference chairperson then introduced me, and I guess he couldn't resist adding how, "this next program will show you that peer tutoring works even in schools and with kids who usually don't!"

It was a great line, I had to admit, but kind of a dig at the same time.

"We'll be waiting for him outside after the conference," I whispered in Leland's ear before taking the podium. For the next 45 minutes I described our student-tutoring project and some of the struggles we faced, including getting both administrators and fellow-teachers on board. The main difference between the first school and us, was that my program was designed to mainly benefit the tutors. It turned out, I explained, that everyone showed growth, and demonstrated gains. This included the tutors, their younger students, the cooperating teachers, and in fact, the entire school. After a Q&A session, Leland took center stage to deliver the knockout punch.

The entire hall of more than 100 people suddenly became very quiet. For many, I thought, it was probably the first time they were formally addressed by a teenage African-American male. Although a supreme athlete on the field, Leland has kind of a shy demeanor, especially in public. Someone came up to raise the volume on the microphone.

"Thank you for inviting me," Leland started. "I'm not used to speaking like this. You know, in public and all."

He looked at me for some reassurance. I gave him a quick, subtle thumbs-up sign.

"My background is, well, not exactly like those other student tutors you heard from. They are great. I wish I had even one of their awards. But I never taught anyone before. Never thought of myself as being able to teach anyone anything, except maybe how to play ball, or catch, run, make a move, you know, outside, outdoors away from school. In fact, I never really liked school either. Always hating it, and getting into trouble."

The audience shifted somewhat nervously in their seats. I was amazed at how composed and relaxed Leland was. He had no prepared notes, no official text to read from. He was speaking straight from the heart.

"When Dr. Laz told me about the project and how he wanted me to be a teacher for other students, I was, well, kinda surprised. I never figured I could do it, or that I would like it at all. But right from the start it was cool. I work with three different kids at our school during the day and they really like learning with me, too. It flips me out but I've become a pretty good teacher."

I almost started crying when the audience broke out in spontaneous applause for him. They were truly moved by this tough inner-city kid who couldn't get a break if he tried paying for one. Now here he was - a successful tutor/teacher with some positive direction in his life. The Q&A part with Leland went on for over 30 minutes, until they announced that lunch was being served. They simply couldn't get enough of him.

Everyone can be a tutor!

It's an educational gold mine that's not just for the well off, the well to do, and the well respected. Individuals with special needs can and should be placed in the role of tutor.

Remember: If one person knows their ABC's and another doesn't, then the former becomes the teacher, and the latter becomes the student. Any skill can be emphasized. I've had wheelchair-bound, non-verbal students teach others, including myself, how to use their communication devices. I should say, "try" to teach me. It's an absolute riot to watch them become utterly frustrated and start cracking up, because I'm a mighty slow learner when it comes to these pretty, sophisticated devices - especially the ones that can conjugate and do verbs. After 10 hands-on sessions I still cannot explain to someone else how those expensive, complicated, communication machines work! But it's a wonderful role-reversal for them to try teaching me, their teacher. Now remember that the whole time they're teaching me, they are actually using their head or knee switches to operate the devices. I, on the other hand, am able to use my fingers to push all the buttons. So, you'd think it would be easy for me to get the skills down. Oh well. For my students it's an exercise in patience. For me, it gives me gut-level, emotional frustration, and thus, a newfound sense of empathy for what my body-trapped students go through on a regular basis.

As mentioned briefly in the previous chapter, a peer-tutoring program also features one other component that is seldom used in a traditional classroom. Verbalizing! In plain English, talking out loud. Not that the sound barrier has to be broken here, but this paired, interactive learning style means that you're verbalizing the concepts you're learning about. You're not just sitting in a quiet corner somewhere thinking about the periodic table. In the peer-tutoring format, you're enunciating the elements out loud. Your ears get to hear what the subject matter is, which stimulates and actively fires other areas of the brain. I think this energetic process helps facilitate the magical bridge from short-term to long-term memory. Listening is, after all, passive, and might very well need some sort of kinetics to help facilitate learning. Speaking for myself, I know that I cannot learn new skills, or even new facts, by simply listening to someone describe them, whether he or she is giving a public lecture, or I'm listening to a CD in my car on the way to work. I need to do something more concrete for the material to sink in. This means I say the fact or piece of information out loud as I hear it, or I actually write it down on paper.

Allow your students to verbalize

— (say out loud) —

the facts or information they're hearing or reading about.

It's usually frowned upon in educational circles, but pay this no heed, folks. In fact, I remember my primary grade teachers telling us to do the very opposite. "No reading out loud," they demanded. "That's poor reading!" It is no surprise that most teachers use this strategy. They want quiet classrooms. To have 20 or 30 little buggers reading out loud at the same time picks the decibel level up a few notches. But research has shown that it's actually very effective reading. Verbal rehearsal, saying those words out loud, does a better job of tickling those long-term memory brain cells than the common practice of silent reading. I invite you now to come to Scotland with me, where I had the opportunity to present at the First World Congress on Special Education. This impressive conference, sponsored by CEC , (the Council for Exceptional Children), was held at Stirling University and featured some incredible sessions by educators from all around the world. The conference also hosted some wonderful ambiance, including a bagpipe band and really powerful Scottish beer, served of course, by men in kilts. The first night of the conference I found myself wandering the campus at four in the morning, holding an open umbrella! And no, it wasn't raining a drop. Just how I got that umbrella remains a mystery to this day, but suffice it to say that one should definitely not drink dark Scottish beer on an empty stomach. The miracle was that I somehow made it to my 8:30 morning session, and for the most part, sounded somewhat coherent.

One of the featured speakers at this worldwide conference presented on the connection between learning and memory retention. He was from a team of three educators who had investigated various techniques to improve memory recall. It was a very thorough study, with more than a thousand students in the experimental group from all across the United States. Thus, their sample size was mighty impressive, as most educational studies are conducted with a much smaller population, usually fewer than 100. These researchers looked at all sorts of methods to enhance memory function for our special kids, including: color-highlighting the material, verbal praise, tangible rewards, repetition, using various symbols, and real-life objects, etc. During their presentation, one of the researchers uttered the following words, "The best way for kids to remember something they're learning is actually a two-fold approach. We found that using a peer-learning approach combined with verbally saying the material out loud, is an unbeatable system."

I was so taken by that innocent statement that I actually exclaimed in my own verbal-rehearsal style, (somewhat loudly), "Oh wow!" I was, of course, immediately "hushed" by several colleagues in attendance. But I simply could not contain my amazement and joy over such a proclamation. This was the very approach I was involved with at the Rabbinical College back in Morristown, NJ and it had indeed, worked wonders. Sitting in the audience at Stirling University, I was privy to hearing about the valid, educational legitimacy of it all. Upon my completion of rabbinical studies, I was more than anxious to put this educational doozy to the test.

Would peer tutoring work with inner-city kids? What about students with behavioral and emotional problems? Could it help people with special needs? I ended up doing my Master's thesis on various studies that put this unique learning strategy to the test for students with behavioral problems. Published in the Journal of Learning Disabilities (1980), the study is called "I Must Be Good If I Can Teach! - Peer Tutoring with Aggressive and Withdrawn Children." The results of this study show that both the tutors and the tutees made significant behavioral gains. Those classified as having aggressive oriented behaviors and authority issues seemed to calm down by functioning as student teachers for their peers. And those kids who demonstrated withdrawn behaviors seemed to come out of their shell when working with their peers. They eagerly looked forward to working with their "cool new teachers."

My Ph.D. dissertation took things a step further. This study utilized peer and cross-age tutoring for students who were habitually truant and who, for the most part, arrived tardy when they did show up. You can read the full article at the SAGE Journals Online website at: http://ldx.sagepub.com. Simply search my name and you'll find the complete study for your perusal. It's called "The Effectiveness of Cross-Age Tutoring With Truant, Junior High School Students with Learning Disabilities." (Lazerson, D.

Journal of Learning Disabilities, 1988.) This particular study was most encouraging, because the tutors demonstrated significant increases in their on-time and school attendance behaviors. Simply put, they now liked coming to school, and felt that they had a good reason for being there. They also made notable gains regarding their self-concept, and felt more positive about themselves. Tutors were quoted as saying things like "I am worthwhile," and "for the first time in a long time, I feel like I matter to someone." Both study projects were highly successful and gave me the encouragement and ammunition to spread the word about this awesome strategy.

Many miles away from my rabbinical college in Morristown, NY, and in a very different kind of academic setting, Leland became my superstar student mentor/teacher. He worked with students in the younger grades who needed extra help. It was a system that benefited everyone, including Leland and his students and teachers who lacked paid-professional assistants in the classroom. Leland quickly found his niche as a "teacher," and even offered cooperating teachers suggestions concerning the specific methods and materials that worked with his new students. This cross-age tutoring program also helped Leland break through the self-fulfilling prophecy of his special-needs label. Pretty soon, as the weeks of tutoring went by, Leland's teachers no longer saw him as a student with disabilities, but rather as someone with abilities. More importantly though, Leland began to see himself in this light. We had found, at long last, an open door for him. This student-as-teacher project was his ticket to ride.

My Ph.D. from University of Buffalo is actually in Research & Evaluation, and so I set up the project in a way that I could actually test, and determine just how effective, (or not), the program was. I took data on all the tutors and tutees — yes, that is the correct word to describe the tutor's students, (think of employer & employee), and compared the data on a pre-treatment and post-treatment basis. In other words, I obtained baseline data on all the students involved in the project. How long, on average, could they stay focused on task? How did they feel about themselves? How did they perform academically? Then, a few months later, after they had become engaged in the tutoring program, I looked at these areas again. To my pleasant surprise, (although, maybe shock is a more fitting description), the tutors demonstrated significant growth in all of these important areas, showing dramatic improvement in their ability to stay on task, in self-concept, and in some specific academic subjects. Not too shabby, considering all this was accomplished without having to buy extra textbooks, or hire psychiatrists or therapists. In fact, there were no extra expenses, whatsoever. Yes, I know what you're thinking. It's almost too good to be true.

If it worked for my students with behavioral, emotional, and learning difficulties, it can work wonders for your child or student too. In this day and age, when school systems across the country are experiencing budget cuts, this is an educational gold mine that delivers the goods, and requires no extra money to set up. Although I must admit to a few minor, out-of-pocket expenses. I took the tutors out to eat as special rewards, and brought them with me to present at various educational conferences. The school PTA also sponsored an awards assembly, where the tutors received ribbons and plaques. For many, it was the first time they had received an honor at school. But little did I realize, that the best was yet to come.

Lessons from a Detention Home

O ne evening after a long day at work, I was lying back on the couch with a nice warm cup of mint tea and the Buffalo News. I'm convinced that the first two sections of the paper are there to protect the sports section. One particular article under 'local news' caught my attention. It dealt with a local lock-down detention home. They had a real problem on their hands. After the kids served the required time for their various offenses, and had demonstrated the necessary behavioral improvements, they were released to join society again. But within months, and in some cases just weeks, they'd screw up royally and find themselves back inside the system. They call this particular phenomenon, recidivism. In a nutshell, it describes the tendency to revert back to old, established behavioral patterns — in this case, delinquent, criminal-type behaviors. Thus began round two or three, or four or more, for some of these troubled teens. Something was terribly amiss - and to make matters worse - detention home facilities across the country were reporting similar results. Whatever rehab these kids were receiving behind these locked doors, it was clearly missing the mark. Some had indeed made the necessary adjustments and become successful contributing members of society at large. A significant number of these teenagers, however, were not making it. For those who ended up back where they started, the hole seemed to get bigger and darker each time, as if they were being sucked into an ominous whirlpool of failure.

Wasn't the fear of going back to a detention home enough to keep them towing the line and behaving properly in the real world? Somehow, I couldn't believe that life was so sweet and good behind those locked doors and barbed wire fences that they preferred it to one of freedom, and going about their business as they wished. The article described these kids as, "spiraling out of control". The detention home teens felt as if they had no control over their own lives. Sitting there on my living room couch, the light went on in my cerebral cortex. Could I? Should I? Dare I? Perhaps it was the challenge, but I couldn't help but think that maybe, just maybe, these teens needed some new, magical medicine. It was time to take things to the next step on the ladder. On the first rung of the ladder, (it happened in that rabbinical college), a virtual non-book-learner, (yours truly), was turned into an 8 hour-a-day man. Next, came my Master's degree thesis, where I took kids who were diagnosed with behavioral and emotional problems and put them into a peer-tutoring program. In that study, many of the students demonstrated remarkable gains. On that rung of the ladder, my tough inner-city crew at Dr. MLK flew high within their new roles as teachers and givers. But detention home teens? Don't be crazy, I told myself. Bringing troubled teens from a lock-down detention facility into a public school would be anything but easy. Despite the warnings, I simply couldn't resist. The very next day I made some phone calls and began the long, red-tape process of putting this unique tutoring project into action.

My principal at the time was Dr. Dixon, a true visionary for educational reform who earned this reputation in part, because he would literally do anything for his school and students. He bravely gave me the green light. Somehow we managed to secure the necessary permission from parents, cooperating teachers, and even city officials. Within two months it was up and running. Since it was a trial project that had a number of risk elements, we came up with a plan that allowed three teens from the detention home to be escorted to our school. Adult-escorts not only brought them in and out of the building, but also remained in the classrooms with the juvenile delinquents, (JD's), to ensure there'd be no slip-ups with the supervision. The facility staff told me they weren't worried about these teens becoming violent or anything like that. They simply didn't want the JD's running out the back door, and booking it for freedom on the streets.

After a few short months of engaging in the tutoring project, the JD tutor-teachers had earned enough points, (and trust), to come to our school on their own. It was absolutely amazing to watch their transformation. I'll never forget the day there was a torrential downpour in Buffalo. The tutoring had to be cancelled due to the horrible weather. It was my job to inform the younger students that their special teenage teachers wouldn't be in and that we would reschedule in a day or two, weather permitting. But just as I was making the calls from my desk phone, the door to my room suddenly opened, and in walked John. He was drenched to the bone from head to toe.

"Hi, Dr. Laz," he said with a grin. "Hey, couldn't let a little rain stop me from teaching my students, ya know!"

I could only shake my head in amazement. If only I had such determination and fortitude toward my own teaching job.

Fortunately, I had a bunch of clothes in my closet, and he quickly changed and went off to work with "his" students. The three tutors from the detention home eventually made it past the revolving door, this recidivism that plagues most lock-down and jail facilities. Like Leland, the tutoring project became their ticket to ride, to become positive, contributing members of society-at-large. To this very day, I write articles, and preach to anyone who'll listen, about the incredible merits of a student-tutoring program. You can read the complete study in the UK's Journal of Emotional & Behavioural Disorders (2005). The study is called; "Detention home and a public school - a cooperative peer tutoring trial project."

Many years, (and many projects) later, I've learned some important things about setting up and maintaining these student-tutoring programs. I've gleaned together a top-10 list of things to keep in mind when setting up your student tutoring projects. The sweat and hard work was done. Why reinvent the wheel? You'll probably come up with a few new ones of your own, but I gladly share this list with you.

10 Commandments of A Successful Peer & Cross-Age Tutoring Program

1) Provide training for the tutors.

I tell new tutors that a good teacher has to know two main things:

- One is how to reward & praise your student.

- The second is how to correct a student in a positive manner.

HOW? Role-play these scenarios. "Oh wow, Amy, you did a great job with that." Or when correcting, "Good try Amy, but let's try it again and take a closer look." They always like it when we role-play the wrong way of teaching: "No you bloomin' idiot," Or "Nice try, meathead." This way they clearly see what to do, and equally important, what not to do.

2) Structure the tutoring sessions.

Give the tutors very specific skills to work on with their kids. Provide the tutors with the necessary materials. Eventually, they will grab the bull by the horns, (on their own), and come up with new skills to work on with the tutees. Some will even design their own materials. But initially, give the tutor all the goods to succeed.

3) Control the time of the sessions.

In general, I've found that the sessions are not productive if they're either too short, or too long. Seems like 15 minutes on the short end and 30 on the long, helps maximize success.

4) Allow for tutor feedback.

Although this step depends on the age and cognitive skill level of the tutors, most really benefit from this process: Meet with them at least once a week for no less than 10 minutes. Ask them for their thoughts and feelings on the program. Remember, any time you take the time to ask a student what they think about something, he or she feels valuable and validated. You may just end up being amazed about their forethought and the quality of their input during these pow-wow sessions. After only a few meetings, my tutors began to sound like student teachers from the university, offering practical suggestions and ideas on ways to really help their kids.

5) Meet with cooperating teachers.

This keeps your main players on board. After all, you don't want the cooperating teachers to feel dumped on. It has to work for them, or it doesn't fly. Take the time to hear their thoughts and concerns. A successful peer or cross-age tutoring program, is really a team effort.

6) Initially keep the roles clearly defined.

This is crucial for the child with special needs. Keep the tutor and tutee roles as clear as the mid-day sun in Miami. This enables the older tutor to really be the teacher. If little Junior from pre-school started calling the shots, it would probably not be good for his or her self-concept. Thus, you need to make sure that this is a skill the tutor can indeed teach, and which the tutee actually needs to learn. Eventually, when the cross-age tutoring project proves successful, you can begin to think about initiating a similar-aged tutoring program, but first things first. Set your program up so the special needs kids can experience the magic rush of becoming successful teachers and tutors.

7) Set up a point & reward system.

This can be for both the tutors and tutees. How well did they work together? Did they both show up to the session on time? Is the tutor exhibiting proper teaching skills, i.e., giving verbal praise when appropriate? Correcting in a positive and appropriate manner? These points can go for a grand prize, or even a weekly prize, (or in some cases, a daily prize), to help insure maximum success.

8) Not just for the elite corps.

Try out various tutoring roles for your child or student with special needs. It's not just for the high achiever. Allow the underdogs to experience the magic of becoming tutors for other kids.

9) Earn the privilege to tutor.

For the first round, you may want to start off with assigning only one or two kids to this new role of being a tutor. Once the ball gets rolling, allow other kids or students the right to teach! They'll soon see what fun it is for the tutors and they too will want to participate. You might use this as a reward that they have to earn. Choosing what constitutes reward behavior will depend on the individual child and his unique situation. The other kids will, in all likelihood, want to join the program and try their hand at teaching. They'll work hard to earn the right.

10) Provide for continuation, if possible.

The biggest problem I found is the letdown they experience when the program stops. In a nutshell — withdrawal symptoms! They've gone to the mountaintop and suddenly, if they move on to a new teacher or school, they're back in the swamp again, where it's business as usual. You may have to be part teacher, part sales person, and part preacher, as you push for some sort of continuation of your tutoring program.

Here are some selling points for your arsenal:

- *Student tutoring programs are flexible and can be adapted to any type of academic or social setting. Students can work with one other right in the classroom, or with other students in different classrooms.*
- *Student tutoring programs have been lauded for increasing academic skills, building self-concept, enhancing positive social skills, improving behaviors, decreasing truancy and tardiness, and an entire host of other important benefits.*
- *Tutoring programs are essentially freebies. They don't cost a teacher or school an extra penny out of the budget.*
- *Student tutors have proven themselves to be wonderful extra hands for teachers who lack paid-professional assistants.*
- *Student tutoring programs are a win-win situation for all parties involved, including the tutors, the tutees, the teachers, and ultimately the schools and communities.*

The notion of peer tutoring applies to all facets of learning. Don't limit this incredible approach to the realm of academics. Pretty much any skill can be taught and reinforced from one peer to another, whether it's doing some Hip-Hop maneuver on the dance floor, identifying star constellations, playing a smooth double-stroke-roll on the drum pad, hitting a baseball, or hitting the high notes of an opera aria by Mozart. Peers, fellow students, and colleagues can become your best assistant teachers. They'll guide and push you, if need be, with love, patience, and usually a lot of laughs.

Not too many people I know became teachers looking for the lifestyle of the rich and famous. Comfortable, for the most part? Probably. Own a yacht and two vacation homes, one for winter skiing in the Alps and the other for snorkeling in the Bahamas? Not too likely. Unless, of course, you hit the lottery or have some very well-to-do and very close relatives who love you immensely. Teacher complaints are nothing new. Class sizes are too big. Not enough assistance is provided. Budget cuts keep getting bigger. Materials and supplies are dwindling away. Teaching is being put to the test. No more fun in education. Gotta work two jobs. Oy - and the list goes on! Whatever is to be done about these seemingly insurmountable problems?

We have one goldmine that remains untapped, sitting right at our feet. Well, let's make that right in front of us. I refer to the very students in our classes. From these kiddies of all sizes, shapes, ages, backgrounds, and levels, come some really great and helpful teachers.

Topping, (2008) enumerates the wide range of benefits in the very useful, "Peer-assisted learning: A practical guide for teachers." Topping writes that the "benefits of peer-tutoring for students includes higher academic achievement, improved relationships with peers, improved personal and social development, as well as increased motivation. In turn, the teacher benefits from this model of instruction by an increased opportunity to individualize instruction, increased facilitation of inclusion/mainstreaming, and opportunities to reduce inappropriate behaviors."

It's time you put this awesome powerhouse technique of peer tutoring to use.

TEACH ME IF YOU CAN!
CHAPTER 5

*The Tower of Terror - Teach 'Em
The Ropes*

> *"I believe I can fly.*
>
> *I believe I can touch the sky."*
>
> R. Kelly

"I can't do this!" Paula screamed out loud. "I caaaaaaaaan't!"

"I got'cha, girl. You're not gonna hurt yourself. Promise."

But Paula wasn't at all convinced as she simply shook her head back and forth.

"Please, lemme down. I beg you. Don't do this to me. I wanna..."

"No problem. Can you just reach the next step?"

"Ahhhhhhhhhhhhh," came the yell back. "Noooooooooo. I wanna come down. Now!"

"Okay mate," I responded. "I'll let you down nice & easy. But you're so close to that next step. You sure ya..."

"Ahhhhhhhhhhh, noooooooooo, ohhhhhhhhhhh moooooooooommy!"

Paula was nearly 20 feet above the ground when her cerebral cortex started firing away frantic messages like "this is not what any normal Homo Sapiens is supposed to be doing!" and "if you were meant to be in the clouds, the Good Lord would have made you with wings!" She was stubbornly fighting these desperate pleas, until the brain waves got really fierce and simply demanded, "put me back down on Terre firma or lunch shall be blown upon the unfortunate victims below!" She was slowly inching her way ever skyward on a solid and very safe climbing tower, although Paula & her classmates grimly nicknamed it the Tower of Terror. She was heading towards the 40-foot mark where the main challenge lay. Two thin cables were waiting for her. One she would use as the bottom wire to walk on. The other, about 10 feet above the walking cable, was used to cross over what we affectionately called the "Sea of Screams." To make things really interesting and exciting, it was of course impossible to reach that high cable since it was a good five feet over the climber's head.

There was only one way to conquer the wicked Tower and Sea of Screams. Dangling from this high wire were several pieces of ropes. One could, in theory, grab onto these dangling ropes and gingerly make your way across. A nice secure platform awaited the victors upon successful completion of this doozy. To make matters even more complicated and downright terrifying was the fact that these little pieces of dangling ropes were spread apart — a good six feet apart. This was a station that required two people to complete. You needed your partner to hold your hand as you reached out to grab the rope hanging from the high wire. Then, once you held onto that bit of rope, you could help your partner by holding his or her hand, assuming of course you could hold on to it despite all the sweat. This high ropes activity was designed to foster teamwork and trust. There was no way you could make it across alone. Once you climbed the pole and reached the 40-foot mark the real work was yet to be done. Despite being connected to a safety line at all times, your cerebral cortex works overtime to convince you that only birds belong up at this height doing such maniac things like balancing on a thin wire.

To make matters a bit more difficult, Paula was quite overweight and she was clearly struggling to just climb the telephone pole.

"Don't worry," I yelled back. "You're on the safety line Paula. I gotcha. You're not gonna hurt yourself."

"Easy for you to say," she shouted back. "You're standing on the ground! I'm up here in the sky! Ahhhhhhhhhhh! Heeeeeeeellllllllllllp!"

Some of her classmates laughed, but others shouted up words of encouragement, all of which fell on deaf ears, of course.

"Lemme down! Now! Pleeeeeeeeeeease!"

The rule was climb-out-of-choice, not force. As I slowly gave her more slack to let her descend, she suddenly had a change of heart.

"No wait! Stop. I can do this. Really. I think I can."

I was totally surprised. In all my years of taking students and groups on high rope activities, I had never seen anyone go from the panic mode to making another attempt. Once the body systems go into overdrive, the hands become clammy, the heart is racing, sweat starts covering the face, (making it almost impossible to see), and there's usually no desire to press onward, (or upward). The brain that has already reached panic mode interacts with the body systems in some mighty strange and powerful ways. Many times the individual simply freezes, temporarily paralyzed and unable to move up... or down! While stuck in this manner, they are definitely in no mood to trust the safety line by to stepping off and rappelling down.

Over the years, I've had the fun and challenging task of designing and building ropes course activities. I started putting them at various summer camps, including at Camp Mesorah, in the beautiful rolling hills of NY State. I think our ropes course is truly unique in that we are one of the few, if not the only camp in the country, that actually utilizes real rope! The "ropes" courses today are usually made of cables - often thick, strong airline-quality cables that are super, since they last for years and require little maintenance. But they have very little "give" to them. Rope, on the other hand, wears

147

& tears easily, needs to be replaced every few years, and has lots of built-in give when holding up objects - particularly heavy adults. It'd be mighty hard to build a zip-line out of rope, since it gives so much to the weight. The more weight, the more "give" to the rope. The angle going from top to bottom would have to be very steep to make it work effectively. People love the fast zip-lines, but if made out of rope, it would be closer to an elevator drop.

Now don't get me wrong. I'm not talking about rope that your grandmother used to use for a clothesline. Come to think of it, those clothes dried in the fresh, outdoor air had a special feel and sweet smell to them. (There are some things that modern technology can't replace). Anyhow, the climbing rope is professional mountain climbing gear, and is reinforced with tubular webbing. It'll probably hold up your family car. Professional climbing gear can be purchased at several outlets. I wouldn't recommend used ropes, since one never knows what sort of weather and abuse it has been through. I usually get my ropes and gear at Eastern Mountain Sports. They also have great sales, and the staff is friendly and knowledgeable. They usually have several pro climbers on staff to help guide you through the process, and they often offer courses so you can brush up or learn the skills involved.

Mookie, a camper at Mesorah, tries out the real McCoy rope bridge. Life gets interesting 30 feet up in the trees. And yes, that's a safety line attached from her harness to a belayer down below.

So why go with rope — even the Mt. Everest stuff — when cable seems to be the way to go? There are a few good reasons. First, it's a whole lot cheaper. A professional ropes course with cables often runs well over $30,000. Most programs require training, along with certification, to set up a course. I've put in some exciting rope courses with over four different height stations for around $2000.

This figure includes goodies like the harnesses, safety lines, D-rings, carabineers, and even some helmets. That's quite a substantial savings. The second reason is that they're a lot easier to build. Once a proper area is selected, I can usually have the course up and running in a few days. Whether a course is the high-end cable style, which is always a preferable option, or the professional quality real-ropes course, both share some important points. Both require extensive knowledge and training. You've got to know your knots, equipment, and how to ensure the safety of the patrons at all times. The second thing they have in common is more basic. Both can inspire fear, terror, struggle, and profound elation!

Right now Paula, who was one of my FIU - Florida International University students, was wavering between the terror and struggle modes. She very slowly and cautiously reached out to grab the next step up the pole. This "step" was really a metal ring that stuck half way out of the pole. You had about four inches of the ring to work with - hardly enough to feel secure as you made your way ever-skyward. To my complete surprise, Paula climbed on and we all shouted cheers of support. I decided to not only give her a medal of honor for really going beyond the comfort zone, but also chose to recognize her classmates, who were extremely supportive and patient. Approximately 45 minutes later, Paula was back on the sweet, nice & firm surface of Mother Earth - shouting for joy, pumping her fists into the air, and giving everyone massive bear hugs! She had successfully completed both parts of the high activity - the climb up, and the two-person walk across the Sea of Screams. About a week later, I received an email from Paula, which I've saved to this very day. I'll share just a few lines from her letter.

"I just wanted to thank you so much for bringing our group to the ropes course. It was, without a doubt, the most amazing and important experience of my life, so far! I learned a lot about myself - more than any regular class could have ever taught me. I learned that I can face difficult challenges, and somehow find the strength to carry on and overcome!"

Everyone, from the very young, to the young-at-heart,

can benefit from the innate challenges

and built-in successes of a ropes course program.

For some, it will be the satisfaction of successfully completing every station. For others, it might simply be reaching up and touching the next highest step. The point is, that nearly everyone experiences some moment(s) when they have to step outside their comfort zone and dig deep within to get the job done! The feeling afterwards is sweet success - exhilaration!

Safety, of course, is the number one concern when setting up any ropes course. Once the safety factor is accounted for, then get ready for some eye-opening experiences. Even though I've been involved in low & high ropes courses for many years, the surprises keep coming. One time I brought a young teenage boys group from the

Manhattan Day School, known throughout the Big Apple as MDS. I was running their special education department at the time, and we had arranged for an all-day outing at incredible Ring Homestead, about a 90-minute drive from NYC. This facility wooded forests, streams, and even large ponds. I've known the director Arnie Ring since ancient history. His son currently runs the program. They're equipped to take large groups of participants, since they have a variety of low and high rope stations. I think they have close to 40 different activities. They do overnight camping trips, so folks can get a real outdoor nature experience complete with tents, cooking fires, the whole nine yards. For my motley crew of 13 and 14 year olds with learning and behavioral issues, the adventure meant rooting them from the confining wilds of the concrete jungle known as the big city, to the refreshing, liberating sensations of the open forests. For city kids, this feeling of freedom diminishes as the sun goes down - but more on this phenomenon later.

We broke up into smaller groups, and my particular gang of about six students was at a climbing wall. To make things a bit more interesting, this wall stretched nearly 35 feet straight up, and the higher you got, the less hand and feet grips were available. In other words, it started off easy, and got progressively harder, throughout the climb. Like all high rope activities, the climber was always attached to a safety line. There was no such thing as falling. If you lost your grip for whatever reason, you'd simply dangle in mid-air like a spider. Adam was the first to make the attempt. That was no surprise, since he was the biggest kid of the bunch and liked to throw his weight around. The other students saw him as a nothing less than a bully.

"Hey you mug-heads," he called out to his fellow classmates. "Who's your daddy? Huh?"

The others laughed, but it was definitely forced. No one really stood up to Adam, other than the staff. He carried on with his jive ribbin' while he started his climb up the wall.

"That's right you wimps!" he continued. "Watch and learn from the master! Your master and daddy! I'll be by after this stupid thing to collect daddy fees! Yeah... I should be up and down in just a minute so don't run away you rejects! Losers!"

A few guys laughed. Some just shook their heads back and forth. Adam was not too shy about letting us know that it was his world, and we were plain ol' lucky to even be in it.

I was a bit concerned, since my group also had another hormone-crazed 13-year-old named Nate. But unlike Adam, Nate was on the short side, spoke in a high, squeaky voice and had a particular knack of bugging the heck out of the other guys - especially Adam. Nate was really a sweet, harmless kid, and I affectionately called him Nathan Detroit. Google search that name if it doesn't sound familiar to ya. Adam was pretty much at the zero-tolerance threshold level with Nate. The combination was like oil and water and I did my best to keep one away from the other. Back at MDS, Adam seeking Nate was like a great white shark stalking its prey. Nate would have been the seal pup, sun-bathing on the beach. I was concerned that Nate would internalize that victimization mentality, which often serves to further empower the bully.

But then, a really strange thing happened at about the 10-foot mark. To my utter shock, Adam started freaking out. At first, I totally thought he was kidding.

"Ok," he said in kind of a gruffy whisper. "I'm done. You can let me down now."

"Oh right," I joked back. "You still got about 25 till the top, Mister Spiderman! C'mon bro. Keep on climbing!"

"Nooooo," he answered, clutching the foot and hand rests as best he could. "I mean it. Let me down! Now!"

Everyone started laughing in the group. We all thought he was being his usually wiseacre self. The guys started yelling up things like, "Go on!" and, "C'mon man, we ain't got all day!" And even lines like, "yeah sure we believe you - I can jump up and almost touch you!"

But then his cries of desperation got louder, and more demanding. He had left Comfort Zone City and entered the Twilight Zone of Terror. I figured he'd have been up and down the entire activity by now. It was one of those purely unexpected moments, part & parcel of any ropes course adventure.

"I wanna come down! Pleeeeeeeeeeeeeeeeeeeeeeeeease! Nowwwwwwwwwwwwww!"

At first we all just stood there, with our mouths open.

"Ok, no problemo," Mr. Ring responded. "I'll let you…"

"No," I quietly interrupted him, whispering in his ear. "No. Not yet. He needs a bit of a workout here."

At first Ring looked at me with that "huh?" expression, but then he winked his eye and understood. This was kid who needed a bit more coaxing and, in my humble opinion, to be put in his place. I clearly did not want to embarrass him, especially in front of his classmates, or should I say his class, "wimps?" But at the same time, I didn't want him to let him off the hook so easily. Always easy to talk the talk, but walking the walk - especially on the ropes, is an entirely different matter.

For a good 10 minutes we all kept yelling out words of support. "Don't worry, you won't fall!"

"You got it, Adam."

"This one's all yours."

"Just reach up and touch that next hand grip."

"You can do it."

Absolutely nothing was getting through his climbing helmet and into the cerebral cortex. Despite our coaxing, he started to cry some real tears. I instructed Ring to slowly lower him back down.

None of the students said a word to Adam as he touched back down on Planet Earth. It wasn't that they were scared. I think they were in shock. Adam threw off his helmet and sat down by another nearby tree. He wasn't in the mood to speak or even see another person. Ring shouted over to him that it was ok, and that he had tried and that was the main thing.

"This is all about trying," Ring told us all. "Not what you can or cannot do. We all have some things we're good at and other things that give us a rougher time. Got it?" Adam just sat there with his head down. I decided to let him be for now, it was none other than Nate's turn. I figured if Adam flipped out at the 10-foot mark then Nate might make it to about three feet off the ground...with me holding onto him.

I could not have dreamed-up a better or sweeter scenario than what took place. Nate shot up that wall like Superman! Forget Spiderman, who would proudly have turned over his costume to Nate. Nate climbed like a spider monkey chasing his mate. We all totally freaked. Some of the guys started laughing and cheering at the same time. I think my mouth just stayed in that wide-open position for about an hour. Nate came down in record time, and we all hugged our new hero.

One can never underestimate the carry-over from the ropes course to the participant's reality world - whether it's back in the job place, or home, or at school. But something extraordinary took place. Adam never dared pick on Nate again, at least not in front of the other guys. Nate had shown he was not Adam's mug-head or wimp, any longer. He knew that if he ever tried his former bullying shtick with Nate, all we'd have to do is mention two words: Ring Homestead.

Expect the unexpected.

The episode on the high climb with Adam and Nate could not have been scripted any better in Hollywood. It taught Adam a lesson he needed to learn - that he wasn't always king of the castle, and that he didn't need to be. For Nate, our trip to Ring Homestead was a gift from above. He no longer saw himself as the weak, feeble one. After that successful climb, he began to see himself in a completely different light. He had gone from Nate the Wimp to Nate the Conqueror. Some of his classmates nicknamed him "Nate The Great."

The beauty of a ropes course adventure is just that — it is a true adventure and experience that, due to the nature of the activities, contains unmapped surprises. No one can predict what surprises will play out. Nearly everyone who participates is "fair game," and thus becomes part of the process of challenge and self-discovery. It's often said that the hardest journey is one that leads to the discovery of one's true, inner self. The ropes course process of struggle and redemption is but a single key in this drama. On a recent outing to a local ropes program, this surprise hit home pretty hard. I had falsely assumed that after all these years of running a ropes course and climbing, I was kind of immune to the process. It was dark and I just had to open my big mouth.

"Hey Clay," I said just loud enough for my Nova University students to hear, "I know it's late, dark, and all that. But what d'ya say we do that Leap of Faith?"

"Well," he said, clearly mulling it over, "since there's only three of you left, I think we could make that happen. Especially since we just did that big gig together."

"You de best, mon!" I responded. "Hey, next gig you get a raise!"

I had actually met Clay by the FIU, (Florida International University), ropes course about a year before when I was jogging past it with my dog, Fluff-Boy. We schmoozed ropes talk for a good while, and then I found out he was a harmonica player. About 15 gigs later, all I can tell you is that maybe there's one or two who are better blues harp players on the entire planet. Maybe. And so we hit it off big time, with our similar outdoor and music backgrounds. When I found out his last name was Goldstein, well let's just say we shared some Passover goodies as well.

My two remaining, brave "marines," cheered for joy. It was definitely a case of ignorance is bliss, for the leap of faith was, in my opinion, the hardest challenge of all the activities. It was a mad-crazy doozey in broad daylight. I could only wonder what it was going to be like in the dark. The Leap of Faith required you to climb a 25-foot telephone pole, stand on top of the darn thing, turn around and jump outwards and upwards to grab a trapeze bar, dangling about six feet away and two feet higher than your head, in mid-flippin-air. Sounds easy right? Wrong. You see the problem was that there was absolutely nothing but air to grab onto as you tried to stand on top of the dang pole. You can't hold onto your safety line, since it's behind you at a good 45-degree angle to your back. The safety line runs from your chest/back harness to a high wire that's probably 20 feet from the pole. Thus, holding onto this safety line will actually serve to pull you off the pole!

To make matters even more interesting, the top of the telephone pole is round, flat and maybe a whole six inches wide. So, the maneuver is something like this: As you're dangling from the pole, you reach and up put your right hand on top. Then you put your left on top. Actually, only your thumbs are on the top surface and your fingers are on the side of the pole since you need room to bring your left foot up first and carefully place it on top. You actually have to lean forward somewhat, to allow your leg to squeeze underneath your body. Of course, if you miscalculate that lean by a degree or two, you fall overboard, into the abyss. Once you manage to squeeze your leg on top, you've then got to get your other foot on the top surface. Assuming you've made it this far, you stand up, blowing ever so slightly in the wind, try your best to keep your balance as you slowly and carefully turn around to face the trapeze bar. All this, without thinking too much or too long, for then, the "freeze" mode strikes big time. You count to three and make that jump into the dark, night sky, hoping and praying that your hands meet up with that metal bar.

Mia went first. She's a wife, a mother of two girls, and a former Broadway actress, singer, and dancer. She had just begun her Master's degree program at Nova, and had the utter good fortune to take my course in Expressive Arts & Therapies. It was her "mazel" that her professor insisted on the ropes course as part of expressive therapies. I forgot to mention one other thing. Mia is also fearless. She not only conquered the Tower of Terror in dazzling style, doing ballet maneuvers 45 feet above ground, but she also went first on the Leap of Faith, and a mere 30 seconds later was dangling from that trapeze bar up in the night sky! I was amazed. Even in the daylight this one always took me a good five plus minutes to work out.

"C'mon Laz," she and my other student Liza yelled out. "You can do it!"

I was at the top of the pole, but hit that semi brain-freeze position when I felt I simply could not figure out how to go from grasping the pole to standing on top of it.

"I really don't think I can do this," I shouted down. "I can barely see the darn thing!" It was true. I had actually broken my glasses a few days before at the gig Clay and I did together in Ft. Lauderdale. Two years in a row my band, known as Dr. Laz & The CURE, did this event for the King David Bikers group. And yes, two years in a row, my glasses went M.I.A. and were later discovered in pieces on the ground. Go figure. Next year I'll add that cost to the bill beforehand.

"C'mon Laz, man," Mia shouted back. "Channel your inner frog!"

"You got this, Dr. Laz!" Liza chimed in. "Make it good. You're on film."

Fortunately, I knew it was way too dark for anything to come out on the video camera. Or maybe that was on the unfortunate side, since the camera might have motivated me to put on my best.

"I can't do this right now," I muttered back, hoping no one would hear me.

They carried on, doing their best to inspire and cheer me on-and-upwards.

"Don't think too much, Laz," Clay added. "Just slowly get your left foot on top of the pole. You got this, bro."

A long two minutes later I was indeed standing on top of that telephone pole, holding onto absolutely nothing but my prayers and the night sky. About the only other thing I could feel was my heart beating. The top of the pole was so narrow that my feet stuck out a bit on each side. Very slowly and deliberately, I began the 180-degree turnaround to face that ever-elusive trapeze bar. Turning took another long 30 seconds - which felt more like 30 minutes - to complete.

"I can barely see the dang bar," I yelled out to my buddies all safe and secure on the ground. I dared not a look downwards into the dark abyss. "Even if I had my glasses on, I couldn't see it! Anyone got night vision goggles?"

Clay reminded me not to think too much, as that would be a mighty bad and trying spot to have brain-freeze kick in. "Count to three and leap," he shouted from the darkness below.

Three seconds later, my hands grasped that sweet feel of cold metal. I had made the Leap of Faith! Clearly, I would not have succeeded without the encouragement of my colleagues.

Later I discussed my emotional reactions to the activity with Clay. Quite frankly, I was surprised it was so hard for me. Clay reminded me that it was a natural, physical reaction since, "we don't have feathers." In other words, the emotional reaction of feeling uncomfortable is perfectly natural, as one begins climbing up, up & away from Mother Earth's reassuring embrace. It's how we deal with this reaction, this response that matters most. It's the classic psychological mechanism of fight versus flight. The ropes course teaches a person to stay focused and fight through it.

Against an ever-darkening sky, I grasp sweet metal on the Leap-of-Faith.

But the real benefits begin long before the adrenalin rush of a zip-line, or a 55-foot Tower of Terror. It all starts on the ground floor.

There are grand benefits to be had on that hard ground.

Make sure you do the lower activities first.

Most professional ropes courses, and their instructors, utilize a variety of low activities way before patrons begin clinging desperately to a safety line high above the earth's surface. Although these lower activities might not have the attractiveness and glamour of the high stations, nevertheless, they are the meat & potatoes of any decent ropes course. If the high ropes activities are likened to the wide receivers and quarterbacks, (who get most of the glory), then the low stuff can be considered the offensive & defensive lines - who do most of the hard work, but often go unnoticed.

These low activities are done either directly on the ground, or close to it. What, you might ask, can possibly done here that's so important and critical? Here, it's not so much the personal challenges, but just as importantly, and for some even more so, we're talking team and group-building skills. Corporations, school groups, and all sorts of business groups have taken trips to a ropes course to foster a true sense of togetherness and cooperation. Some groups find the lower activities so important, that they divide a typical four-hour program into three hours on the ground, and only one hour on the more-exciting high goodies. Most typically, a four-hour program will be divided in half; two hours building team and group skills on the low activities, and the last two hours climbing and screaming bloody heck in the air. The lower activities cannot be underestimated for their value and benefits. I have found this to be particularly true for classes with some sort of special needs. One common concern, expressed by both the parents and teachers of special needs kids, is that the realm of social skills is a tough one to navigate. Individuals with special needs often have a rough time interpreting facial cues, body language, nuances of speech, etc., all of which most folks really tend to take for granted. This being the case, many individuals with special needs may tend to shy away from group and interpersonal activities, whether it's a weekend dance, or a game of volleyball. These individuals may simply not "get it," and may wander away from the group, or engage in inappropriate self-stimulation behaviors. A low program on the ropes course can be a tremendous way to teach, and boost, group functioning social skills. Here too, you're in store for surprises. By now, you should be mighty familiar with the phrase "expect the unexpected".

At my alternative high school program, I'd always make sure to take my crew out of the concrete jungle of NYC and into the sanity of the forest of Ring Homestead. I promise you, I'm really not getting a cut of the action every time I mention this place, although I may just bring this up to the Ring board of directors. We too, always had a whole bunch of biz to take care of at ground level before we ever hit the high stuff.

Many individuals have a rough time when it comes to working cohesively with others. The etiology of this phenomenon incorporates an unending conglomeration of factors. Suffice it to say, you get people together to accomplish something and it matters little,

Two of my students learn the value of teamwork from 40 feet up.

at this point in time, how others picked on him when he was in elementary school, or whether he wasn't nursed long enough. Or, how he was never quite fast enough to make the high school track team. Now, something needs to get done. In the here & now. Time to forget the past and move forward-and-onward. Just to throw a little wrench into the pot, some kids also have a rough time when it comes to social skills. For a whole variety of reasons and possibilities, they tend to be loners and shun group activities. In the realm of special education, social cues can be a royal doozey for these students. All those subtle facial expressions combined with voice inflections can be interpreted, and thus misinterpreted, in a zillion different ways. So the low ropes activities can be highly beneficial, because it focuses on fostering group effort and teamwork.

In fact, nearly every time I bring a group to any ropes course, it's these low stations that are the most difficult to accomplish. Here, it takes the entire team's cooperation to solve a problem. Sometimes it's done verbally, that is, the team can speak to each other to help solve the task or problem at hand. Other times, the activity is deliberately accomplished in silence, so people have to find other ways to communicate effectively. Like a solid music band, all the members have to look and listen to each other.

The Spider's Web is a good case in learning teamwork-building skills. Although this activity is usually only three feet off the ground, it can cause groups a lot of difficulty. The idea is to get all the members of the team through the hole in the webbing without touching the ropes at all. If they touch the rope, this person is officially caught by the spider, and unable to escape. Then...the entire group has to start all over. Sometimes this activity includes a tire suspended in the air. If you touch the sides of the tire at all, the spider's got ya! The trick is that the team has to physically work together to lift each member, and pass him or her safely through the opening. It's definitely easier with a thin person, but no guarantee. If the other team members don't really cooperate, work together, and stay focused, then even a skinny-minny hits the webbing and is trapped. Our major success was passing Sruli, one of my larger students, safely through. He tipped the scales at around 250 pounds, and was taller than me. When we got Sruli safely past the spider's jaws, we all shouted for joy.

Next, there's the Whale Watching Cruise. This one is basically a large platform, called the Mother Ship, which has a fulcrum in the middle. It's like a very wide and long seesaw. If you were to stand on the right side, well the right side touches the ground. Same thing is true for the left. But if two people go on at the same time and slowly work their way to the opposite sides, the ship stays perfectly balanced and neither side hits the ground. Touching the ground in this activity means that the ship has tilted way too much to one side, and the people have been thrown overboard in shark-infested waters. Help! Then the group has to start all over again.

This is a fun one for large groups, and you'd be amazed at how many people can accomplish this daring feat. I've seen it done with more than 30 group members. That means there are more than 15 people on each side, and nobody has messed up the balancing act. For the Whale Watching Cruise, two people go up into the middle of the ship and slowly work their way to the sides. Once safely there, the next come aboard. This process continues until all members of the group are safely on board the "ship." Once everyone is on top of the large platform, the entire process is reversed. They all have to get off the Mother Ship in one piece. If someone gets too anxious and simply doesn't have the patience to wait, he or she can mess it up for the entire group, which would then have to start over. During a recent visit to the FIU TRAC program with my

Nova students, we totally nailed this one in our first attempt.

Another interesting activity that plays into promoting group dynamics is called, "Snake Rings". There are five long circular pieces of various-colored climbing rope. Only one of these completely goes through the other four. In other words, by lifting just one of the five ropes, you will actually lift the others. If you pick the wrong rope, it pulls out all by itself. For this activity, the facilitator tells the group that they can look and examine the ropes, now lying in a pile in the middle of the group. Looking is permitted, but no touching allowed. The entire group must come to a mutually agreed decision regarding which is the correct rope. This requires that the group members listen to everyone's opinion. Before the final decision is given, the facilitator goes around to each team member and asks for his or her final verdict. The group can decide that majority rule will prevail, but each member is allowed, and must voice an opinion, one way or the other — or can even express that he or she is not sure, or simply doesn't care. This one is rather fascinating, because it requires no physical effort whatsoever. It's all based on reasoning and observations. While my Nova students got this one correct, it was interesting to see the dynamics that took place. Some people, right away, took charge and voiced their opinions. Others were more laidback, and waited longer to figure things out. One of the students told Clay that she didn't really care how this played out, and which was the correct rope. I asked her to explain, since I was curious to learn whether she simply didn't have the patience to stay on this task and help solve the problem. She told me later that she was just anxious to get to the high ropes activities, and "get moving."

Another, more-active ground-based activity, is the Desert Lifesaver. This one is lots of fun, and also has a rather high difficulty factor. Here the group is given all sorts of tubes, usually PVC piping, which has been pre-cut into different shapes, sizes, and lengths. Along with the PVC goodies are some other interesting objects, such as a can of water, a large coffee-size cup, and a Ping-Pong ball. I kid you not. The object is to build a contraption that will transport water from the can, into the tubing, and eventually into the cup that now has a Ping-Pong ball inside. Enough water must reach this cup to float out the Ping-Pong ball. There are a few things I should point out. First, the cup has many holes in it. Second, the team has to use every single object to properly complete the activity. It usually takes several attempts to float out that Ping-Pong ball. The group soon realizes that too much water escapes from one place, or not enough flows through another, or that another person is needed to cover all the holes in the coffee mug. The awesome thing about this activity, is that it's real hands-on group solving - in the literal sense. The group soon discovers that everyone must use both hands to help complete the Desert Lifesaver. Since arriving at this conclusion often takes many attempts, it's often the quiet, shy one who comes up with the best ideas to achieve success. After all, the first six tries didn't work, so the group at last turns to others for advice and direction.

My NOVA graduate students lend a helping hand. Teamwork and trust begin on the ground before moving skyward.

If the group is large, this activity may be split up into two competing teams. This adds another element to the picture. If the group is five to eight people, then very often, the facilitator will give them a 15-minute "Beat The Clock" time limit to complete the task.

From team building skills, to fostering cooperation and trust, to overcoming personal fears and challenges, there's a ropes course nearby just waiting for you. The awesome organization known as "Outward Bound," sponsors a whole variety of exciting and challenging outdoor adventures, and some include wonderful ropes course activities. Check them out at www.outwardbound.org. In many locales, you'll be surprised to find that your local Scouting program has a ropes course just waiting for you and your group. Take a look at their website www.scouting.org and contact your local Scouting agency. Your only regret will be that you didn't hit the ropes sooner. So get out there and reach for the stars.

TEACH ME IF YOU CAN!
CHAPTER 6

Lights, Camera, Adaptive Bubble
Machine - Drama!

"Tell me and I'll forget.

Show me and I may remember.

Involve me and I'll understand."

— Chinese proverb

"Ten minutes, Quest!" the voice rang out, after a quick and deliberate tap on our dressing room door.

"Ten minutes," I repeated unnecessarily. "Yikes."

I took another look in the mirror, brushed my hair, (yet again), straightened out my bowtie, and even smoothed over the outline of my beard.

"Do I look okay?" I asked.

"Yes, for the 100th time. You look fine," Zippo called out from the back of the room. "I think you're more nervous than your students."

"I think you're right," I responded, taking a quick glance at my crew. A few were making obnoxious noises and giggling. Others were sitting quietly along the wall of the narrow dressing room.

Gathering my students for one final pep talk, I made some last-second adjustments.

"Oh, you guys look awesome. Don't worry about a thing, ya hear? You're gonna blow the crowd away!"

It was completely true. Zippo was right. I was a walking, basket-case, and my students, the ones who were supposed to be out of control and needing all sorts of last-second supervision, coaxing, prodding, pampering, etc. - well, they were just fine. In fact, it was almost as if they simply weren't aware of all the ramifications involved in walking out on stage in front of 2,000 people. To make matters even more intense, they would be performing before hundreds of their own peers. Kids, I well knew, can be tough on each other.

"Showtime, y'all," Brian, AKA-The B-Man said, as he headed out of the dressing room. "Good luck, everyone. You'll be great, I'm sure." Giving me one last good luck pat on the shoulders, he added his wishes of "break-a-leg," and headed to his seat to catch all the action on video. Both Brian and Zippo, also known as the Zip-Man, were our professional videographers. They'd been to many a Quest function, catching our special performances. And special they were — in more ways than one.

Our choir from the Quest Center, part of the Broward County public schools, was giving a performance at the prestigious Broward Center for the Performing Arts. The hall was absolutely incredible. Brand spanking new, with hundreds of state-of-the-art speakers and mikes, dangling from the ceiling, surrounding the stage floor and sides, hidden within columns, under various seats... it was a performers paradise, indeed. Isaac Stern was quoted as saying that everywhere in the world, music enhances a hall, with one exception: Carnegie Hall enhances the music. The same could be said for the Broward Center for the Performing Arts.

Imagine for a moment that you're standing center stage in front of a sellout crowd, numbering well into the thousands. You've already bowed humbly to three standing ovations, and these came during the main performance, not at the end of the evening! Well, then you decide to do something way beyond the norm, something so gutsy that it boggles the mind of every person in the place. You decide to sing the next tune without a microphone! That's right. The acoustics are so totally awesome in this place, you simply can't resist. Your guitar backup musician strums quietly as the entire crowd becomes completely silent. You lay the mike on top of the piano and walk to the front of the stage. Now, just to make things a bit more interesting, let's pretend that you're in your mid-80's, nearing 85, to be exact. I'm talking about the icon, Tony Bennett, who recently performed at the Broward Center for the Performing Arts and, to my utter amazement and pure delight, sang the iconic "Fly Me To The Moon," without a microphone, to a sellout crowd. It was his 4th standing ovation during his two-hour performance. His voice is better than ever. Growing up, I always saw him as someone from my parent's generation. I was into the Beatles, the Stones, and all those awesome 60's groups. Tony Bennett was not in my record collection. But you can be mighty sure that he's now a major player on my iPod and the Pandora Radio feature on my cell phone. I am in awe of his charisma, charm, and incredible voice that just seems to get better, over time. His daughter Antonia, by the way, is a superb jazz singer, following in her dad's footsteps.

I couldn't help but marvel at the amazing set of circumstances that had brought us, brought me, to this incredible venue. It had been a long, crazy haul, and the teaching gods had at last smiled upon me. After 25 years in special education, I was doing music therapy for students with profound special needs. My principal put it bluntly and told me, "Laz, you found your niche." My choir was not your regular run-of-the-mill performing group. You know the kind...top-notch students. Honors classes. Perfect-pitched voices singing harmonies right on the money. Not exactly my crew. Many in my group were completely non-verbal. I'd do reverse cartwheels if they could verbalize a note or two.

We started off as the Quest "Sing & Sign" Choir. It seemed a pretty decent name, since the non-verbal students used American Sign Language, (ASL), to communicate and "sing along" to the live music the band played. I would sing and they would sign. But as our group expanded and we began to play larger venues in the community, we started getting more students involved. Some with other special needs, such as autism, could carry a tune pretty well. Ryan was in his early 20's when he first started with the band. Besides his social difficulties, he was also diagnosed with autism. He was one of the few readers in my program. He spoke in a rather high-pitched voice but, needless to say, I was thrilled to have someone on board with some verbal abilities. For several weeks he sat in my music class, not interacting or saying very much. But one day he asked if he could hold the microphone. I was singing the tune "Locomotion," and the class was rocking away to the beat, using tambourines, shakers, wood blocks, and assorted percussion goodies. Ryan first started mouthing the words to the song, then suddenly let out a loud, piercing blast from his vocal chords that sounded much more like opera, than some R&B Motown hit.

"C'mon baby," he belted out in falsetto that would've made the Four Seasons mighty proud. "Do the locomotion!"

He held the last syllable, "shun" for a good 10 seconds, complete with hitting the high note about 16 octaves up there, all the while using some dramatic, stunning vibrato. I was totally floored. It wasn't the fact that I had never heard the Motown tune "Locomotion" done opera-style before. Ryan could sing! He could not only sing on key, but had this very unusual, high voice. I later found out that his mom is a semi-professional opera singer. Ryan immediately became one of our soloists on the road. Unfortunately, for this big gig, Ryan was unable to attend. He had graduated from the Quest Center a year prior to this important event.

At some point, although I'm not exactly sure where and when it happened, we were dubbed by the media as "Dr. Laz & The Sensations!" That p'zazzy name won out over the rather boring title of the "Sing & Sign Choir" and, like they say, the rest is history.

"Five minutes, Quest!" came another tap on the door. "You all need to take your places by the side of the stage area, now."

"C'mon mates," I said, adjusting their brand new Quest choir vests. "Let's rock this joint!"

We quickly made our way behind the huge stage with all its' myriad of curtains and dim lights, to our position, and waited for our cue.

The supervisor, a very nice lady who had called me months before to set this up, came over to us. "We always show off the best of the Broward schools to our audiences. But I really think that you all are the best of the best!"

I raised my hand in clenched fist and pounded the air above my head, whispering our chant of "hooo, hooo, hooo, hooo!" They all followed suit, of course, and to my pleasant surprise, did it all in a whisper. One by one, I gave them a warm, supportive bear hug.

Standing right next to me was our one-and-only Sandra, the most verbal of all my students. Sandra had asked me many times during our 90 minutes prep in the dressing room to, "Please Dr. Laz... pray for me!" I was more than happy to oblige, but asked her to do the same for me. If anyone had a direct line "upstairs," it was definitely my students. Sandra was turning 22, and thus had graduated from the Quest the year before, but I often brought her back to help out with the choir. She was one of my best signers. She was also a real social butterfly.

Next was Osvin. 18 years old, full of energy and life, and a serious rock star wannabee. Since his social awareness was higher than most of my students, he was a tad-bit nervous about standing in front of a huge audience, including all sorts of Broward county and school board officials. Thus, he spent a great deal of time in the dressing room making all sorts of gross sounds with his hand and mouth. Comic relief, I suppose. I would have to keep an eye on Osvin during our 10-minute performance, making sure he actually did some signing, instead of just mimicking my guitar movements. Osvin is an air-guitar player, extraordinaire.

"Dr. Laz," Michelle said, "my turn!" I quickly embraced tall, sweet Michelle. She had a way of keeping me on my toes. Whenever I would innocently say something like, "okay guys" at one of our choir practices, she would immediately respond, indignantly, "I'm not a guy, I'm a girl!" I had to beg for forgiveness. She kept one close watch on Sandra for the appropriate signs.

I then gave Raymond & Daniel a big hug, while the clock ticked down to curtain call. They often went as a pair. Both were nearing birthday number 20. Having Downs-syndrome, they were on the short, stocky side, and were extremely limber. Daniel could easily put a leg behind his head. Raymond could do both — at the same time! They were both verbal, but with slurred speech, and to an outsider, very difficult to understand. Both were excellent signers and Daniel, it seemed, never forgot one sign, even from a song we had done two or three years prior. I often asked him to demonstrate the signs to the rest of the class. "You guys are the best," I said, still hugging 'em like crazy. "You ready for this?"

They immediately responded with another "hoooo, hoooo, hoooo" call, complete with fist over their heads.

Then there's our superstar, the incredible Danielle, who you met briefly in chapter three. In that chapter, I shared an incident that happened to me and the band, well let me be a bit more specific, where I had totally blanked out the words to a song. The problem was that we were in the middle of the tune in front of a hundred-plus good folks in the audience. The only person who caught my mistake was that bright, sharp as a whip, Ms. Personality, Danielle! She's basically non-verbal, although she does laugh and make various verbal utterances to get your attention. She has a severe case of cerebral palsy, and has poor control over her arms and legs. Yet she can completely drive and steer her wheelchair on her own, using her head switch. She's absolutely awesome with her knee switch — as long as her legs are strapped in good to the chair. She also has an awesome sense of humor, something I found out, courtesy of her adaptive communication device. On more than one occasion, mind you.

This particular time I was teasing about taking her to the movies after school. She started hitting that knee switch connected to her communicator. I knew some words or sentences were on the way, so I waited patiently for the "beep, beep, beep" of her knee switch to fire out some response. Finally she was done, and with a broad smile on her face, she clicked the switch one more time. The communicator put her time-consuming efforts into a verbal sentence. Speaking in a monotone, the machine's voice said, "Bug off, Dr. Laz. You're too old!"

"Ouch," I told her unable to control my laughter. "You really know how to hurt a guy."

Danielle was now a main part of our act, operating the audio-visual goodies totally on her own, with that incredible knee-switch that fired its wireless messages to the computer. Our songs had an added dimension of special-visuals going on, that were geared and appropriate for our songs. They really took on meaning when Danielle was making it all happen. She has the cognitive ability to know when to hit her switch, which in turns communicates wirelessly with the computer, and advances the next picture or short video clip. Let's say we're doing that awesome tune, "Wonderful World." As I sing the words, "I see trees of green" - Danielle hits her switch and shows the picture of the green trees. "Red roses too" - she hits the knee or head switch again, and the PowerPoint slideshow moves to the picture of red roses. Other students of mine who are wheelchair bound and don't have this high cognitive ability, operate slideshows where the pictures and visuals aren't so time-dependent. In these circumstances, the students know that when they hit their switches it causes a new and different picture to come up on the screen. They've learned this cause & effect mechanism, something that most of us take for granted, and it's completely up to them when and how often to change the visual background while the song plays on.

With Danielle, I was a glutton for punishment. I'd tease her about some nonsense and she'd always come back with great responses using her communication device. She was living proof of that powerful statement - "you can't judge a book by looking at the cover."

I was hoping this big show at the Broward Center would be a really positive experience for these awesome kids, and, just as importantly, for all those in the audience. Hopefully, it would be a learning experience for them, as well. Perhaps it would help break down some of the stereotypes people have about individuals with profound special needs.

"We'll show 'em," I thought to myself, "that you guys can make meaningful contributions...that you can give to others." After months of preparation, and hours and hours of hard work, I was anxious to get out there and let my students shine. Our students with profound special needs don't have to be passive observers. Given the chance, they can be active participants, and they can truly give so much to others.

Within seconds we were standing in our proper places, the choir arranged in a sort of semi-circle. Me to their right side, slightly in front, so I could keep tabs on them all, and our keyboard player, Zahava, in the same position on the opposite side. I gave them one last thumbs-up sign.

"Been a long time comin' with this, eh Dr. Laz?" one of the stagehands remarked in a whisper.

"No doubt, my brother." I nodded. "A few years of hard work for this 20-minute performance. Kind of mind-boggling."

"Yeah, that's how they all are, pretty much," he added. "But I think yours may have had even more work involved."

"You can't imagine,' I responded, "what it took to get us to this point."

It was a remarkable process indeed, and I was pretty overwhelmed just thinking about what it had taken to get to this point. Many said it was a waste of time. Others said it simply couldn't be done. And then again, there were the teachers and administration members from the Quest Center who gave nothing but encouragement, and their full backing. Visually, we made a mighty big impression. Four young adults with Down syndrome and one with profound autism were the signers. They looked mighty sharp in their black and white outfits with matching vests. Two students with multiple conditions, including physical challenges, formed our percussion corps - all running the adaptive instruments from their wheelchairs using their switches. Danielle, in charge of the visuals for each song, gave me a broad smile as she sat in her wheelchair, ready to take her place on center stage. We put in a lot of classroom prep-hours to get to this gorgeous performing arts center. Tony was full of excitement, as he stood at-the-ready to do his thing, and run the large bubble machine using his head switch.

We finally heard the dramatic announcement.

"Ladies & gentlemen, boys and girls. Welcome the Quest 'Sing & Sign' Choir!"

The curtain rose, and so did the transfixed gaze of everyone present! Although this very large and well-attended event featured Broward's finest and most talented students, it was our crew that stole the show. They got a standing ovation, and I don't think there were too many dry eyes in the place. The only issue I had was Osvin playing some wicked air guitar at different times during the songs, but the audience fell in love with him. They kept cheering him on despite my desperate whispers behind the microphone of "no air guitar now - just sign... sign!"

Our group, dubbed by the media as Dr. Laz & The Sensations, at the awesome Broward Center for the Performing Arts in 2007, for the Arts Teacher of the Year event. The group featured three students using American Sign Language, and three wheelchair-bound students using their head or knee switches to run adaptive drums,

The magical show at the Broward Center for the Performing Arts was a huge success for us, and my brain-wheels started turning. Perhaps it was the taste, the feel, the whole Gestalt of the stage experience. Whatever it was, I wanted more for our very special band. If singing and signing and performing for others were so beneficial for my students, why not go the whole nine yards and have them do real-McCoy, full-fledged dramatic musical productions? Why not full performances, complete with music, lighting, scenery, costumes, and acting - the whole exciting, stimulating, engaging medium of live theatre? First, a bit on this powerhouse strategy, known as "drama therapy."

What is Drama Therapy and what can it do for you?

Broadway Vs. Broad Way Approach

Like every other major term discussed in the realm of education, drama therapy belongs to a rather umbrella-like phenomenon which includes many mediums; and its description will vary, depending on who you ask and what their area of interest and expertise is. It runs the gamut from the very large, time-consuming, involved productions; to the very small, short, impromptu-style experiences, often running only a minute or two, (or less). The major theatrical productions involve song, dance, scenes, costumes, lighting, timing, choreography, hours-upon-hours of rehearsal, and the hundreds of other details that follow this "Broadway" model.

Educators and therapists espousing this approach, claim that you simply have to have the "real" thing, in order to reap the "real" benefits. They might argue that there's really no comparison to having a tiny morsel of dollar-store chocolate, compared to a full-fledged banquet that finishes with your choice of 12 different lush desserts - including the flowing Godiva chocolate fountain. Both satisfy, but only one memory lasts a long, long time. The process is long, and highly involved in the Broadway model, but the product, the end result, produces all sorts of "oohs" & "ahs."

Other therapists and educators take a much more open view. I refer to this as the, "Broad Way" approach. Each component of theatre and drama is valid and meaningful, and in fact, produces a myriad of positive benefits, many of which we haven't even articulated or put our finger on. In this approach, simple role-playing, (acting out a feeling or thought), is valid, and often leads to further rewards, such as emotional release, a sense of freedom and growth, and even resolution. In this model, it's the process that outweighs the product.

I usually begin each Nova class-session with "circle" time, which gives us an informal opportunity to share with one another. During one such session, Mary, one of my former students from Nova University, who runs a drama and stage program at a South Florida high school, told us about a remarkable incident that occurred during one of her recent drama classes. Her student, Joey, had burst into her room, chucked his book bag against the wall, and cursed out loud as he kicked over a desk. Mary held out her hand, calmly walked up to Joey and said, "act out what's going on!" Joey, at first, didn't want to hear it. "C'mon man," she said. "What better time and what better way than this?"

Joey then proceeded to do a live, one-person theatrical performance that dealt with how someone had "keyed" his car, scratching up the entire driver's side of his newly-acquired set of wheels. The other students in his class sat mesmerized as Joey acted out not only the culprit, but also himself, and how he had initially reacted. Then Mary came up with a brainstorm. She suggested that he act out the role of the car itself! Joey gave a brilliant performance of the car shouting to the guy with the key. "Ouch, what the heck are you doing to my side?" and "Hey idiot, why don't ya scratch your own side up?" and "Wait'll my owner finds ya, you'll be mighty sorry, ya flippin' fool!" Toward the end of Joey's impromptu five-minute performance, the car was actually laughing at the fool-of-a-criminal, saying things like, "Ya know what, I can touch that up with some paint and look all sweet and cool again — too bad you can't do that with your face!" He finished with the car getting the last laugh and Joey getting a standing ovation.

"This method," Mary continued, "was not just release for Joey. It gave him a new way of seeing the situation, not from just his prior perspective of anger, but also from the car's imagined perspective. It was incredibly powerful, and enabled him to move on in a much healthier and more productive way."

Mary was actually utilizing a few different approaches, within this broad field known as "drama therapy." At first, Joey was engaged in role-playing; both the culprit's role as well as his very own reactions. These mini-dramas, played out to his classmates and teacher, were about a reality-based scenario and responses. Then, Joey moved into a different venue of role-playing, that of assuming the imagined, and thus fictional, reactions of the car. Both of these scenarios played out and helped provide Joey with some emotional and psychological healing, as well as the opportunity of seeing the situation from a new, expanded view.

Role-playing can assume all sorts of formats, and some occur in very spontaneous ways. I once came in the front door of my home after a long day at work, and it seemed like everyone inside was in a foul mood. I wasn't sure who had the blues worse - my oldest daughter, my youngest son, my better half, or me! It mattered little. The decibel level was rocking, and it seemed as if I had somehow missed my house and ended up in the Twilight Zone. I don't even know where all this came from, as it all happened spontaneously, but a light went off in my head.

"Okay," I shouted above the noise level. "Why don't we all just take this from the top? Like one mo' time. Ready?"

The whole Laz gang turned their heads toward me, ready to pounce, but I continued with my plan.

"Look. I'm gonna go outside and pretend that I never came in yet. We're going to start this whole process one more time. I'll ring the bell. Knock on the door. And this time you're all come greet me with smiles, laughs, and even some hugs! C'mon! We'll pretend we're just one big happy family!"

They were all speechless, as I gathered my backpack and jacket and headed out the front door.

To my surprise, it worked like a charm. I rang the bell, knocked on the door, and this time they put on their happy faces. And yes, I got a few hugs, as well. Later on we all laughed about it, but it certainly was a form of drama therapy in action. Technically, one wouldn't call this role-playing. This little scenario was closer, perhaps, to a mini-psychodrama, or a drama type game. But we see from this example that drama therapy can be beneficial, even on a small scale. The important thing was that re-entering the house allowed my family to backtrack and restart the train again. It was a fun method that enabled us all to use a different emotional strategy. The kids, who at first were whining, cranky, and in miserable moods, suddenly had the chance to take a new approach. They put on some smiles, and found them much more to their liking. Like that, the turbulent waters became calm, peaceful and user-friendly. It reminded me of that oldie-but-goodie tune, "Put On A Happy Face." One of the verses goes like this: "Take off that gloomy mask of tragedy, it's not your style. You'll look so good, that you'll be glad ya decided to smile." Sometimes, just changing the external way we do things or brightening our appearance, can have an effect on our internal makeup as well.

There are so many different forms of drama that it's almost unlimited in scope and thus, in definition as well. To make matters even more interesting, this field is far from being a new dimension within the human experience. It's been around since people first started inhabiting Mother Earth and hanging out together. While they didn't use sophisticated soundboards and lighting equipment, they sure as heck danced to the moon and sun; and they used dramatic reenactments to share stories and adventures with fellow tribe and village members. They acted out battles, hunts, and other important ceremonies. Some pretended to be animals. Many wore elaborate costumes. Others used masks. Some were deliberately quiet. Others screamed and made primal noises. All these techniques are used in drama therapy to this very day.

Here too, I would suggest to the reader that you contact any of the professional drama therapy associations for more detailed information on these, and other approaches and styles. There are several wonderful programs throughout the world, many here in the United States, where one can take courses and become a certified drama therapist. It's an exciting and meaningful approach to helping others, and you'll have a darn good time doing it. Like the saying goes: "Do what you like - like what you do." Check out the National Association of Drama Therapy at www.nadt.org. They keep an updated list of programs that offer accreditation, resources, and conferences on this exciting aspect of the expressive arts therapies. Another wonderful organization worth getting involved in, is the International Expressive Arts Therapy Association at www.ieata.org. Besides all the great resources listed, they also maintain a list of national and international programs that offer advanced certifications in the expressive arts. Both of these organizations sponsor annual conferences.

Perhaps I should have mentioned the awesome Lovewell Institute first, because they are extraordinary in their vision, outreach, influence, and simply at getting-it-done! Besides, my department head at Nova S.E. University, Dr. David Spangler, is not only a personal friend and mentor, but also a founder and artistic director of Lovewell. You'll definitely want to check out their site at www.lovewell.org. In fact, I strongly suggest you contact these good folks and make every effort to attend one of their awesome programs. They sponsor theatre productions for youth and the young-at-heart throughout the world. Many of my graduate students from Nova attend the Lovewell's unique summer program in Sweden, which is also under the direction of Dr. Spangler. I personally feel a deep connection with the Lovewell model. We are kindred spirits, because their focus is on providing a medium, (the expressive arts), through which our youth can become more active participants in life. Lovewell has produced many successful artists that have advanced to careers in the arts, including singers, songwriters, choreographers, dancers, actors, painters, and more. For those of you living closer to the south Florida area, I suggest you register at Nova and take a course with the awesome and always inspiring, Dr. Spangler. I'll be expecting your thank-you card. While you're at it, register for my Expressive Arts Therapies course. Don't forget to bring your journal, colored pencils, comfortable dancing shoes, and your favorite drum.

Back at the ranch, I mean the Quest Center, it was time to bring in the troops and take things to the next level. Enter the "Dream Team."

Collaborate. Get your colleagues on board.

No need to go it alone here, folks. Once you start digging behind the scenes and asking around, you'll probably be amazed at the hidden talents of your fellow staff members. Often your administrators will get involved, especially if they can play an instrument, sing or act. Whenever administrators participate in teacher-made productions, it gives a tremendous boost to staff morale, and fosters a sense of group cohesion. There are benefits galore just waiting to be tapped into, by working on a school-wide production that involves faculty and students. A few conversations between you and other teachers, and pretty soon the entire place will be buzzing like a beehive in July.

The Quest was no exception. Well, let me rephrase that statement. The Quest was exceptional, in more ways than one. I began with our tech man on campus, Larry Bisceglia. He was the person I turned to on a zillion different occasions for help with the adaptive switches, the wireless technology, and for ideas on how to get my students more involved. Larry recently retired from teaching, and he is sorely missed. He was a walking/talking encyclopedia of technological resources for special needs. His knowledge and practical skills was incredible, and he was a main player in our "dream team." Next I schmoozed with Deb Kalitan, our school's autism coach. Deb is another dynamo, filled with exciting ideas and ways to implementing them for individuals with profound special needs. She's very professional yet, at the same time, a warm, caring person that people simply love being around, students included. She knew both the technology end, and each child's strengths and challenges. Deb is a valuable asset to our drama program. Next, is the dynamic teaching duo of Cindy & Dean Frost. I quickly made friends with both of them when I began working at Quest. Cindy has a self-contained class for older students with autism and other needs. Dean is a behavioral management person, and he is mighty busy on campus. To my pleasant surprise, (although shock may be the better word), both have serious backgrounds in the theatre. Talk about good fortune! Cindy is artistic, specializing in visual arts and set design, and Dean is a lighting specialist. Both worked for various theatre companies prior to teaching.

With my background in teaching and music, the Quest dream team gelled enough to begin applying for grants, and set their sights on more than 10 major productions. It was a match made in teaching heaven. We secured more than a dozen grants during a five year stretch, and our special needs drama theatre program took off like the North American X-15, which by the way cruises along at the outrageous speed of only 4500 miles per hour. Yes, you read that right. I could have compared us to NASA's X-43A scramjet, which recently set a new world speed record for a jet-powered aircraft at Mach 9.6, or nearly 7000 mph! We're talking unthinkable, unimaginable, mind-boggling speed here folks. But the X-43A was not built for landing and thus, crashed in the ocean after setting the record. Bad example for my special needs theatre program. We're much better off with the X-15, which unlike the X-43A, is a manned aircraft. The X-15 can only get better, and I am always rooting for the same when it comes to any expressive arts endeavor for individuals with special needs.

Things did get better for our full drama productions, when we began to network with the incredible Deb Lombard. She functioned as our artist-in-residence for several projects and brought her zest, enthusiasm, and professional skills along. Debela, as she is known to her many friends and colleagues, runs the Exceptional Theatre Company, an after-school performance-oriented program that caters to individuals with special needs. It's been a fun and productive two-way street, as I've gone over to help her with some programs as well. Check out her amazing work at www.etcsfl.org.

Everyone loves a good show. Like the saying goes - "there's no business like show business." This same mantra applies for those with special needs, and perhaps, even more so. There are so many skills that drama therapy affords, from reinforcing academics, to building self-esteem, to fostering positive social skills. And there are probably about 16,000 additional reasons, beyond these top-three. Students learn to operate various forms of assistive technology, to take turns, to wait patiently for their spot to shine, to sing, dance, act, say a few lines or more, and sometimes to overcome challenges on a very personal level. Take Ryan, for example:

He had a difficult time performing for others, particularly for large groups. He knew the Locomotion song cold, but he got very shy in front of others. We spent several months working our way up the ladder in small, tiny increments. At first, Ryan had to get used to singing without the mike, in a classroom by himself. A few days later, I was able to enter the room. Eventually, he was able to use the mike, and belt it out at school assemblies. But as I mentioned earlier, this is all about process not product, and so the surprises keep us all on our toes. During one of our major performances at the school, complete with parents and various dignitaries in attendance, a curveball came our way in the middle of the show. The stage was set - literally - and it was Ryan's turn to shine. He stood in the middle of the stage holding the microphone at his side as I started his song.

"C'mon baby do..."

This was, of course, Ryan's cue to take it. Instead, there was total silence. I repeated the intro line one more time. Again, complete, utter, and extremely uncomfortable, silence. The audience shuffled nervously in their seats.

I sang the first part of the phrase one more time, and finally Ryan put the mike to his mouth. I breathed a sigh of relief, not so much for me, but for him.

But he had something else to verbalize.

"I don't think I can do this," he finally said, dropping the mike to the floor as he exited stage-left in a hurry.

In this business, one learns quickly to go with the flow. Adapt, or take a walk into a different profession. We moved quickly into the next act. Ryan stood off to the side in the cafeteria/auditorium and watched the rest of the show. To my amazement, he walked onto the stage toward the end of the show, asked for the mike, and crooned out Locomotion to a standing ovation. Afterwards, the Quest "Dream Team" gave all the performers a massive group hug.

"Been a long road getting here," Deb remarked to me. "Real long." She was right, but it was worth every little step along the way.

It's important to start off in small, very small, steps. Our first theatrical production was performed in school, and for just the school. No outsiders to this baby. We wanted to see how it all went. It was one thing to practice with the students, but quite another when they had to perform in front of an audience. We had a lot of questions. Could they handle it? Would any of them lose it, and have, what we politely refer to in the world of profound special needs, a "major meltdown?" It wouldn't look too good to suddenly call for the behavioral specialists, aka- the big guys, who handle kids experiencing major "behavioral difficulties." When the call comes booming out over the school's P.A. system: "Code B! Code B!" you know "B" is for behavior, and that some student, somewhere in the building, is in that freak-out mode, possibly endangering him or herself, as well as fellow students and teachers. This urgent message is immediately followed by the exact location, such as "In the hallway by the front door!" Or, "on bus #64!" And then our behavioral policemen, yes - they're usually big, strong males - come running from all directions to the hot spot to handle the kid, and the situation, in a professional and safe manner.

The idea is to control the situation and to prevent any physical pain to the student. In addition, the behavioral specialists are trained to minimize even the psychological impact of the event on the perpetrator. It's all done in the most sensitive way possible, to help the student maintain his or her dignity. It's called PCM, which stands for Professional Care Management. Once I took a good look at my students, some of them close to six feet tall and well over 200 pounds, I too decided to get those three little letters after my name; David Lazerson, PCM. It means that after a kid comes up and sinks his fingernails deep into your forearm, well, you hopefully won't bust his jaw with a right hook. Rather, you'll stay focused and together, and won't lose it, and react emotionally. You may have to "mat" the student, (place him or her face down on a large, thickly cushioned mat), but they won't be body-slammed there by Stone Cold Steve Austin. Not unlike CPR, which is rather technical and demanding, you have to get recertified every year in PCM.

While we're here, let's discuss classroom management. There are a zillion books out there, and a similar number of courses, seminars, conferences and lectures that deal with this huge, sometimes overwhelming topic. Having spent 30-plus years in the field of special education, not as an administrator, but as a teacher on the "front lines," I'll simply offer here what has worked for me.

Behavioral Management — A Few Tips of the Trade

Like good dentistry — it's all about preventative medicine.

Fluoride beats drilling any ol' day.

There's no doubt about this one, folks. You're much better off going for a cleaning than a root canal. But after years of downing 4,986 gallons of soda - or "pop" as we like to call it in Buffalo - it's a bit late to think that brushing and dental flossing will keep the dentist far, far away. Added to the barrels of colored, sugar-water are 756,419 candy bars, truckloads of that awesome chocolate mint chip ice cream, too many doughnuts to even begin listing, and the fact that all these are all washed down with buckets of our favorite Starbucks lattes, that are simply too sweet to be true. Even our ketchup is loaded with sugar! We usually start making our new year's resolutions during those trips to the dentist. And we get mighty religious on the ride there. "Dear Lord, I'll be good. I promise. Please! Just let it be a small cavity, not this astronomically priced, mortgage-my-home implant! And even though the dentist desperately needs my salary to pay for his brand new Maserati and 12th vacation home in the Bahamas, still, I'm going cold turkey on the corn syrup and the licorice and the candy bars. Just one more chance. Pleeeeeeeeease! I'll be soooooo good!" By this time, of course, the heartfelt prayers are kind of a waste. The dentist's drill is warmed up and waiting, and you may just end up in that hot seat for quite a spell. It's simply a matter of way too little, way too late.

In my opinion, the same applies to behavioral management. Like dental flossing, gargling with Tom's mouthwash, and good hygiene are preventative strategies. Use the rules of good teaching and, for the most part, in fact for the 99.99% part, you won't leave the teaching job with a repetitive migraine, (and you won't want to ship your kids off to military school). Although a bit trickier, it also applies to parenting. For the most part, we simply have to out-smart the little buggers!

Part of your classroom or behavioral management strategy involves using some of the techniques already mentioned in this book. For one, get them moving as quickly as possible, first thing in the morning. If you can, get them running, as I did in my very first teaching assignment at Dr. MLK, Jr. Community School in Buffalo, NY. I ran with them outside, for close to a half hour. If it was lousy weather outside, then I used the school gym. If the gym was unavailable, then we did aerobic exercises in the classroom. To this very day, I still start off my morning experiential music class with movement exercises.

This strategy is particularly crucial for individuals with attention, hyperactivity, and behavioral issues. Unfortunately, many schools have cut what little there was of physical education and other fun-oriented activities, such as music and art. Students today have very few opportunities to just get up, stretch and move their bodies. There's this push to make them sit all day long. No wonder there's been a huge increase in reported ADD and ADHD, accompanied by all sorts of behavioral and anti-authority problems. What sort of individual is even capable of sitting that still for hours at a time? This backwards, outdated, militaristic approach is heavy-handed, and backed by threats, pressures, testing, and punishment. And all too often, when the kid fails to comply with this system, they bring out the "experts," who issue the call for drugs and medication. Nothing like some hard-core meds to make 'em sit still all day.

Enter the Floating Brains

This ineffective and highly abusive system has taken its toll on both students and teachers. It's a bizarre approach that views the child as this weird, floating brain. Like a strange Sci-Fi movie, imagine that you open the door to your classroom and in floats 10 or 20 brains that somehow find their way to, and hover over, their individual desks. The brains are not even attached to spinal cords, since the spinal cord is only really necessary for picking up and conveying signals to other parts of the body - which doesn't exist anymore. This sort of educational system doesn't see the whole child; one that has a heart to express emotions and feelings, and a body that responds in wondrous ways and needs to move, and a soul that longs to do good and reach for the stars. This brutal system views children this way because, in and of itself, it is heartless, lacks soul, and has no body, (substance), whatsoever. The only way to even try to overcome such a dreadful situation is to buck the system, and offer your own gym, music, and expressive arts programs. If the school system doesn't offer these "insignificant" components, then the onus is on the poor, underpaid teacher to somehow put these vitals back into his or her repertoire. But doing so will help maintain your sanity, as well as your students.

Even under the best of circumstances, a teacher or parent will have to deal with some inappropriate behaviors. But that's our job, and that's why we became parents and teachers. The kids who never seem to act out, or become defiant, would probably do just fine without us. So here are some practical strategies to help you get through those tense and tricky moments, and more importantly, to turn them into victories for everyone involved.

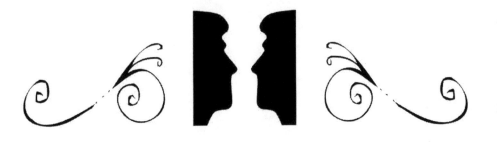

Practical and effective Behavioral Management

Pick your battles!

Not every infraction is worth the effort of engagement. Some things you can let slide off your back. You might not feel this way inside. Your guts might be telling you to stand your ground and fight! So remember, a good teacher is often a good actor. The same goes for parenting. Play like it doesn't bother you one teeny little bit. This often pulls the carpet right out from under their stinky little feet!

Theresa was simply called "T" back at my days at JFK. You remember this school from previous chapters. And you probably recall the meaning of those three letters. I'll refresh your memory just in case you skipped ahead to this chapter. JFK had nothing to do with a former US president. My students gave me the real definition. It stood for Jail For Kids. Anyhow, Ms.T was a student of mine for three years in a row. She was 12 when I first welcomed her, and 15-plus when she finally graduated to bigger and better things. She also had a mouth that could make a sailor blush! No, let me rephrase that. She could make a dang pirate blush. Basically, every other word out of her mouth was a candidate for censorship. The only problem was that she was doing it in school, not just out on the streets. She would also never, ever, back down from a fight. It didn't matter if it was two against one, or even if the other party was a big guy. She stood there, claws out, teeth in the ready position, ready to kill. Not too many took her up on going into battle. The third day I had Ms.T, she simply couldn't control herself anymore.

"So Ms. T," I asked. "What do you think this science word means?"

Her response was something like this, although I have to add the "bleeps" or they'd never publish this book!

"I don't give a bleepin bleep what the bleepin bleep means!" she responded.

"Ah, I see," I answered, with a tad-bit of a twinkle in my eye. I knew full well that curse words, especially those used in school and at home are used as "triggers." Words students often use to get your goat! Their goal is to get your heart pumping and your pulse flying, while they watch the color leave your face. In other words, they're said for effect. This is often related to the real issue, that getting some sort of attention is better than getting none: "If I can't get positive attention, well I sure as heck will do my sweet, ever-loving best to get the other kind." But I was hip to this game. I figured it was worth a shot a diffusing it through humor. This is my 2nd big commandment in the art of behavioral management:

* Things getting hot?

Lower the temperature through humor!

Okay, before we get ahead of ourselves, you're probably wondering just what exactly happened during the incident with Ms. T. Fair enough. Of course, she said her line in the middle of class, where all the other students could hear it...they all giggled nervously, and most probably wondered if I was going to give her the good ol' "pink slip." (This is where you send 'em to the office and the administration decides whether to impose an in-school or out-of-school suspension). But I figured that since this is what T was probably expecting as well, I simply wouldn't buy into this silly game. I also decided not to react emotionally, and get all hot and bothered, because a student had cursed like a maniac in my classroom.

"Nice," I quickly responded to T's outburst. "Do you know how to spell that juicy curse word?"

At this point, most of my students' mouths fell open. Ms. T gave me a startled look, but quickly regained her composure.

"I don't need to bleepin spell the bleepin bleep word! I just bleepin say bleep when I bleepin wanna say bleep!"

The other students looked at her, and then back at me. A few giggled nervously.

I ignored her statement and walked to the board.

"In my room, Ms. T," if you're going to use certain words, especially words you use a lot, I mean a real lot, well... you're just gonna have to learn how to spell 'em!"

I then picked up a piece of chalk and began to write the word on the board.

"Okay," I said continuing, to my students' utter astonishment, "let's sound it out, Ms. T."

She couldn't take the game to the next level, which of course was what I was totally hoping for. And she actually stopped cussing out loud for that entire period. I would love to tell you that she never cursed again in my room. No, it was simply too much a part of her being, at that point in her life. But all I had to do was pick up a piece of chalk and head to the board and she would restrain herself.

In our business, we educators like to keep track of our victories. It's good to know what works and what doesn't. I had another major victory using this magical touch of humor, at the same school, in fact. It's a line that I've used often, and it's worked every single time. It's one that you'll want to keep in your teaching/parenting arsenal.

It was during a math lesson with one of my very large V.E. (Varying Exceptionalities), classes. I had well over 20 students, ranging in age from 12 to almost 15, and the special needs ran the full spectrum from behavioral issues, to learning problems, to psychological disorders, to emotional difficulties. I also had no assistants, which made the job just a tad-bit on the challenging side.

I was in the middle of explaining something, and one student let out with some very loud, obnoxious sounds, Let's just say, it was a masterpiece coming from both ends of his body. The loud belch was followed by an even louder blast that the author Roald Dahl referred to as a "whiz-popper!"

The entire class burst into hysterical laughter. I waited the 20 seconds it took them to calm down, which of course felt more like 20 hours - then it was my turn.

"Ya know something," I said staring straight at Devon, the class clown, "that's the smartest thing you've said all day!"

This time they burst out into even louder and longer laughter. Only now they were on my side, laughing at the perpetrator, not me. Like good ammo, keep a few good lines in your response repertoire. They will come in handy.

* You Vs. The Terminator

My regimen was something that rivaled the local Marine unit. Every day. Not one day missed. My very survival might depend on it. And so, each day after working at Dr. MLK Jr. Community School in Buffalo, NY, I hit the gym for some iron pumping, rope skipping, pull-ups, sit-ups, crunches, and some work on the heavy bag. My reasoning was pretty simple. I figured that I had to be in top shape to make it as a teacher for an all-male class composed of teenage boys with special needs. I even wore a protective cup to work, as if playing in a football game. I kid you not. More specifically, I thought I had to be Schwarzenegger Junior to have any chance whatsoever.

But that realization came to a stunning halt one day while I cruised the school's hallways during my break period. Our principal, Dr. D, had an open-door policy. Unlike many other schools, MLK teachers had to keep their doors wide open. As a teacher, it was rather embarrassing to have a noisy class, and so we all did our very best to keep the noise level down to a dull roar. Two rooms down from me, I couldn't help notice how one teacher's class was completely quiet. You could hear a dang pin drop in her room. And no, there weren't two or three students receiving private tutoring. She had a packed-to-the-gills class, in this rather tough, inner-city school. To make things even more interesting, she was not only Caucasian - she was old! I don't mean that in a derogatory manner, it's just that it totally surprised me to see this cute, petite, white-haired lady standing in front of all these tough, hip, and often-wild students. What knocked my socks off was that she had total control over the class. How did she manage to pull that one off? I stood in the hallway and simply watched her operate, my mouth wide open.

She was pretty much the exact opposite of my teaching style and yet, she never, ever, raised her voice. In fact, she spoke in a whisper! Here, I was basically eating nails and garlic for breakfast and working like a horse to pump up my pecs and biceps, and this teeny, older white lady, with a bad case of laryngitis, was teaching her class in complete silence! Something clearly was amiss here. What did she have that I didn't? Was it an Uzi submachine gun hidden under her long, totally unfashionable skirt? Was she disguising Quaaludes as M&M's for her students?

After the bell rang and the hallway came bustling to life, I decided to have some words with her. How the heck did she do it?

"Excuse," I whispered to her. "Do you mind if I ask you…"

"Why are you whispering?" she responded in a regular speaking voice.

"I'm sorry," I said. "I just thought you had a problem with your throat."

"Oh that," she laughed. "No. That's just my teaching voice."

"Your teaching voice?"

"Yes," she said gathering up her papers and supplies. "I figure if I speak quietly then they'll have to pay really close attention to hear me. Works every time."

I was speechless.

"Oh, and one more thing," she winked. "Never ever discipline when you're all hot and bothered! The calmer the better. Getting all emotional just teaches a kid that it's okay to freak out. Plus, then they know what buttons to push, to get your goat!"

I knew as a parent that this last bit of advice was way up there on the top of the effective management ladder. Never discipline from anger. Stay cool, calm and collected! I realize it might be easier said than done, but like good ol' William Shakespeare commented in the classic work, As You Like It, "All the world's a stage, And all the men and women merely players." So even if one feels like yelling, screaming, and chucking the student/child out the window, well, keep it under control and play-act! You're in a play with your child or student, so act the part of a smart adult! Pretend you're not flipping out inside, and keep a calm voice. Then, and only then, is discipline effective. Besides, people do really stupid things under the influence of red-hot anger. Things they often regret, after the fact. Don't put yourself in that awful position.

I decided right then and there to try to emulate this superstar teacher. She became my mentor during my first three years of teaching at Dr. MLK Jr. Community School. One of the things she had over me was 30-plus years of experience. I could only marvel at her amazing skills in the classroom. She also had two other things going for her: First, she loved and respected the students, and her students in turn knew this, and respected her all the more. The second thing was that she was that rare combination of fairness and toughness. She set high expectations for her students and did everything possible to make sure that they worked hard enough to meet these expectations. She often went to visit their homes or apartments, to speak with family members. When I say often, I mean it was two or three times a week! She did this mostly to bring good news, but also made the trips to urge more family involvement, because she knew it would result in better student performance.

I still kept working out and pumping iron, but I realized that one doesn't have to become the Terminator or Predator to be a good teacher. You simply have to become yourself! Go with your own unique skills and personality. Like the Fab Four sing in, "All You Need Is Love": "Nothing you can do but you learn how to be you in time... it's easy!"

Find a good, solid teacher in your school,

and take some lessons!

This mentoring partnership will fortify you with good direction while on the road to becoming an effective and happy educator. The same notion applies to parents, as well. It boggles my mind...parenting is the most difficult and demanding job on the planet, and yet, most of us do it by osmosis. To make things even harder, the little ones don't come with how-to manuals. One day we go from being foot-loose and fancy-free to having this bundle in our laps. It's responsibility with a capitol R. Parents new to the game would do themselves and their kids a huge favor by hooking up with good, effective parents. Many places offer PET courses, or, Parent Effectiveness Training. Don't be swayed by the negative naysayers who tell you it's too little too late. To become more effective individuals, especially as teachers and parents, it's never too late to improve. More important than the so-called professional courses, is hands-on interactions and learning with a solid teacher or parent. Besides, this help is usually offered free of charge.

- ### *Student Helpers Do The Job!*

Like the saying goes, necessity is the mother of invention. Since I often had no assistant teachers or adult helpers in my special needs classrooms prior to the Quest Center, I often turned to students to help fill this role. We previously discussed peer and cross-age tutoring, but don't stop with academics alone. Students are particularly useful when it comes to behavioral management. In fact, they're not only effective, but also often tougher with their peers than the teacher would be.

For many individuals with special needs, behavioral reinforcements often need to be tangible, and occur more frequently. Grownups know all about delaying gratification. They might wait a week or two, or more for their paychecks, but nonetheless, they still go to work. They see the light at the end of the tunnel. Students with special needs have a rough time with this concept. Many have difficulty seeing outcomes at all, and thus, the rewards, or behavioral modification techniques, are critical to growth and development. Besides appropriate praise, such as, "catching the child being good," my arsenal also includes popcorn at the end of class, and little candies or pieces of cereal during class.

For my students with higher cognitive functioning, I appoint a few from each class to be the behavioral point sheet monitors. These sheets simply contain the names of the students. I work it like baseball. Three strikes, and he or she is out of the popcorn party at the end of the period. A student who disturbs others, or engages in some sort of negative behavior, receives a "w" after their name. The "w" stands for Warning. Two "w's" and the students know that they're close to striking out and need to make some behavioral adjustments. Exceptionally good behavior, such as sharing, and working nicely with another student, can eliminate a "w." In this simple manner, a student can mess up a bit in class, especially if it's a long period, and still know that it's possible to make amends and come out on top. Popcorn is relatively inexpensive. A little goes a long ways. Plus, it's a pretty healthy snack if you avoid the oil, melted butter, and heavy cheese toppings. I use a hot air popper right in the classroom, and have my two point-sheet monitors, pass out the goodies for our end of class party.

I usually start the year off with a popcorn party after each long period, or at the end of the day, if it's a self-contained class. Once this system kicks in and the students become used to it, I gradually wean them off the daily parties, to every other day, and then to an end of the week party, which includes other special foods and drinks, besides popcorn. To make it fairer, I switch point sheet monitor assignments, so everyone gets a chance to be in this position. I've found that some students enjoy this role more than others. On the one hand, there are some who don't want to be put in the position of what they see as, judging their peers. The big, tough kids usually have no problem with this role, and they'll help you run a quiet, effective classroom. Some individuals with special needs have trouble listening and following the teacher, but they'll shape up mighty fast when their peers are put in charge of the behavioral point system. Don't ignore these extra helping hands sitting right there in front of you. To sweeten the deal, I usually bring in an extra treat or two for the point sheet monitors. It gives a little added incentive, and helps insure the success of your behavior modification program.

- ### *Keep the rewards exciting, something with pizzazz!*

Besides the daily or weekly popcorn parties, I also put in place a grand monthly contest. The prizes include tickets to local sporting events, appropriate movies, and after-school dinners. All these types of activities have to be approved by your administration, and the parents/guardians. Anything done outside of school, (or after school), must have the parent's permission. To insure this happens, I simply have the parents become part of my behavioral support team. They help me plan the extra trips and events and come along to help chaperone and provide needed supervision. The main point here, is that the rewards have to be exciting, in order to motivate the student to respond. Very often these type of special outings and adventures are easier to implement in private schools. But many public schools take their students on exciting and meaningful trips, including extended overnights. You'll need to consult with your administration, and PTA, etc., about the best way to organize these awesome experiences. I've often used an afternoon scuba diving and snorkeling trip as a motivational prize. For this one, though, it's an end-of-semester excursion, and they have to earn the points as a group. This means they have to work as a team and learn to help one another out. Here too, classmates and peers become tremendous motivators, and help galvanize those students who seem more asleep than awake. As in academic peer tutoring, students often respond better to their classmates than they do to other adults and authority figures, (such as teachers).

I keep their progress as visual as possible and have different sorts of large displays right on the classroom wall. One of their favorites is the large football field that runs clear across a side wall of my room. Student names are written on brown-colored paper footballs. All the students start in one end zone on the "field" and each football moves across the large paper turf. The object is to score a touchdown by reaching the other end zone. The individual footballs slowly make their way across the field by earning points in my room for homework, class conduct, working together, helping out in the room, etc. This visual aide helps them see and monitor their own progress as the days and weeks move ahead.

- ### *Keep your cool.*

One final thought here on classroom and behavioral management before we get back to the main topic of this chapter. A good teacher is not only flexible, fair yet firm, and in charge of the classroom, but is also prepared. For special needs, it's always better to be over-prepared than to simply walk in and try to "wing" it.

Being well prepared means having all sorts of backup plans when Plan A, or Plan B, or Plan 439 fails. The more prepared you are before the students walk into the room, the less likely behavioral issues will occur. When they do, the trick is not to get emotionally fired up and react like a marine soldier engaged in hand-to-hand mortal combat. Keep the emotions cool, and have your behavioral plans at-the-ready. I've seen teachers totally lose their cool and start getting physical with students. Even those who won the battle, lost the war. They got more than fired up. They got fired.

The same strategies, by the way, apply to parenting. It's never beneficial to get physical with your own children, unless of course it means dancing, throwing a ball, or working out together. When you have to resort to physical violence against one of your own kids, you end up losing his or her respect and trust. There are all sorts of ways to deal with kids and teens in trouble. Physical abuse is not one of them. Speaking together, group and individual therapy sessions, even walking away from an escalating argument, is a far better option than fighting. If things are near the boiling point, then it's important to seek outside professional help. It's never a good idea to dish out negative consequences when the mind loses control over the heart. Anger can quickly turn from a low burner to a raging, destructive forest fire. Raw emotional anger is a tough one to overcome, but it has no place whatsoever in the classroom, or at home for that matter.

There are several management plans that highlight the positive, while dramatically reducing the focus on negative behaviors. Results are compelling, and several districts throughout the country have already introduced the Nurtured Heart approach. These schools have reported significant gains in a wide variety of areas, including: reduction of anti-social and anti-authority behaviors; improvement in student participation and self-concept; greater interest in school; improved attendance; and students who are happier with themselves and their learning. My wife's school, the Hebrew Academy in Margate, Florida, utilizes this positive-driven approach. She reports that it has tremendous benefits and notes that both she and her students seem happier and more self-assured than before. For further information about this promising approach, check out "Inner Wealth Initiative: The Nurtured Heart Approach for Educators," by Block, Glaser, & Grove (2007).

Ain't No Business Like Show Business

Let's return to the awesome use of theatrical drama productions for individuals with special needs. Whatever magic occurs on the stage in the "regular" world is nothing compared to what happens to individuals with special needs. It's their chance to shine, and they do - like the midday sun in Arizona. You'll have to pass out sunscreen to every member of the audience, because these productions are a rare mixture of incredible, time-consuming practice, and wonderful spontaneity. For individuals with autism, Downs-syndrome, CP, and other profound challenges, this is their time to take center stage. But be forewarned, along with the SPF 45 lotion, you'll have to pass out tissues to everyone. There won't be a dry eye in the place, and I'm not talking allergies here.

Peace, Love & Happiness.

Dust off the 60's Posters and Turn On The BLACK LIGHT!

One of the easiest - and totally coolest - mediums to use for a theatrical production is a black light. C'mon, surely you remember those awesome black light posters of Hendrix and Jefferson Airplane and Big Brother & The Holding Company from back in the day? It didn't take much to turn a plain-ole looking room into something really special. "Close the window shades and turn on the black light." All those amazing posters from the late 60's came to incredible life under a black light and this same notion applies to theatre for special needs. Make it something really awesome for the performers, as well as those in attendance. Give 'em an experience they'll never forget. Put Black Light Theatre to work!

*Any academic concept is brought to life through the medium of black light.
Students cut out and learned about a variety of shapes before putting on the
"Shape Roundup Black Light" drama production.*

Like everything else in special education, it all starts way before the culminating production. Black light is a powerful medium that can be extremely helpful for students who have trouble focusing and staying on task. When the room gets dark and the black light comes on, their attention automatically turns to whatever is highlighted via fluorescent paper or paint. Black light is extremely easy to use. You have to make sure the room can get really dark, and this means covering windows and possibly doorways, as well. At the Quest Center, we use black light to teach a variety of academic skills, including reading and math. This medium also becomes a vital component of our theatrical productions. It works the same magic with audiences, who become mesmerized by this special technique, and focus on whatever we

*Adam & Raymond get ready for the black light theatre
performance on shapes.*

highlight in white or fluorescent paint. It's often part of the scenery, or costumes or props that suddenly stand out. Students who are too shy to perform in public often shine brightly, you'll pardon the expression here, during a black light performance. They're able to "hide" beneath the cover of darkness while their costume props suddenly stand out and come to life. It provides anonymity, a veil from which to participate, that can be so important for individuals with special needs while they are new to this adventure.

Multi-Sensory Environments

We hear a lot of talk in the special education scene about multi-sensory environments or MSE. Black light is a wonderfully effective technique that can easily be a major part of any MSE. Areas, centers, or zones, depending on what the state is calling them these days, often have a wide array of switches that activate all sorts of lighting and visual effects. Others energize sound machines. Many MSE centers simply have pleasant "new-agey" sounds that help students chill out and feel calm. I put comfortable cushions and beanbag chairs in my room. This way the student doesn't have to sit in an uncomfortable chair, or stand. MSE areas also have stations that enable the student to touch certain elements, such as beads, water, sand, etc. The important thing is to create an area that the students are really interested in coming to. Here too, as in pretty much all other main areas of education, motivation is key. Black light makes for an exciting and visually engaging area. This black light medium, combined with music, singing, use of sign language, body movements, props & costumes, other lighting effects, and adaptive instruments, becomes a MSE, par excellence. It's one that is highly engaging for both the performers and the audience. Make sure to utilize each and every student in your black light productions. Wheelchair bound students can use adaptive switches to help run the lighting effects, the soundboard, and perform in the show.

A student uses her wheelchair to dramatically show the round shape of a wheel. Note the shapes on the stage and how the black light brings them to visual attention.

The "WOW!" effect

One doesn't have endless opportunities to catch that magical moment when teaching/learning occurs. Some refer to this special time as the "MTM" - the Most Teachable Moment - when all the cards are in the right order, the stars are lined up properly, and Bingo, real learning takes place. This book is about maximizing these "windows" of learning and getting the odds on your side as a teacher and/or parent. The "wow effect" is something I put to work in my classroom and is, in fact, very similar to using a black light. I use the "wow effect" from the very moment my students step into my special music room. The room is darkened, and I have special lighting effects already operating, such as colored spinning balls and butterflies with optic lighting. But the main component we've spoken of before...my awesome screen saver that simulates an under-the-sea adventure. This constantly changing imagery is taken from a scuba diver's perspective, as if the camera were built into the diver's mask. It's very beautiful and colorful, and is even accompanied by the sounds and images of underwater bubbles. I project this wonderful slow-moving screen saver onto the ceiling, and an entire back wall. To do this, I simply move the projector as far back as possible, to allow the greatest amount of surface for displaying the underwater adventure. I'm pretty certain this simple technique is magic, because the next class is always lined up outside, eager to enter my undersea world - the hands on music classroom - where they experience all sorts of interesting sounds and images. Put the "wow" effect to work in your own specially designed MSE for your child or students. Once they're engaged and interested in this unique "outside" environment, you have opened the door to introducing anything you want for teaching, and the acquisition of important skills. The trick is to get them motivated and engaged. Commence this "wow" effect the moment they enter this special area known as the MMSE; the Music Multi-Sensory Experience.

Students gaze at the fish swimming on the wall and ceiling of my room. I turn off the main lights and let this wonderful screensaver grab their attention.

Let's Get "Physual"

This section of the chapter deals with expressive visual arts and its adaptation to individuals with special needs. Here too, as highlighted in previous chapters of this book, the techniques and strategies discussed are highly appropriate for our "regulars," as well. I have purposely avoided using the term "normal," for, as anyone who's ever been a parent or teacher knows, that's one label that belongs in the circular file. Normal? Riiiiight. No such entity, no such creature. In light of what we discussed before, regarding the FID Factor, (Frequency, Intensity and Duration), this notion of "normality" is as subjective as one can get. It varies from country to country, from culture to culture, from sub-culture to sub-culture, and ultimately from individual to individual. My use of regular, therefore, implies a description of the teaching mode. It covers approximately 68% of the population as depicted in that lovely statistical model known as the Bell Curve. This grouping includes all those who fall within one standard deviation, from either below or above the median. It's also what most teachers end up teaching to - this sort of grey, uniform blob of students in the middle. Those on either side, the "fringe elements," usually get lost in the shuffle.

At the risk of sounding redundant, many of our schools are based on an archaic model of education. One that stipulates that all kids, the same age, learn the same thing, in the same way. It almost sounds absurd to even write such a statement. But it is, nonetheless, the continued practice and policy enforced in the "system" at large. Some dinosaurs just don't know when to get out of the way. In today's rapid paced environment, where one can immediately-access-everything from a 3-inch 3-D cell phone, kids often view traditional schools as ancient T-Rexes miring about in a tar pit. Let's be honest here. Most kids today are far more computer and tech savvy than their supposed "teachers" and parents. I know whenever I have a problem with something on my website, or with a certain function on my iMac, I turn to my 16 year old grandson Mendy, for some assistance. If he's not available, his younger brother by two years is a darn good substitute. Mendy is a lot cheaper than the Best Buy Geek Squad and shows up at my door a heckuva lot quicker.

Further compounding the public school downhill slide, is the fact that many schools continue to cut their arts programs, and other "extra-curricular activities," such as phys-ed and music. These "specials" are often the only periods of refuge, (and movement), a student gets during the long hours comprised mostly of sitting at a desk. Despite this bad news, the teacher or therapist can introduce many visual arts techniques that can be of tremendous benefit to individuals of all sizes, shapes, colors, and needs.

What are the Visual Arts & What Can They Do For People?

The phrase "visual arts" is another of those broad, umbrella-like notions that encompasses a tremendous variety of focuses and activities. The nerve center here is one that deals with the act of creating some type of art form that can be shared visually, such as paintings, drawings, and even three dimensional art, such as sculptures, ceramic pieces, etc. Thus, we're talking about an art form that can be seen by both the artist and others. In my opinion this tends to be a rather narrow definition, since I also utilize these art forms with students who don't "see" in the traditional sense. The visual arts have worked magic for my students who were designated "legally blind" - a term which means they have very limited visual capacities and may only sense things such as shadows, lines, faded colors, or peripheral imagery, etc. A legally blind person can't get a valid driver's license or operate any potentially dangerous mechanical equipment. I've also used "visual" art forms with students who were completely blind, and for them, the experience becomes more of a kinesthetic/tactile & body movement exposure.

Perhaps a more accurate description of this general art from should be the "physical arts," since it requires a lot more than simply looking at something and processing visual information. The title of this chapter could very well be, "Let's Get Physical." After all, think about the process involved in painting or coloring. The artist must pick up and hold some sort of coloring utensil, decide where and how to begin painting, put the brush or marker to the paper, and then move his or hand in some sort of deliberate action. But the hand and arm are often not the only body parts moving here. Very often, as the person connects with some inner emotion - particularly in response to certain background music selections - the entire body begins responding. The artist may sway back and forth. They may "throw" the paint onto the paper to the beat of the music. Some artists even paint with their feet, and thus, the entire body is actively involved in the process labeled mere "visual arts".

In case you were wondering about the descriptor of this section (Let's Get Physual!), I'd like to suggest this new term because it more accurately describes the incredibly powerful process involved in visual/physical arts. It does a nice job of combining the terms Physical & Visual.

Now that we have a better working definition here, we can move on to the crux of the matter. What do the Physual Arts do for people? The list of benefits could be a mile long and is, in fact, probably limitless, well beyond our feeble attempts to put into that nice, neat box of descriptors. The "physual arts" have been successfully used in a wide variety of situations. The list below names a few of the uses and benefits of a "physual" arts program.

- *Treating Alzheimer patients and others suffering from severe psychological disorders*
- *Physical rehabilitation*
- *Improving on-task behaviors for individuals with ADHD*
- *Providing therapeutic benefits for those suffering from psychological and emotional disorders*
- *Improving gross and fine-motor coordination*
- *Allowing for nonverbal communication*
- *Provides opportunities for personal fulfillment*
- *Gives a sense of enjoyment and pleasure*
- *Provides a calming and often meditative effect*
- *Encourages self-expression*

As we mentioned, the medium for the Physual Arts is even more varied than its definition and benefits. The Physual Arts may be as intricate as the time, effort, inspiration, and expertise that went into creating Michelangelo's statue of David, or the famous Sistine Chapel. Conversely, it may be a simple as playing with sand or shaving cream on a table. The important thing is to start utilizing the expressive arts with your children and students.

My big sister Sharon, whom I affectionately call Sr. Walker since she refers to me as Jr. Walker & The All Stars, helps run an incredible program in the Berkshires for Alzheimer's patients. She uses all sorts of expressive arts with them, including Physual arts, singing, dancing, body movement, exercise and often, a combination of the above. She also uses a lot of humor-therapy.

This rather unique program in the Northeast part of the United States, utilizes an approach called "Habilitation." This philosophy focuses on maintaining the functional skills the clients have, without trying to force them into a predetermined system. It means entering into the individual's personal sense of reality and working from there. Sharon frequently has them listen to music, or a poem by Frost, while engaging in painting.

During one session while painting with watercolors, Sharon noted that the process was almost magical. "A calmness enveloped the entire room when they would paint." Together with her clients and staff, they put on several art shows, displaying the unique talents and perspectives of the patients. Some of the artworks on display were beautiful depictions of nature, such as ocean waves, or trees. Nevertheless, they all served the purpose of helping the artists connect, on a deeper level, with themselves. Perhaps a buried memory emerges through the act of painting. Or, perhaps the very act of engaging in the physual arts helps stimulate brain cells and triggers events retained in long-term memory. Either way, it's a win-win situation for both process and product.

Sharon has some delightful, heartfelt, and humorous stories about her work with these wonderful people. Sometimes these events happen when you least expect it.

Sharon, leading a group in some singing & chair movement exercises at the Kimball Farms center in the Berkshires.

One time she was telling someone at the assisted living facility how a former high school teacher of mine told me I would amount to nothing. To my face, on the day of high school graduation, this teacher came up to me and poked me in the chest and remarked "Mr. Lazerson, you'll amount to nothing! You'll be behind bars one day." As Sharon was describing this incident to a fellow worker at the home, a client, who usually sits quietly in his wheelchair all day, suddenly burst out with "What? Let's go and spit on her grave!" We really have to watch what we say, because one never knows what they're processing. Always assume that they can process anything and everything. We definitely don't want our words to come back and haunt us one day. Sharon and her colleague cracked up at this client's sudden outburst that was, in my humble opinion, very cool and right on track.

The art shows are a wonderful way to display your students and children's masterpieces. It's an awesome way to boost their self-esteem. Although at Sharon's place, it's not so easy. Due to their current mental state and challenges, they often have poor memory recall, even when it comes to their own handiwork. She told me about an older man with Alzheimer's who simply couldn't believe that he had created a certain painting of a sunset. "No, I didn't do that," he said. "I couldn't have." It was a bittersweet moment, as Sharon tried to convince him that he actually had done this wonderful painting a few days prior. The more you use the expressive arts the greater the benefits. So get in there and "express" yourself. Design your own MSE environment. Turn on the black lights. In doing so, you will help turn on the "turned-off" learner.

Drawing by one of my former students, Edward Solares, when he was pushing 13 years old. I never realized he was so talented until he had some free time in class for the "physual" arts. You gotta love his attention to detail —the NY Yankee logo on my skullcap!

I often give my students some free time for drawing or painting -anything that allows them to get "physual." It's a tremendous way for them to tap into their creative side and learn to express themselves through whatever visual arts medium they decide to use. Sometimes the results are quite extraordinary. In one of my Varying Exceptionalities classes, the students were busy putting this free time to good work. Some used colored pencils. Others brought out watercolors. A few even started working with clay. I put on some nice classical music and simply told my students to "let it flow." One 13-year-old student brought me a drawing that knocked my socks off. I had no idea he was so talented in the visual arts. I told him that one day I would use his amazing picture for an album cover of mine.

200

Putting Technology To Work.

What is Assistive Technology and what can it do for my student or child?

The area known as assistive technology is an ever-growing one in special education. What we have available today is a far cry from what we had 20 or even 10 years ago. As computers get faster, ever smaller, and more powerful, today's innovation is quickly relegated to the status of, a "dinosaur" of the technological world. While this process usually means a year or two of validity, in some cases it applies almost overnight. However, the goal and objective essentially remains the same: to help individuals with special needs achieve their full potential. This applies on all levels, from basic physical needs, such as movement and walking, to expression and communication. I recently saw an amazing project from Israel, where they're working on a kind of Iron-Man-type suit that will help wheelchair-bound individuals stand up, walk, and even climb stairs. In a similar vein, Guitar Hero now has a version that students can use with adaptive switches, such as knee, head, eye-blink and even puff switches. Thus, the goal is to take those with disabilities and turn them from disablers to "ablers" through these enabling devices. As discussed in previous chapters, this area of assistive technology helps bring the child with special needs from the usual role of passive observer to one of a more-active participant. The only limitation may very well be our imagination.

By utilizing assistive technology appropriately, an ever-increasing number of individuals with profound special needs can participate in your dramatic musical productions. The use of adaptive switches and assistive technology helps even the most profoundly challenged child become a more active participant. We use this dynamic combination to help our wheelchair-bound, non-verbal students become part of our drama productions. Some help regulate the lighting effects. Others "sing" duets. A few students run the visuals or backgrounds and various scenes that go along with the songs. Some run adaptive drumming and percussion instruments. And some even tell jokes, and function as the show's MC - Master of Ceremonies, announcing the next act. It's a simple, yet powerful combination, accomplished by using the child's adaptive switch and a communication device. Eventually, through trial & error, you'll discover what role your child or any specific student prefers to assume. Yusupha, an older male student at the Quest Center, has really taken to his role as our production's MC. He welcomes everyone to the show, and announces each act before it takes place on stage. He even tells a few jokes! Not bad for an individual who's basically non-verbal and requires a wheelchair for mobility.

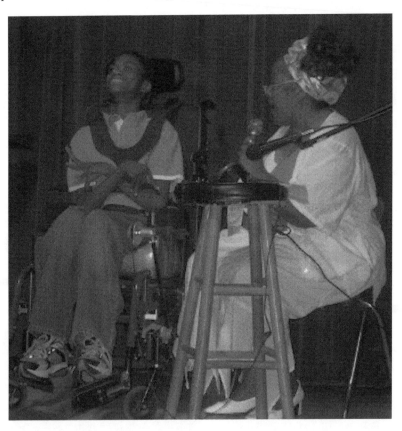

Dynamic Duo! Yusupha and his teacher Debra Kelly, rock the Talent Show. Using his adaptive switch by his left knee — which is connected to the Step-by-Step communication device on top of the stool, Yusupha "sings" his part of the duet. Needless to say, he stole

One last point to mention here, and it involves showing appropriate and highly motivational visuals in your room's MSE, whether at school or in your own home.

These are easy to do, and can make a world of difference for your student or child. Start producing your very own PowerPoint (PPT) presentations. Once you get the hang of it, you'll soon have to join the PPA for your addiction. (That's the Power Point Anonymous group). I currently use over 50 different PPT slideshows that enhance all sorts of academic skills, from counting, to colors, to holiday themes and everything in between. There are a variety of computer programs that gather various pictures or animations and merge them together in a slideshow format. So, whatever is easier for you. For a nice personal touch, put pictures of your own students and children into the various presentations. Let's take the T-Man for example. You will recall that he absolutely loves the song Day-Oh. (If you need to refresh your memory cells, visit the chapter on music). I put together a PPT that went along with this tune, and added some pictures of Tony to the mix. Needless to say, he smiles ear to ear whenever we play this tune and show the PPT slideshow with it. It's not only easy to make PPT shows, but many pictures have built-in animation. They move or glitter, and do all sorts of tricks on their own. You can also add a variety of special effects to any picture you use, from expanding in or out, to spinning and flashing, etc. The added benefit of using assistive technology, is that students with special needs can run the shows on their own. Tony operates the Day-Oh PPT by using his adaptive head switch, which in turn communicates with the computer, wirelessly. Every head movement translates into hitting the return button on the keyboard, which of course moves the PPT show along to the next slide.

I've turned to two companies in particular, for their help and expertise in this ever-expanding area of assistive technology. Check the Internet for their latest products and updates, and certainly, do yourself and your students a favor by requesting their latest catalogue. These two companies have names that are easy to remember:Able-Net at www.ablenetinc.com and Enabling Devices at www.enablingdevices.com. In lieu of the expensive PowerPoint program, try the reputable OpenSource software called, Open Office, and use their "Impress" slide-show creator: www.download.openoffice.org. Turn your classrooms and your musical drama productions, into real, "equal-opportunity" employers. You'll be amazed at what you and your students can do.

TEACH ME IF YOU CAN!

CHAPTER 7

Teachers & Administrators — The Good, The Bad, & The Really Unusual

The Good, The Bad, & The Really Unusual

"The best principals are not heroes; they are hero makers."

— Roland Barth

Before we continue with other exciting strategies for your students, we need to deal with a most important issue: working with the school's administration. You can have the most glorious ideas in the world for stimulating learning and participation, but if there's no "green light" from the powers-that-be, they won't see the light of day. This chapter could very well be called, Staying Happy As A Teacher, Through a Cooperative & Helpful Administration.

Some may wonder if these two positions can even jive together. Perhaps the most famous, (and currently-hot), system of teacher training and school improvement, is the Marzano Causal Teacher Evaluation Model. Marzano lists administrative/teacher relationships as one of "the most significant contributing factors to teacher growth and development". Many school districts throughout the country have adopted Marzano's research-based principals. For further information about these highly effective strategies for professional growth, start with the following source: www.iobservation.com/Marzano-Suite.

In light of the above, the opposite is also true. A miserable educator usually has a principal, (or assistant principal), breathing down his or her neck. Simply put, the administration can make or break a teacher. But unlike books and articles that talk about the need to exercise and be good to yourself by taking daily foot massages, this one gets right to the crux of the matter. All the after-work health spas, vacations, rollerblading and rope skipping, yoga meditations and chamomile tea, won't do your stress level much good, if Monday morning, your boss is back on your case, shattering what's left of your ego to smithereens. Some principals and AP's seem to thrive on this sort of nonsense and that, in my opinion, is nothing short of bullying.

What makes the situation even wackier, is that most school districts now have strict anti-bullying policies in place. These are important, and necessary steps for protecting students. But educational departments seldom explore the very real problem of administrators who unfairly push their weight around with teachers. It's an issue I've seen play out all-too-often in schools. Many teachers feel picked on, threatened and abused, and leave their schools for what they hope will be greener pastures. Some, especially newer teachers, leave the field of education altogether. It's a sad loss that can and should be prevented.

I must share a little secret with you. The truth is, I was very hesitant about taking the job offer at the Quest Center. I was certainly qualified and not at all ashamed of my Ph.D. or 20 years experience. It had nothing to do with ego, whatsoever. It wasn't even about changing those humongous diapers on very large bodies. It wasn't class size. Or lack of supplies. And it wasn't even the salary that had me bugged. My reluctance to teach at the Quest was based on old battle scars obtained on the frontlines of the education world. Wars fought, not with out-of-control students or irate parents, that's easy stuff. These hardcore battles were fought between teachers and administrators. I wasn't wimping out on the Quest offer, instead, I was just battle-weary, and my last teaching position, (prior to the Quest offer), left me with a serious case of the pits. Let's put that in capitol letters: PITS. Ahhh, much better. This lovely term stands for the following: Post Irritated Teacher Stress. It describes the residue that remains behind after multiple confrontations. Before we discuss the ever-crucial role that administrators play in the lives and well being of their teachers, let me share with you two such battles, with two different administrators, in two different school districts, in two different parts of the country. The common thread is that both led to bad blood, and both were totally unnecessary. They should never have happened.

The first major brawl took place in my very own neighborhood school. It was always fun to see my students, known as "the motley crew," to the hood. I wish I could say the same for the administration.

Collision Course

"Step outside please."

His finger motioned me to drop, (ASAP), whatever I was doing — a hot game of chess — and attend to his almighty-important business, which no doubt, spelled trouble. It also meant leaving my students alone in the classroom for a few moments, always a dangerous notion. After all, this was a VE — Varying Exceptionalities class for 20-plus wild teens. VE basically meant that the county was saving a whole lot of money by dumping kids together who had been diagnosed with emotional problems, behavioral problems, attention deficit/hyperactivity disorders, learning difficulties, and my favorite label, "issues with authority." This last one was always the doozy, especially since the VE teacher, me, was in the position of authority here.

Still, he was the AP, Mister Assistant Principal. I knew what the letters AP really stood for, "Always Power-hungry!" His finger told me to move a bit quicker, his head now a fixture in the doorway.

"Excuse me everyone," I said to my students. They nodded their heads in what seemed to be a gesture of sympathy for me, as if to say, "good luck".

"Be right back."

I entered the doorway, and with the door opened just enough for us to communicate while still eyeballing my crew, I simply said, "What's up?"

"Come out, and shut your door."

"Leave them unsupervised?"

"It'll be less than a minute."

"Unsup… I mean I thought I was never supposed to leave them."

"Just shut the door for a moment," he demanded.

Reluctantly, and somewhat slowly, I followed his directives.

"What are you doing in your room?" he demanded.

"We're in the middle of a break. During this time, I give them some thinking-type games, and activities. You know, chess, checkers, Uno. Stuff like that."

I was sure this type of innovative thinking would earn me some Brownie points. "Not bad," he must be thinking. "Laz, the brand new teacher on the block, gives 'em structure, even during their break time! Educational games, no less!" But for some reason, he didn't seem all that impressed. In fact, his face reddened and his jugular veins became more visible.

"Not here, Dr. Laz. Not in this school. Not in my school."

"Not what?" I asked, in all innocence.

"No games. No breaks."

"It's not like they're in there gambling over a hot Uno game."

"None."

"But the periods are almost two hours long," I protested. "And on their IEP's, you know the Individualized Education Plans, it says they have to have frequent breaks."

"That's not our school policy."

"Isn't the IEP law?" I responded, still trying for reason here. "You know, federal law…heavy duty stuff?"

"Yeah, well, put that aside. Here we teach bell-to-bell. They're supposed to be sitting on their butts working, from bell-to-bell."

I looked at him with that "huh" sort of expression. IEP was indeed law. It was something set up for every child and student placed in a special education environment. To the diehard followers of this paperwork, IEPs are referred to as, "living documents." Each IEP is supposed to be monitored throughout the school year, as you note any changes, developments, accomplishments, etc., towards the student's individual goals. Nearly everyone in my VE class had the words "frequent breaks," underlined and highlighted, (in fluorescent pink or bright yellow colors), on their

208

IEP's. In fact, they were probably initially written in neon, flashing lights. Hey, I can't sit still for an hour and 50 minute session. I'd be real happy if I could make it for 20 minutes. How could anyone expect it from my students? (I also knew that Mister AP couldn't sit on his backside for more than ten. He was always jumping around the school).

"And what's considered a frequent break?" I asked. "The five minutes they get walking to their next class?"

He tried to verbalize, but seemed a bit in shock. He began to turn a variety of colors. (I thought the madras one was a particularly nice effect). I guess I was supposed to roll over and play dead here. But even though I was a new kid on this block, (it was my first special education assignment in South Florida), nonetheless, I was coming in with 20-plus years of hard-core classroom experience: Approximately 5 inner-city years back in my Buffalo days. Over 15 years in NYC with some seriously challenged adolescents and teenagers. Plus, I had just survived a bunch of wild and crazy years living in multi-ethnic Crown Heights, Brooklyn, during the turbulent urban race riots. Quite frankly, I wasn't all that intimidated by a greenhorn administrator on a power trip.

"Look," I continued. "I'm not trying to rock the boat here. I just wanna know how I should regard the directives on their IEP's. Do I pay attention to them or ignore them? What are you requesting me to do?"

He was treading on some very thin ice, and I guess in terms of job security, so was I.

"Imagine if the rest of the students find out what's going on your room?" he said shaking his finger. "Imagine the chaos it would cause. That's not gonna happen at my school. Is this clear?"

The students told me that the letters JFK had nothing to do with an American president. To them the letters meant "Jail For Kids." I was beginning to understand what they meant.

"Why not have other teachers try the same thing?" I said, trying to give it one last desperate attempt. "I think they'd have fewer behavioral problems. I mean, this way, the kids would focus more during…"

"No breaks!"

"No breaks?"

"Not a one!"

"Not a one?"

"Bell-to-bell."

"Bell-to-bell?"

"On their butts in their seats."

"No problem," I said, shaking my head in disbelief.

But I was really thinking, "No way. Not a blooming chance." Chalk up another brilliant, "do-it-cuz-I-say-so-cuz-I'm-the-almighty-administrator-here-and-you're-the-lowly-lowlife-peon, mere-teacher rule. Doomed from the start. This was one rule guaranteed to create lots of violators, and lots of ridiculous punishments, as well. It was the absolutely perfect example of the negative snowball effect.

I always try to work with others, get along, and follow the game plan. To be a team player. But this was something off-the-dang- wall. Besides, this guy wasn't the one standing in the classroom for these extra-long 110-minute blocks of time. Nope. He was safely out of the classroom, just giving orders. I knew that this absurd request wouldn't stand up in court. Many moons ago, back in my beginning years of teaching in my hometown of Buffalo, NY, a veteran teacher advised me to never ask permission. I wasn't sure what he meant, but he spelled it out rather clearly:

"It's easier to ask for forgiveness, and get it, than ask for permission, which you usually never get anyhow," he told me. In other words, you just carry on, do the right stuff, and do whatever it takes to get the job done. If you did something you weren't supposed to do, then you'll find out. Mighty quickly, in fact. Then, say you're sorry and move on. If you do something good, well most likely you won't hear too much, but most teachers aren't in the business for pats on the back from the higher-ups. We get our highs from our students. Watching them grow, learn, and develop holds some mighty intrinsic rewards.

Unfortunately, I no longer had the luxury of claiming innocence. The "school policy," or probably more accurately, the AP's policy, was clearly laid out on the table.

"If that's what you want," I said slowly. "Can I go back to my room now?"

He nodded his head and walked away.

My students were unusually quiet. I suppose they had been trying to catch some words of our conversation. They gave me that "what-the-heck-happened," "what-should-we-do-now?" look.

"Carry on mates," I shouted joyfully as I made my way back to my hot and heavy chess game. A good teacher is also a good actor. I had to put on my happy face, although I had a much different feeling in my gut. "Now, where were we?" I had some fine chess players. One of my Russian students could play five classmates simultaneously - and whoop 'em all, hands down.

This special ed teacher was not going to ignore their IEP's, or good common sense, for that matter. Come what may, job or no job, my chess and card games were on. It was the only way I could actually get them to focus on our class unit. Knowing that they would get a break for good behavior seemed to be working in my room. They also liked working toward special rewards, and my end-of-the-period homemade popcorn. I never had to send a kid to the office, or push my emergency bell, (sending the security guards rushing to my room). Perhaps my techniques were actually working. My professor and mentor, Dr. Bernie Yormak, AKA — BBY, from Buffalo State College where I pursued my Master's degree in learning & behavioral disabilities, had a way of putting things: "The head can only take as much as the rear end can sit," he told us teacher wannabes. "Don't ever forget that!"

I think Dr. BBY was smiling over my shoulder, that very moment. I figured it was cruel and unusual punishment to force these students to sit still for almost two hours straight — only to repeat it five minutes later during their next period - and to resume the position, one mo' time, after lunch. "No normal kid can do such a thing," I thought to myself. No wonder the other teachers were sending their students to the office like moths to a spotlight. You would've thought the AP would appreciate me not filling up his office, and time, with a zillion detentions.

Who knew what the day would bring. A "pink slip" perhaps, in my mailbox? A hearing with the administration for ignoring a directive, and not following internal school policy? For the time being, he either assumed I was enforcing this sitting bell-to-bell rule, or he let it slide, not choosing to pursue a legal fight against state and federal law. Nonetheless, he was determined to make my life as miserable as possible in "his" school.

That hallway discussion was one of many battles to come. The AP's next step was to ban popcorn making at the end of each period. I told the administrator that my students worked nicely in the room, and needed this sort of behavior-mod program to help them stay focused and on task for that hour and 50 minute block of time. "But the other special ed students are jealous," the AP told me. "The whole school smells the popcorn. We just can't have this going on here!"

"Why not tell the other teachers to do something similar?" I told him. "It works. It's dirt-cheap. Popcorn's even healthy. They'd have a lot less headaches and behavioral problems."

Fat chance. This was another glorious blunder into the realm of sinking to the lowest common denominator. Since everyone else can't be bothered with these "new" ideas, well boy, neither will you! When he couldn't respond to educationally based "proofs," (my students were never sent to the office, and my room was basically quiet during instruction time), he simply said, "popcorn brings bugs...it has to stop."

Now I was forced to buy more expensive, ready-made treats to use as class rewards. This was done on the sly. Like Rabbi Nike says, "just do it!" It is an expression I've always tried to emulate. "Got something good to do — well, indeed, just do it." The Nike logo was even emblazoned on the top of my skullcap. I put it there myself, using special glow-in-the-dark, fabric paint.

I had my toughest, biggest, baddest, guys and gals running the point system each class period. And what a job they did. Tough as nails. Much harder with the points than I would've been. But it worked like a charm. All I had to do was give out prizes to our daily winners. This was one system I was determined not to have the other teachers or the AP find out about. For sure, they'd put a stop to it, as well, finding some ridiculous reason to support their own lack of imagination. They always seemed to be on the warpath when anyone rocked the system or demonstrated a bit of creativity. Next on the chopping block was team-teaching with my dear friend and super social studies teacher, Marsha Neuberger Katz. We taught the civil war and the holocaust together. It was a wonderful system for both her "regular" students, and my VE kids. But this too, for some crazy reason, bothered my AP.

"Not good," he told me in the hallway. "Learning takes place in your room. That's where you get paid to teach. The team teaching has to stop."

I cringed when I heard that statement. It not only signaled more of his narrow minded, power-trip nonsense, but, on a more personal note, it brought back some mighty bad memories from yet another deep battle scar:

Major incident number two goes back to my teaching days in my good ol' hometown of Buffalo, NY. I was in the hallowed grounds of my very own alma mater high school, Bennett High. This was a large public high school - composed of more than 2500 students. I was the special education resource-room teacher. It was hard to believe that I was teaching at the high school I used to attend. Our school anthem said it all: "Bennett, Bennett, lead us onward, for the best is yet to be." I always loved our school song, because it seemed so upbeat and optimistic. But here too, the ever-power-hungry assistant principal lurked the hallways.

Each 50-minute period was different. I had anywhere from three students, on the low end, to more than 15 on the high. Some came for tutorial-type help, others for remedial assistance, working on a specific learning issue. I've always been a big believer in experiential education - real life experiences - and since I love scuba diving, I decided it was high time to expose my kiddies to the amazing undersea world of Jacques Cousteau. Since I'm not yet a billionaire, I knew I couldn't bring the whole crew to the Bahamas, or even the "Coin Pile" in Buffalo's Niagara River.

Scuba diving lessons always begin in a pool, and since the high school pool was both large and beautiful, and came complete with seating for 100 plus, it was a perfect fit. I did my lesson plans and prepared a handout for every student. I even arranged it with the gym and swim teachers, indicating that their students could attend, as well. These teachers were thrilled, because it meant a break from their regular routine. Besides, we all felt it would be both educational and motivational.

My handouts were a true work of art. Complete with pictures, drawings, and all sorts of heavy-duty science questions.

*What's in the air you inhale?

*What's in the air you exhale?

*What's the main component of air?

*What's the air pressure on your body right now?

*What happens to air and pressure as you descend underwater?

It would be a lesson they'd never forget. It was also a lesson that I would never ever forget, but unfortunately not for the same reasons.

Enter once again that equation: The administrator > the lowly, (submissive, know-nothing, those-who-can't-do-teach), educator. Like an idiot, I asked for permission. I had forgotten "ask for forgiveness not permission." But I must admit, I was not just seeking approval, but trying to score some "brownie points." I mistakenly figured he'd be completely thrilled about my exciting proposition. "That's awesome," he would say to me. "Keep up the great work! So wonderful to have teachers going out of their way to educate and inspire our students!" Right. Fat chance.

"You get paid to teach in your classroom," Bennett's AP told me. "That's where learning takes place."

"Hold on," I argued. "That's where learning usually takes place. I just wanna give them something different. Something to turn them on, get them excited about something. And besides, they're not jumping in the water with me. It's just a hands-on, live-science kind of demonstration."

He looked at me like I was totally off the wall.

"Like I said, learning takes place in your classroom. If you want, do it on your break period."

I felt like the wind had been taken out of my sails and the ship was suddenly sinking.

"But Mr. Z," I begged, "it takes me 20 minutes to get suited up and another 15 to put it all away. That leaves about 10 minutes for the lesson!"

"That's your choice," he responded, and turned and walked away.

My self-imposed Scout's Oath of Teaching was coming back to hit me in the face. It was the one I made to my inner-most, deepest self: "I hereby promise not to do to my students what most of my teachers have done to me — Bore The Living Daylights Out Of Me! I will do whatever it takes to inspire, motivate & stimulate my students To Grow & Learn." Within reason, mind you. The live scuba demonstration? It seemed well within the boundaries of sound reasoning.

Did I have the guts to keep my teaching oath here? It would not look cool for me to be fired in my hometown, let alone my Alma Mater school, (that I graduated from only nine years prior)! Not great headlines for the local Buffalo News. On the other hand, like at JFK, the AP's decision was not based on whether educating was taking place. Was he simply old-fashioned? A tad too much military training in his background? Lacking in self-concept, so he compensated through power trips? Jealous of the more-creative teachers on campus? A bit anti-Semitic, perhaps? A weird combo of all the above? There are actually administrative certification programs that teach principal and assistant principal candidates how to intimidate, and put the "fear of the Lord" into teachers. They reason that fear is a mighty big motivator for adults worried about losing their jobs, their sense of security, and their self-esteem. In my opinion, you get a lot more from the bee's honey than from its stinger.

Come hell or high water, I had to be honest with myself. I had to be able to face myself in the mirror each morning — and especially in the late afternoon, when I was done teaching.

And so, that particular day in good ol' Buffalo, found me in the chlorinated water of the high school pool's deep end. Not only for my 50-minute break period, but also for every period of the school day. Hundreds of students saw the live demonstration. They all got my handouts. During that last period, when all had gone even better than expected, the swim teacher motioned for me to come closer to the side of the pool. I slowly made my way over to him, (I was in full scuba gear, BC — buoyancy compensator, weight belt of about 24 pounds). While movement under the surface was actually quite graceful, on top of the water it's all very awkward. You kind feel like a large sea lion trying to climb on top of an iceberg). "Laz," he whispered when I finally got in range, "you gotta get out now! Mister Z came by and says he wants to see you immediately!"

"Hey," I responded, "I'm already in hot water, well, deep water anyhow, you'll pardon the expression. Tell Mister Z if he wants to see me he can meet me right here, in the middle of the deep end!"

Dumb move on my part? Perhaps. Pink slip in my mailbox? No doubt. But all they could get me on was not following an even dumber directive. In any sort of hearing, I was the one standing on firm, educational ground — not so, the administrator. Floating in the deep end of my Alma Mater high school pool in front of 125 attentive, interested students, I felt strangely good inside. It was a powerful "Zen-like" moment knowing I actually made the right ethical decision and forced the administration to take a closer look at their educational philosophy. Education is not the military, and schools are not supposed to be marine training camps. And...teachers should not be treated like new GI's in boot camp. We've already paid our dues to become teachers: finished all our course work, our training, and passed our teacher exams. Now was the time for the administration's support and guidance — not this ridiculous "cuz-I-said-so" sort of nonsense.

But now you know why I was wary of that ridiculous line that echoed alarm bells in my head; "Education takes place only in your classroom!" Helllllllp! Makes me cringe every time I hear it.

I survived the scuba demo battle, although the administration convened a hearing about it with the head of special education for the entire Buffalo school system. Since I won the district "Teacher of the Year" award just three years prior, I figured that it wouldn't look too good for them to fire me. I wouldn't be the one to look like an idiot in the news media. I didn't get the infamous pink slip, but the die had been cast. Not unlike JFK's AP years later, the Bennett High School administration's mission became one of making my teaching hours at the school as miserable as possible.

Next up for the chopping block was my awesome Wilderness Club! This was a cheap shot - a hit below the belt. Upon first hearing the idea, the principal told me that these were inner-city high school teenagers who, well, they just wouldn't be too interested in the great outdoors. To his credit, he told me to give it a shot. A month later it had grown into one of the biggest clubs in the history of the school. We had more than 100 signed members. It was an interesting group, to say the least. We had yearbook editors, school jocks, punk rockers, and the druggies. They all wanted in! Our agenda included goodies like visiting recycling centers, outdoor excursions, one of which was snow shoeing - (hey, this was Buffalo) - backpacking, and yes, scuba diving, (and I wasn't aiming for just the school pool anymore). After everyone was signed on and we had held a few meetings, the principal called me in. Once again, I figured it was to give me some badly needed pats on the back. I was expecting to hear something like, "Wow you pulled it off," or, "Super job - it's the biggest club in Bennett's history," etc. Instead, I entered his office to face a frown and a thumbs-down gesture. "The club has to be nixed," he told me. I put up my palms and just uttered, "how come?" I was surprised he kept a straight face when he responded with these words: "It's too big. Too unmanageable." For a minute I thought I had entered the Twilight Zone and was face to face with Rod Sirling. It just couldn't be for real. But it was indeed, and our "too big" Wilderness Club bit the dust. C'est la vie, as they say in downtown Buffalo, although I think I must have muttered a few other choice words for the occasion.

I share these events, (and yes, there are more-a-plenty), only to help prepare other educators and administrators for what I hope will be improved relationships. We can all learn from mistakes. I wouldn't advise new teachers to follow in my footsteps with that decision to proceed full speed ahead with the scuba demonstration. Or, to buck the boss's decree and carry on with IEP-required breaks. My situation was a bit different, in that I was a veteran teacher with a few teaching awards under my belt. Secondly, to be honest, I did have other job offers, so I wasn't in a desperate situation. Thirdly, and maybe most importantly, I was determined to always make that choice of remaining true to my teaching convictions. I knew that if any hearing were to take place I could defend the activities as being highly educational and motivational. I did have to do this at my hearing, by the way. I'll never forget when I came out of that intense, hour-long pow-wow, which included the school's administration, my supervisor, the head of Buffalo's special education department, and a few other biggees from the school board, And by the way, some of my ex-Wilderness Clubbers who had congregated in the hallway. There were about 15 of 'em, mostly the athletes and the punkers, and they were in a mighty foul mood. They didn't take it too lightly that our club had been disbanded. And now, they were looking at the possibility of me getting the royal boot from their school.

"How'd it go, Dr. Laz?" they all asked at once. "Yeah, what's the scoop?"

I told them that I really wasn't sure what decision would be reached, but that it was gonna all work out.

They weren't satisfied with this answer.

"Where are their cars?" they demanded. "They parked outside in the lot?

"Yeah. What kinda cars they drivin'? We'll go and mess 'em up big time, for ya!"

It was nice to know that they had my back. I urged them not to do anything like that. That it wasn't worth getting busted for. But I did slip in "but if ya wanna wait till they're off school grounds, hey!" They all laughed, but by the next day my advisor told me that the decision was not to fire me. She urged me to "tow the line." In keeping with my inner promise, I kept up the wilderness outings during after school hours and thus, we didn't need the official sanction of the school. Unfortunately, for the remainder of the school year, which was about four months, my instruction and crew learning took place "in my classroom," inside those lovely four walls. We barely peeked outside the door or down the hallway.

It was after this last incident that I began seeking other means of employment. I was in the middle of preparing for my real estate salespersons exam when my dad discovered the Manhattan Day School (MDS). He saw an ad in the NY Times that said a private school in the Big Apple was looking for a director for their newly formed special needs program. They were also looking for someone who had some Talmudic background. "Might be a perfect fit," my dad told me. "Maybe since it's private and smaller, they'll be more flexible and let you do your own thing!"

It was a stroke of pure genius on my dad's part. This next teaching assignment was truly a Godsend. It was this individual, this principal, who inspired me to remain a teacher and put my master's degree and doctorate to good use. More importantly, he gave me the opportunity to be open, creative and empowered, as an educator. It turned out that this new position was the medicine I needed to keep me off the streets selling houses and sent me smiling, back to the classroom.

Rabbi David Kaminetsky, known affectionately as RDK, was an awesome principal at the Manhattan Day School, (MDS). It was so fantastic to work for him that I took a job at his summer camp, Camp Heller in the famous Catskill Mountains, aka - the Borsht Belt, in NY State. You may recall the story from chapter 2, where I presented him with a list of student-centered functions, imperative to accepting the job. But given past events, I simply had to test this principal before signing on the dotted line.

As a veteran camper, Rabbi K recognized the importance of bringing in camp-like, real world activities to reach these challenged students. His motto echoed my own personal feelings on the subject: "Do whatever it takes to reach your students, and become all they're capable of becoming."

RDK reaffirmed my commitment to that one essential ingredient in the educational puzzle, the most magical of all, in fact — motivation! When the student feels an impelling drive that originates right from the gut, something mystical clicks on inside them, and then, absolutely anything is possible. Thus, the trick is for the teacher to provide a broad array of goodies to quicken them, make them think and feel, make them inspired. This means one of two things, or ideally, both: Get them out of the classroom &, at the same time, make your classroom an exciting, desirable place to be.

In my 6 years working at MDS and 13 summers at Camp Heller, I got to see RDK in action extensively. I don't think, in all those years, I ever heard him raise his voice. Not once! The man is simply incapable of yelling or losing his cool. We're talking about all the stresses of running a school and a camp, folks. Most administrators I know take off during those precious vacation weeks in the summer, and just get away from it all...(from the students, the teachers, their downtown bosses, the parents)... they don't want to see the school building again for as long as possible. But not RDK. He went right from the MDS 8th grade graduation ceremony to his summer camp position. Somehow, he managed to juggle it all and blend these two separately huge commitments, into creative, successful, and highly desirable programs. Everyone wanted in! Teachers from all over the dang planet sent in resumes to join the MDS staff. Counselors applied from the far corners of Mother Earth to be a part of RDK's summer camp. Like I said before, I was most fortunate indeed, to be part of his team 12 months a year for all those years.

There's one story I'd like to share that is indicative of RDK's style. It happened at MDS, and it was an eye-opening experience. I was walking down the hallway of the school, and at first, all I heard was loud cursing. Then came the unmistakable sounds of glass breaking and objects hitting walls. To my shock, it was all coming from the principal's office and it sounded like a massive brawl was going on. I could only imagine what was taking place behind those closed doors. Perhaps some parent had totally lost it and was physically fighting with my principal inside in his room! I ran as fast as I could to save my boss's life. When I burst through the doorway, I was doubly shocked by what I saw. RDK was sitting behind his desk holding onto Moshe, an 8th grade student. RDK had Moshe in a bear hug, and was repeating out loud, "it's ok Moshe, everything's gonna be all right." Moshe was in the zone, way beyond listening to words of comfort. He had kicked everything, absolutely everything, off the top of RDK's desk. Broken picture frames lay on the floor. Papers, files, pens, pencils, boxes, etc., were scattered all over. RDK continued his chant, and Moshe, quite frankly, kept on with his, using every juicy curse word in the book to describe the "*'n RDK and his *'n school!" RDK motioned that he was ok. I slowly retreated from his office, but stayed within earshot in case it got uglier. This went on for a good 15 minutes, until Moshe finally calmed down. It turned out that Moshe's parents were in the middle of a nasty divorce, and school was the last thing on this student's mind. RDK held on, and kept telling Moshe that he loved him, and that things would be ok.

Now I don't know about you, but I will say, for myself, that I don't know if I could have done such a thing. If a student cursed me to my face for an extended period of time, I probably would have lost my composure and chucked the ungrateful brat out for good. I think many principals would do the same. Cussing out a principal to his or her face and clearing off their desk, (without being asked, mind you), is grounds for expulsion. But RDK was able to look past this present moment. He saw that Moshe's world seemed to be falling apart, and that what Moshe really needed was some TLC. Outside of the home, the school is a child's next-best haven. For some it may be their only true haven. It certainly was for Moshe at this moment, and RDK not only physically held onto him - he held his world together. Years later, I met up with Moshe. He actually came up to me, since I didn't recognize the 19-year old young man he had become. I was at my summer employment, at Camp Mesorah. Moshe was in the kollel at the camp. This meant that he was studying for many hours a day, to become a rabbi. I couldn't help but think what would have become of Moshe if RDK had done what most principals would have in similar circumstances. But RDK had shown him a more powerful force than physical strength. He had gone against protocol, and really, saved this kid's life. Hats off to one incredible principal, and amazing human being! To Moshe, and to me, and to hundreds of other students and staff, RDK is a true hero. Let's recap some strategies for keeping things positive between teachers and administrators.

Hot Tips for Administrators

1) Avoid the "cuz I said so!" situation.

This statement rarely works between parents and their children, why would it work between two professionally trained adults? A principal would do far better to explain his or her feelings, preferences, and needs to a teacher. Simply laying down the law seldom helps foster common goal-setting opportunities. Remember that teachers are much more likely to follow an administrator when treated with dignity and respect. Unless you're teaching for the armed forces, administrators should not relate to their staff like marine sergeants to their subordinates.

2) Foster a sense of family and cohesiveness.

A team approach is the way to go, if any school or organization wants to be successful. The use of fear is a tool that fosters resentment and disharmony. Like good teaching, galvanizing parent/teacher collaboration can only be accomplished through mutual respect and positive reinforcement. Teachers are a loyal bunch, and will do anything for their students, their schools, and yes, their administrative team - providing they feel appreciated and respected. There are many practical things administrators can do to make this team philosophy a reality. Staff-versus-student sports games are an easy way to foster a sense of togetherness and lighthearted fun on campus. Faculty luncheons, potluck meals, picnics, even after-school social events that foster open conversation, help encourage those good, positive vibes. I am, as you already well know, partial to taking the entire faculty, administrators included, to your local ropes course. Their entire focus is on team building skills. With today's budget cuts, job losses, and other big hits affecting the world of teaching, administrators need to extend themselves, and make teachers feel wanted, needed, and appreciated. Our entire first week back at the Quest Center, the administration, along with the PTA, provides special breakfasts, lunches & treats for the teachers. They encourage us to share our plans and ideas for the upcoming year. We also have a once-a-month luncheon where everyone brings in some goody for a joint, get-together luncheon.

3) Empower teachers.

Give teachers enough "breathing space" to allow their individual strengths and personalities to shine. Kids don't learn skills in the same way, (even when the same age), and the same applies to us bigger kids. Teachers have their own unique styles. Some move a lot. Others talk a lot and have bubbly personalities. Some are more reserved and need their lesson plans all spelled out. They run the gamut from the over-retentive to free spirited, go-with-the-flow partakers of life. As long as each teacher is doing his or her job, getting the paperwork done, and moving the students along, the administration should allow them to "simply be".

4) Use the peer-tutoring model for new teachers.

Administrators need to realize the crucial role they play in the lives of their teachers. If a "greenhorn" teacher is having trouble getting it all together, it is preferable not to ride this teacher, (right out the "revolving door"), but rather, as administrators, to take a positive role. The new teachers can be paired with older, more-experienced teachers utilizing a mentor/advisor format. The veteran, successful teachers can help guide newer educators and help them navigate through the "landmines" of teaching. This model has been used quite successfully in many schools throughout the world. This is yet another example of a highly appropriate use for peer-interactive learning. This time, however, the peers are not students, but teachers.

A list of options

If a veteran teacher feels mistreated by his or her administration, there are many steps that can be taken. First, don't sit back and do nothing. This often encourages aggressive, bullying-type behaviors not only to continue, but very possibly, to worsen. Sometimes there's simply been a misunderstanding. Make an appointment to meet directly with the administrator, and in a non-threatening manner, state your feelings and thoughts. This lets the principal or AP know that you're both aware of, and very uncomfortable with, the current situation. Administrators are people too. They are under pressures from their "higher-ups" to perform and deal with a zillion things that most teachers are blissfully unaware of. Very often a direct, face-to-face meeting can go a long way toward clearing the air. If this personal meeting doesn't resolve things in a satisfactory manner, there are other options you can pursue. If you belong to your teachers union, ask for their advice and help with the situation. It's always best to try and resolve things in a peaceful, civilized manner. Sometimes a little scare from the local teachers union is enough to get the administration off a teacher's back. Another option that I've seen many teachers utilize, is to ask for a transfer to another school. Both the teacher and the administration might happily agree to such a move. Obviously, the best scenario is to try to resolve things in a productive manner. The teacher may have to make some changes and show some sincere efforts to adapt, and the administrator may have to try different strategies to help the teacher grow.

Tips for New Teachers

1) Stay upbeat & positive.

This may mean hanging around only a "select bunch" of your colleagues at school. It may also mean eating lunch with just a few, or even on your own. In other words, for this step to translate into reality, you may have to avoid the infamous teacher's lounge. Ah, the place of wrath, sarcasm, depression, anxiety and fear! Ok, so I exaggerate. At the Quest Center, it's actually a pleasant and fun atmosphere, most of the time. But let the point be made that sometimes teachers can be a vindictive and cynical bunch. I don't blame them - not with all the difficulties they face on a pretty constant basis. But it's vital for new teachers to keep that chin up, and stay positive and happy. Otherwise, they'll soon join that horribly sad statistic of those exiting stage-left during that very first, difficult year. Better to be a loner and keep that smile than a card-carrying member of the melancholy crowd of deep, dark, depressed educators.

2) Do what it takes to keep that smile after school.

This means working out, swimming, playing tennis, taking walks, playing drums, strutting your stuff at Jazzercise - whatever it takes to maintain your fitness on all levels - physically, emotionally, psychologically, and yes, spiritually.

3) Hook up with one happy veteran teacher.

Let this more-experienced teacher guide you through the often murky and turbulent waters of education. If need be, hire this person. He or she will make sure all those hours put into your teaching certificate and degree isn't for naught. I was quite fortunate to have found my mentor during my first year of teaching in the Buffalo public schools. I was under the misguided impression that I had to be like Bruce Lee to survive at Dr. Martin Luther King, Jr. Community School, until I met this wonderful cute older lady, probably in her 70's, who was about half the size of her students and taught in a low, quiet voice. (I mention her in greater detail in Chapter 6). I made it a point watch her in action during my break periods. I probably learned more from her in one hour than from any of my Master's degree textbooks on special education. Part of working with a fellow teacher is the important benefit one gets from peer observation. It can be a real eye opening experience to have a colleague come and sit in the back of your class and watch you in action. Since the corresponding critique comes from a person who's in the same boat, the analysis is always done with genuine care and friendship. Take things a step further and videotape yourself teaching. Parents, by the way, can do the same thing at home. In a way this can be even less threatening, since no one but you has to watch the videos. I once taped a class of mine just to see how I was doing. I set the camera on a tripod and let it roll. In reviewing the short 10-minute video, I was totally shocked at my posture. It was a little thing perhaps, but I noticed how my shoulders seemed to hunch over. I saw the same issue while reviewing a tape of one of my gigs. Right then and there, as Santana would say, I vowed to change my evil ways. Good posture conveys a sense of readiness and confidence, which I think is important for both teaching and parenting. The peer observation is best when done as a two-way street. You and your fellow teacher, (or parent), observe each other in action and discuss any concerns afterwards.

4) Demonstrate that you're a team player.

You may have to go out of your way to show the school administration that you're on their side and working for the betterment of the school. If a principal, (or assistant principal), complains about something you did or didn't do, and it's legit, then ask for their advice about what you can do to improve this situation. Generally, once the school bosses see that you're not getting defensive, but are making a serious attempt at growth, they will be supportive, and not just ride your back. Institute a "best practices" forum at your school where teachers can share creative and practical ideas with one another. This will help create a real sense of teamwork at the school.

5) Do something extra for the school.

This can translate into many things, such as writing grants for your program, or volunteering to help with a school play, or parent event. Bring in an exciting program that other teachers and classes will benefit from! Any of these help the administration to recognize your efforts and view you as an asset to the school. In other words, doing something extra for the school will help you stand out in a positive way. While we're at it, since obtaining grants is probably the most productive "extra" thing you can do for your school, let's discuss some important points about them:

Grant Writing Tips

Your first grant will go a long way toward helping build positive relations with your administration. First, like they say about the lottery, you gotta be in it, to win it! The same, of course, applies to grants. There are lots of grants out there, with lots of good people and organizations with money to be dispersed. I'm not really sure why most teachers don't apply and take their chances. You've really got nothing to lose except a few hours work, so there's really no reason to be intimidated. Why shouldn't you and your program, (or school), get some of this action! There are no shortcuts here, but you might just hit the jackpot. You may get rejected more than once from the same organization before finally being awarded that pot at the end of the rainbow. The important thing is to keep at it until you finally get that sweet, first grant. Take a lesson from J.K Rowling, folks. Does that name ring a bell? Or more like about a billion bells by now? Yes, she wrote the famous Harry Potter books, which have now been made into movies and gazillion dollar rides at Disney World. But many people do not know that she was rejected from many publishers before hitting the jackpot. It may take several shots, but keep plugging away with your grant ideas and applications. Eventually you'll land one, and then the fun really begins. You'll get to implement your ideas without worrying about the cost!

Use your internet search engine and get the train rolling. Many school districts even have a special grants department. Get in touch with these good folks. They are trying their best to help you secure extra funds. Grant writing can become addictive. All it takes is that first victory and soon you're back at the computer firing out a bunch more. I have discovered that the area of special needs is wide open for grants. Let's be honest here. Special needs can really pull on the heartstrings. In my 11 years at the Quest, I have secured more than 18 grants for the school, in excess of $500,000. Most have been $5000 and under, but all of this adds up to more equipment, more creative projects, and a much happier you and your administration. And most importantly, lots of wonderful goodies for your students that you don't have to lay out a penny for. If you go out of your way for your school, the administration will, in all likelihood, respond in kind.

1) Keep it creative.

Think of a new way you can utilize your educational strategies. You obviously have an arsenal of verbal, physical, and experiential tools at your disposal. Can they be applied toward a specific subject or learning mode? Share that goal and get funding organizations as excited about the potential as you are.

2) Keep it short & sweet.

Use some descriptors in the title of your grant that will capture someone's attention. If it starts off with long-winded, dissertation-style lead-in and an utterly boring title, chances are the grant readers might not get to page two. I like to use catchy sounding acronyms. For example, in the realm of profound special needs, we often use adaptive switches with our students, such as a head, knee, or puff switch. Our students use these to access all sorts of important functions, such as communication devices, adaptive drums, lighting effects, etc. I called one of my grant projects "S.W.I. T.C. H." - See What I Totally Can Handle! It was a play-on-words that also brought out the notion of switches and how my students, with the assistance of this grant, could indeed do much more on their own. The grant was worth over $5,000 and it focused on my students with special needs putting on several drama productions. We got the grant and not only did they put on an awesome show, but we now had all sorts of new switches, lighting effects, and adaptive percussion instruments that could be utilized in the months and years to come.

3) Make sure your grant idea is doable and testable!

Testing doesn't have to be done using complicated statistical analysis - just provide a record that demonstrates accountability. The easiest methods utilize a pre & post-test analysis. This could be done with both quantitative, (proof by numbers), and qualitative, (proof by methodology), measures.

4) Thank the organizations you apply to...

and keep them informed about the progress of your grant implementation. They love seeing pictures, and often use them for their own PR. By the way, make sure you have permission to photograph your students before anything hits the press.

As mentioned before, there are lots of people and organizations out there just waiting for you to get in touch. Special education is an area that truly needs extra funding and support, so don't hesitate to toot your horn and share your creative ideas. The wide world of grant writing is often viewed as a land mine, and many regard it not worth the effort. Most of the hardware in my music & drama program has been procured through these wonderful grants. As a result, our school now has three sound systems, recording equipment, drum sets, guitars, amps, percussion goodies, keyboards, assistive technology, specialized lighting equipment, and all sorts of very cool adaptive musical instruments. Don't look upon grant writing as a land mine. Not a chance. It's a gold mine, and it's waiting for you to dig in.

Lessons from The Quest Administration

My journey to the Quest Center was not an easy one, and I've often wondered why it took so long and was filled with so many ups & downs before I found this awesome place. After the negative experiences at my previous schools and a rocky relationship with the school's AP, I made yet another noble attempt to sell houses. Maybe this teaching business wasn't for me after all. But there's a famous Yiddush saying that my grandma used to tell me; "A mentch tracht un Got lacht." Literally it means; "man thinks and God laughs." But in her wisdom, she always reminded me of the hidden, deeper meaning. Pinching my cheek, she would say with that knowing smile, "Listen Mister Big-Shot, just remember that God's the boss, and He's got a way of doing things His way." Whenever she said that remark, she would stress the word His. And so, just when I was thinking I was finally free of the trials & tribulations of being a teacher - well, along came a surprise phone call. I thought I heard my grandma and the "Boss" laughing.

"Can you come in for an interview?" they asked. "We got your resume from the Broward Public Schools placement office."

I hesitated just long enough for them to continue.

"Oh thanks very much, but..."

"We're a special ed center," the lady on the phone told me. "Very small classes."

"It's just that my real estate..."

"Oh, you're selling your home. Best of luck. We also have a very small teacher-to-student ratio."

"No, not selling."

"Oh buying. How nice. I wish you success. The ratio is like one-to-three."

"Not buying. It's this course. I'm... did you say one-to-three?"

"Yeah. But in some of the classes, like the medically fragile classes it's more like one-to-two."

"One teacher for every two... three kids?"

"Yes. I know we should probably have one-on-one, but, well, you know, budget considerations and things like that. But it's special education so we have a workable ratio with the one-to-three."

Was she actually apologizing for not having a one-to-one ratio? I was more used to the notion of 1-to-25. Small ratios were not even on the distant horizon. I had to pinch myself to make sure I wasn't lying in bed in the middle of a bizarre dream. I was more than intrigued.

"What did you say the name of the school is?"

"The Quest," she responded. "We have an exciting and creative approach to education. So can I schedule you for an appointment?"

The Quest, I thought to myself. No doubt about that, darling. Seems like I've been on a quest ever since I got into this crazy field.

Now hold on a second. Did she use the words exciting and creative? Could it really be true? Did such a school really exist? I simply had to find out and could only answer the sweet secretary of the Quest with one simple word. "Please." It was not just a polite response. It was more of a plea. "Oh, if it could only be!"

That, dear friends, was about 12 years ago, and to my pleasant surprise, I'm still hanging out at the Quest. Longest I've been at any school. Education is often called the 'revolving door" field. Teachers come and go, always looking for a better placement. Administrators come and go. Moving up the ladder, perhaps, but always on the lookout for something better. Somehow, for most teachers at most schools, it feels like the glove just doesn't fit. The Quest Center is one of those incredible places that fit like the finest silk PJ's. And my tenure is far from the record. I'm working with many teachers and Para-professionals who have been there over 20, and some over 25. Let me repeat that — that's 25-plus years at the same school. What's their secret? How has this school managed to buck the odds and retain the same teachers year after year? What are they doing right that other schools could emulate? What's the administration doing, and not doing, that makes the teachers want to stay and not look for greener pastures?

I'd like to suggest several factors. First, it's the teachers themselves. To do what needs to be done at the Quest - such as changing those big diapers on really big individuals, or watching the increments of growth that progress in very slow and tiny steps - it's obvious that more than just a paycheck claims their loyalty. I think the teachers who have stayed on, feel that working with kids with profound special needs is much more than a job; it's a calling. They've found themselves, and their niche. When folks find out that I work with students who have profound autism, (or Downs- syndrome or cerebral palsy), or who are classified as medically fragile, they often say things like "Oh, that's so nice of you" or, "Wow, you must have a lot of patience" or, "I could never do such a thing."

I never thought I could either. But I absolutely love working with these students. They're a lot of fun to be around, and I find them inspiring. Their challenges and successes are as exciting as climbing Mt. Everest, and I am truly blessed to be a part of it all.

The second factor here, and it's just as important as the first, is that the administration at the Quest has been, in a word, amazing. I've worked with three different administration teams in my 11 years so far at the Quest. The first two principals retired. The critical element here is that they are supportive of their teaching staff. Yes, there's always the nitty-gritty's to work out...in order to make sure business is carried out in a professional manner. But they view and encourage a sense of family and belonging. In this manner, they not only guide teachers but more importantly, empower them. A new teacher would do well to begin his or her career in such a school. He or she may actually end up retiring 30 years down the road from the very same school.

In order for you to appreciate this statement, allow me to introduce you to my first principal at the Quest, Ms. Linda A. Walker, aka - the LAW! Ms. Walker was the medicine I so desperately needed in order to overcome my depressing case of the PITS. She was the reason I stayed in the field of education and didn't start selling homes in South Florida. With the current housing slump, I guess she was a bit of a prophetess too.

It's high time you met Lady "LAW" for yourselves. She is an example of one of the finest administrators I've ever worked with. Even more importantly, she's a remarkable human being. Teachers who worked under Ms. Linda A. Walker followed her like moths to a bright light. Where she went, teachers followed. There's no better sign to indicate an administrator supreme. Let's be honest here. Principals, like teachers, come and go. Some retire. Some are urged to retire. (Some should do the world a favor and retire early). Most folks in education are hoping that the next assignment, the next placement, will be better. Whether they're in the classroom, or in the front office, they keep looking over their shoulders for that better situation, out there. When teachers beg to be placed in a different school just because their principal is going there, something mighty powerful is going on. These teachers know they truly lucked out with this principal. Where Ms. Walker was headed, so were they - if it could be arranged with the powers-that-be, downtown. I'll never forget one of my first verbal exchanges with Ms. Walker at the Quest Center.

"Doctor." she said with a slight smile, "Take this. Look it over, and prepare it for tomorrow's meeting."

"Sure," I responded, with just a tad bit of doubt. "Tomorrow's meeting."

"Yes. The faculty meeting. Make sure you're there on time!"

Could she really know me so well so soon? I mean, here it was, my first day on the job, (the students weren't even coming till next week), and my principal was already worried about me not showing up on time! Was it possible she knew about LST? You see, JST, or Jewish Standard Time, usually runs anywhere within an hour or two of a meeting time, or date. You show up within 30 to 45 minutes, hey, you're way ahead of the game. But there was yet another dimension at play, here. I'm talking LST or, as my dear friends are ever so quick to remind me, Laz Standard Time. This is very similar to the Native American culture that often translates as "Yes, we shall meet. When? Ahhh, when the corn is about yea high." And so, I couldn't help but wonder that, after just one day at the Quest, my principal, Ms. Walker was already putting in the word about me showing up on time. Did one of my buddies call her up and mention LST?

I looked at the book she put in my hands. It was called "The Present" and I took it home to read. It was a wonderful, lovely story about a boy looking for the most awesome present he could find. He went through all sorts of physical gifts, accumulating one after another, tiring of each, until he realized that the here & now, this precise moment - the present - is a tremendous gift. That's why, in fact, it's called the present, for indeed it is.

I wasn't sure what Ms. Walker wanted me to prepare, but at least I had read the book. At the faculty meeting, (by the way, I arrived early), she actually had me read the whole book to the entire faculty. It took a solid seven minutes or so to do this. I didn't know why she picked me, perhaps I was new and thus, low man on the totem pole, but my mind was boggled, absolutely stunned. It was probably the first faculty meeting in 25 years of teaching that I actually enjoyed. In fact, I enjoyed it from the first minute until the sweet end, which occurred 45 minutes later. Ms. Walker made fun, interesting, and active. I could have listened to her stories for hours. She had a unique way of making sure we were all involved and doing things, not just sitting like robots listening to a speech.

Nearly all my previous faculty meetings were exercises in patience. Watching the clock. "Okay, when will this stupid thing end? Please dear Lord, have some mercy. Make the hour hand jump ahead! And I promise to be good!" At the Quest, Ms. LAW was more than a pleasant surprise - she was a Godsend.

Meetings in the business world are often referred to as "sacred cows." They're big, somewhat clumsy, and untouchable. People figure it's how business has always been done, and therefore, how it should continue. Much of the time spent in meetings is diverted to off-track stuff, and it becomes more of a social scene than one of tending to the business-at-hand. But the staff is generally not interested in social gatherings, particularly first thing in the morning. One prominent businessman even suggested that their meetings be conducted standing up! That's right. Everyone up on their feet. This way they tended to stay focused on the really important stuff, which meant they would soon be out and on their way - ASAP. Ms. Walker's pow-wows were anything but sacred cows. Instead, they were morning wake-up calls, like a stiff shot of espresso combined with Night At The Apollo. Nobody slept through her staff meetings. You couldn't if you wanted to. She had this knack of keeping us focused and engaged in a fun, interactive way. I couldn't help but notice how these were the main ingredients that made for good classroom teaching, as well. Keeping it interactive automatically makes it more fun, because everyone is directly involved in the learning process. They're no longer armchair quarterbacks - they're helping call the shots!

I had the pleasure of working with Ms. Walker for five years, until her retirement. While happy for her, I was, needless to say, mighty depressed. How often does one get lucky enough to work with such an amazing principal? If I had waited 20-plus years to hook up with LAW, how long would I have to wait for the next inspirational one? I had this deep, dark inner feeling of "ugh" combined with an "Oy! Here we go again!" Like Yogi Berra once remarked, "it was that déjà vu feeling all over again. Ms. Walker, noticing my concern, told me not to worry. "You're gonna love my replacement," she said trying to cheer me up. "She absolutely loves music."

Enter Raquel Cobb, who not only appreciated music, but was a player to boot! Within weeks she was coming into my music room to jam, (whenever she had a break from her busy schedule of meetings and paper work). She played great drums, and to my surprise, also crooned out some Beatles tunes on the guitar. Friday afternoon dances at the Quest featured our live school rock band, with Zahava on keyboards, and Raquel and I switching off on drums and guitar. Within a few months, Ms. Cobb was on the road with us doing gigs. Working for two wonderful administrators in a row, I felt like I had hit the lottery for the second time. Back to back winnings, no less. What is amazing about Raquel's story is that she started at the Quest many years before this leadership role. Her first position? Bus driver. Raquel worked hard as she climbed the ladder in the world of education. Eventually earning her teacher's certification in special education and culminating her career as a top-notch principal. During a visit to her previous school, I met so many teachers who told me that they cried when Raquel left. Like Ms. Walker, she was tough but fair, and always went out of her way to support and help her staff. She also kept things on the fun side, since she knew the importance of music for kids with special needs. "It's the best therapy," she once told me at one of our school dances, "for the students, for the teachers, and for us too!" There was no doubt about that statement. Raquel retired after four sweet years, but we still do gigs together. She's been a great spare drummer for my band and we always schmooze about music and the latest music gear. I think my guitar and percussion collection, which takes up a more than one room in our home, is far surpassed by Raquel, who seems to have a matching guitar for every outfit in her wardrobe.

My latest principal at the Quest is Mr. Leo Nesmith. He's younger than most of us Quest old timers, working towards his doctorate, and to his credit has stood by the music program. In fact, he encourages me to write grants and expand my program as much as possible. He inherited a difficult situation. New state and national regulations are affecting things like tenure. Funding is being cut. Massive teacher layoffs and other financial repercussions are daily concerns. All teachers, experienced or not, have a whole new area of concern and anxiety; job security. There's also this tremendous focus on testing, data collection, proving results, and teaching to national tests rather than to curriculum. Mr. Nesmith walked into a situation where everyone is walking around on pins and needles. I truly appreciate his support and encouragement, especially during these trying times in our public schools. He has this quality of being tough but fair, and more than willing to back teachers who put out that extra effort. We do however, disagree on one very crucial area. He's a huge Dallas Cowboys fan. To enter his office at the Quest Center one gets the sense that you're in Texas getting ready for game time. Coming from Buffalo, NY, we lock horns about this. Unfortunately, his team has gotten the better of mine for way too long, now. Why they call the Cowboys "America's team" is a big mystery. After all, my Buffalo Bills wear the read, white, and blue.

Let's return to the notion of bringing some life into your lessons. Just as the scuba doctrine of thirds can fire up any meeting, it can work wonders for your day-to-day units of instruction, too.

The "Rule of Thirds!"

Pizazz your meetings and lessons.

Students hate boring activities and so do teachers. Yes, there's always the tedious, nitty-gritty stuff you just gotta get through, and doing a little something extra can make the boring stuff a bit easier to swallow. Like the song belts out - "a spoonful of sugar helps the medicine go down." One handy formula is what I call the "Rule of Thirds." I first discovered this little doozey while taking a scuba certification course back in my University of Buffalo undergraduate days. It urged divers to use one third of the air for descending and exploring the bottom, another third for ascending to the surface, and the last third as a safety measure - just in case something went wrong. This "Rule of Thirds" translates very nicely into any class-unit lesson, and yes, even those dreadfully long, boring meetings.

Split 'em up into threes.

1) Start it off with some pizazz.

2) Introduce another bit of pizazz in the middle, when everyone's energy level slows to a turtle's pace.

3) And last but not least, conclude the unit or meeting with another high interest point. For the "Rule of Thirds" you're only limited by your imagination.

This notion of starting a lesson or a meeting with some pizzazz has its roots smack dab in the Talmud. It mentions a seemingly insignificant point when it tells us that

Rava, a tremendous Talmudic scholar, would begin his lectures with a joke. This would, in effect, put his students in a good mood, (into a more open and receptive framework), so they could get down to the serious business at hand. The Talmud is giving a brilliant piece of advice here for any teacher or administrator. Put step one of the "rule of thirds" into play. One Talmudic master took this step even further. His pizzazz was to get his students laughing. I'm not sure if he did the ancient version of Johnny Carson's 10-minute hysterically funny roasting monologues, or what...but Rava knew the tricks of the trade. His lectures were about these incredibly, nit picking, profound, intellectual matters. Nothing like a joke or two to get the students on your side and ready to tune in!

The Rule of Thirds applies particularly well to long units of instruction. The teacher should start off with something wild & crazy to get the students attention, and kick off the unit. If the class is studying a single topic for a few weeks, then the middle time slot would require another shot of pizzazz. The unit concludes with something truly exciting that pertains to the studies, such as a class trip, or a drama presentation, etc. Listed below are several examples that either I have personally used, or have seen in action by other educators.

I'll start off with what is often viewed as a tedious topic in the Torah world - the intricate laws of "muktzeh" on Shabbos. For those Torah-observant folks, there's a whole bunch of things that are not allowed to be handled on the Sabbath, which by the way, begins Friday night at sundown and concludes Saturday night. These "untouchable" items include goodies like iPods, computers, cell phones - basically anything electric or battery powered. Since conducting business is also a no-no on the Sabbath, money also falls into this category of "muktzeh." There's extra motivation here to start keeping the Sabbath. It's a guarantee that for at least 24 hours you will unleash from all the wireless gadgetry and monetary matters that seem to clutter your life more and more with each passing day! There are several different categories in this complicated realm of "muktzeh," and when the unit came up for study at MDS, (Manhattan Day School), quite frankly, I was a bit concerned. I figured it was going to be way too hard for our students with special needs. But I should have known better, with the two awesome teachers we had on board. Rabbis Abraham Kaminetsky, (yes, related to the principal - and you get 100 extra points for noticing the connection), and Levi Cash told me, "don't worry - just make sure you're there for our first class!" It was one of the most awesome examples I've ever seen regarding the "Rule of Thirds." It proved that if it works for the intricate laws of "muktzeh," (which can be rather tedious and boring), than it can work for absolutely any topic on the dang planet, whether you're teaching the ABC's or Einstein's Theory of Relativity.

I sat at the back of the classroom as that very first lesson on muktzeh began. After the class was seated and the bell rang, in marched the two young rabbis dressed up like cooking chefs. White aprons, tall white chef hats, and long wooden spoons in hand, the whole nine yards. With dramatic fanfare, they walked to the front of the room and placed two large bags on top of a table. Then they passed out sheets of papers containing the lyrics to a song they had written. It was to the tune of Monster Mash, only the title read as Muktzeh Mash! I kid you not. They sang the tune to the utter delight and astonishment of the entire junior high boys special education class. Each verse dealt with a different category of muktzeh, and during each verse, they dug into the large bags to pull out the appropriate items that fit into these various categories. Five minutes later they received a standing ovation from the entire class for their efforts. But these two pizazzy teachers were just getting warmed up. Next, they brought in a large wooden frame that was previously hidden in the hallway. It was home made, but it looked mighty fine. It was one of those light-up boards. When the metal pin is placed on the correct answer, the board lights up and a red light starts spinning on top. The class was divided into two teams. When one team decided a displayed object belonged into a particular category of muktzeh, a designated team member went to the front of the class, and with great confidence, (or hesitation), tried to light up the board. If the first team got the answer wrong, the other team had the choice of either going for the correct answer, or asking the judges to answer. An incorrect choice was a loss of a point, and a correct response yielded a point.

The game was a huge hit and encompassed the entire 45-minute period. There's no doubt in my mind that the intro song and hands-on game were big hits with the students, because they were fun-oriented activities, and were a complete surprise. These techniques also helped reinforce the curriculum material. They would always remember this information about muktzeh, simply because it was taught with some pizzazz, including song, costumes, props, and an exciting, competitive game. This topic is the sort of stuff that lands in the realm of short-term memory, and never seems to quite make the trip to long-term memory territory. In other words, you learn it for a test and usually forget it days, or even hours, later. Dressing up as chefs, singing their wacky tune, and playing that interactive game, brought the learning to life and really tickled the students' long-term brain cells. By the way, by popular and unanimous demand, the two rabbis concluded that first class with an encore rendition of Muktzeh Match. I made sure the principal, RDK, was there for that encore performance. The students simply could not get enough.

The next example of bringing on the pizzazz for an intro lesson, involves child labor practices. We're not talking China or some Third World country here. This one is part & parcel of US history, when children worked 12 to 18 hour days, during the early days of industrial growth. These kids worked under extremely harsh conditions, and eventually laws were enacted to protect them. This superstar teacher's name was Mitch Goldman, history teacher supreme, at good ol' MDS. I would often stand in the hallway on my break periods and just watch Mitch in action. Despite having large classes - sometimes over 30 -for what is often considered a tedious, cut 'n dry subject; no student ever complained about being bored in Mr. Goldman's class. Mitch gave me a heads-up and invited me to come to the kick-off lesson for his unit on child labor and the industrial revolution. One never quite knew what to expect upon entering his room, and this lesson was no different. Strewn all over the floor, covering it in fact, from wall to wall, were thousands of colored pieces of confetti paper. His students were sitting on the floor, and to my surprise, the windows were covered with black plastic garbage bags. Despite it being late April, Mitch somehow arranged to bring in about 10 electric space heaters that were going full blast. The room felt more like a sauna than a classroom.

"Just so you'll appreciate a little bit of what those kids went through," Mitch told them, "We're gonna crank up the heat. You'll get a small taste, very small, of what kids your age went through before this country had decent child labor laws in place."

He then gave the different groups their special work assignments. Each was responsible for picking up just one color confetti from the piles that literally covered the entire floor. "Group A over here, will pick up all the red ones. Group B gets to pick up all the tiny blue ones. Group C, all the white ones. And Group D, all the yellow ones. You're not done until the job is done! Got it?"

There were many groans in response.

"There will be no breaks for drinks or eating. Nothing, until this is done!"

Mitch wisely stopped the activity after 15 minutes, (before anyone passed out), but this was an intro to the topic that these kids would never forget. When the students were finally able to stand up and stretch their legs, the heaters were turned off and the windows were mercifully opened. Mitch explained that this example was merciful compared to what the kids went through for hours on end, day after day, in horrible working conditions. Back then, it was more like slave labor for those unfortunate kids.

Since I also taught history for many years, I've developed a wide variety of exciting, starter activities to get things jumping - create a sense of wonder - and perk up the interest level of my students. I find that the easiest thing to do is simply dress up as some historical character and talk and act out what the historical scenario was like, back then. I'd dress up as Chief Joseph of the Nez Perce Indians and come proudly strutting into the class, complete with bow & arrows. The students would clap and cheer as I made my way to the front of the room.

"You may wonder about my weapons," I'd start. "First, I'll bet you didn't know that the bow & arrow was much more effective than those long rifles used by the Blue Coats!" This led to all sorts of looks of disbelief. It also led to an immediate question.

"What's a Blue Coat?" they seemed to ask in unison.

"Good question," I responded. "You see, all the US soldiers wore these blue jackets. So us Native Americans, us Indians, always referred to them as the Blue Coats."

I then went on to explain that any decent Indian warrior could get off three or four good shots with his bow, before a Blue Coat could fire a second round. The early guns were a handicap for the soldiers because they took so long to load. I further described how we were able to ride our horses at a full gallop, and shoot our bows at the same time." This took great skill, but the Indians were much better at this sort of stuff than soldiers." The lesson became more and more focused, as I discussed how the US government back then would make deals with the Nez Perce, and then break these promises, time and time again. "Eventually, they tried to force us off our own lands and send us to these horrible places known as reservations."

"I'm now leading my people to freedom," I said in my full Indian dress. "We're heading to Canada, a place where the soldiers cannot chase us!"

This intro lesson would be something my students would never forget. It was used to kick off the unit, and they simply could not stop asking questions. After they went home, some hit the books, some even went to libraries, while others checked available media on the topic. They spoke about visiting authentic American Indians and getting interviews. They also wanted to see where these original Indian lands were. They were totally flabbergasted when I told them "we're sitting on top of their land right now... at this very moment!"

"I thought the Nez Perce were out west, you know, far from here!" one of my students blurted out.

"Yes, that's true. I like the way you were paying attention before! But there were other Indian tribes living right here before the government took it from them. Right on this land where MDS was built."

This was like throwing gas in a fire pit. They all started talking at once.

"That's crazy!"

"That's disgusting!"

"That's terrible!"

"So not fair!"

This led, of course, to some very real, practical, and quick research on their part. They could not get enough information! How could it be that our own country was built on someone else's land? "Isn't that called stealing?" they all wanted to know.

The Middle Unit

Sustaining Interest!

This second part of the Rule of Thirds is to keep that interest level alive and well. A few weeks into our unit on the Native Americans, I played dress up again. This time as an US Army officer. I dressed in traditional Blue Coat garb. I even had an old musket that a friend purchased at a flea market for me. It was time to hear "first hand," so to speak, from the other side, and my students had a zillion questions. What was the US government's position on what they called the "Indian problem?" How had the situation between the Indians and the "white men" gotten so bad? Why was it called the "Indian problem?" Why not the "white man" problem? Do Indians own the land today? What happened to the Nez Perce and all the other tribes? Why was our country so mean to the Indians? They had lots of unanswered questions. I explained to my students that I, (the soldier), was chasing after the Nez Perce Indians who refused to sign a peace treaty and move onto the reservation. The history of this saga in the American experience is fascinating. Once kicked off their ancestral homelands, the Nez Perce led the US army on a 1100-mile chase. They fought more than 20 skirmishes against Howard's men and had several major battles along the way. The US army, although they greatly outnumbered the Nez Perce, could not actually defeat them through military means. Chief Joseph surrendered, in order to put an end to the bloodshed. He was just 40 miles from the Canadian border. Nonetheless, some of his band did make it there. Today, several decades after my MDS teaching, I still run into former students who tell me that they cannot get enough of history. They've become avid readers, especially of American history. Many have purposely taken trips out West to view first hand these lands that were under such dispute and turmoil for so long. It's always gratifying to see that those early, (exciting), classroom activities helped generate a lifelong interest.

The Final Third

Ending With Pizazz!

The last two weeks of this unit featured my students' creation of their own personal projects. This notion of student-centered projects was discussed in a previous chapter, but what a tremendous way to conclude your unit of study! Rather than hitting them with a boring, two-dimensional test - as is usually done in most classrooms - here, the students have an opportunity to really shine when they present their projects to their classmates. In my case, each was more creative than the last. Some chose drama presentations using role playing, and dressing up in costume. Others used songs to illustrate important points about their historical research. Some videotaped simulated TV interviews, with the "real life" characters from back then. A few students built their projects. One was a map outlined in salt that depicted Nez Perce's dramatic escape for freedom. Another was a Nez Perce village built out of wood. It was amazing to see how involved the students got in the learning process. Yes, the topic itself was conducive for learning. But the method, the means of approaching the learning process, is critical here. This Rule of Thirds, together with the student-centered model, allows for maximum participation and actual acquisition of knowledge. More importantly, this process inspires them to want to continue learning! Once the unit is finished and the books are put away, these students will continue to learn - more and more - on their own. Learning is not a static process. It's not about programming in and spitting back information like a computer. True education is inspiring. It is the act of imparting the desire to want more after class is finished. You can quote me on that.

Get this! The exciting class session where they shared their projects was not the end of the unit. The real pizzazz came with a concluding class field trip. Off we went to visit a real McCoy Native American Indian reservation. Since this was NY State, we went to visit an Iroquois reservation, only a 90-minute drive from our school. It was a "wow" moment from beginning to end. My students got to meet and interact with real Native Americans. Suddenly, the words from our books and articles came to life in front of their eyes. The only problem was getting them to stop asking 14,000 questions at once! Our Indian guide, He-Who-Stands-Tall, taught us some authentic Indian games, spoke to us about their history, culture, and their ongoing contributions to American society. As we sat in a large circle in an open field, we learned about the "dream vision" quests, that many Native Americans do to this very day. It requires fasting, often for more than a full day, (or 24 hours). Sometimes, it lasts closer to two full days. According to Indian tradition, the person, if found worthy, will experience some sort of deep, spiritual vision. Our new Indian friends were very impressed that my 13 and 14-year-old MDS students fasted for 24 straight hours, two times a year, once on Yom Kippur and another for the 9th of the Hebrew month of Av. He-Who-Stands-Tall knew about Yom Kippur but didn't really know about the second fast. Our students told them that this fast was in commemoration of the destruction of our holy temple in Jerusalem, over 2,000 years ago. I told our guide that Judaism and Indian culture actually have a lot in common, since we too are a tribal people.

"Your people have 12 tribes, correct?" he asked the kids.

"Yeah," Moshe, one of my students quickly answered. "But we really don't know which exact one, unless you're a Kohain."

"A what?"

"A kohain means a priest," I said. "Someone who served in the temple. This knowledge is passed down from generation to generation. And today we still have people who know that their fathers belonged to this tribe!"

"Having 12 tribes must make things interesting," he said with a smile. "But imagine our heritage and culture. We literally have hundreds of different tribes, and almost all have their own unique language!"

"How do you talk to each other?" Nate asked. "I mean, how can you understand each other at all?"

"We have something that's really awesome," the guide explained. "It goes back, way back, before the white man ever stepped foot on our land. You know what that is?"

We just shook our heads back and forth.

"Sign language! That's right. My people, the Native American people, lived here for a long, long time before it was ever called America, and we developed this way of communicating with each other. Sign language! All the different tribes pretty much knew this silent way of communicating."

(As I've already told you, I used American Sign Language (ASL) in my teaching career, and currently use it quite extensively at the Quest Center with my non-verbal students).

"C'mon," he said standing up. "Wanna learn some?"

He taught us some very cool signs, but we ended up learning a lot more than just signing, that day. Teachers need to get the creative juices flowing and plan their units of instruction. How to start...how to maintain interest during the middle stages...and how to end the unit in style. Think big. Think outside the box - outside those four constraining walls of the classroom. Take 'em into the real world for some real life experiences. These are the kinds of activities that will stay with them forever and will impact their lives in all kinds of wondrous ways. We might not be able to change history, but through these hands-on, real life experiences, history can indeed change us!

The Faculty Meeting Pick-Me-Up!

et's go back to that "sacred cow," the very large, clumsy and very slow moving, (and infamous), meeting! The very thought of it, even verbalizing the word "meeting," can bring an utterly depressing "ughhhhh" from any subjected to this misery. With a little creativity, the usual bored-to-tears meeting can be spiced up. Ms. Walker once passed out a bag of treats for a faculty meeting. I've seen this sort of technique used at conventions, as well. We looked inside to find a rubber band, one paper clip, an erasable ink pen, one Tootsie-Roll and a Bob Marley pin. She explained that the rubber band was a reminder for teachers to stay flexible when it came to our students and lesson plans - that flexibility was particularly important for special education. The paper clip was a reminder that sometimes the smallest thing keeps it all together. The special pen was included to teach us not to dwell on mistakes, especially the little ones. "Erase 'em and move on," she told use. The Bob Marley pin, she explained, was to help encourage us to relax and know that "everything's gonna be all right." The best thing about that meeting, of course, was that we got to keep the pins!

The Tootsie-Roll? Pure brilliance on Ms. Walker's part.

"It's to wish you all a sweet day, week, and year on the job, here. But it won't just dissolve in your mouth like a mint. No sir. A tootsie-roll takes some chewing, some effort, to get to all that sweetness. Same goes for teaching!"

I've seen creative administrators use a wide variety of activities to perk things up. This is especially important at the beginning, to get everyone's attention and interest level up nice and high. Some play a short selection of music and then ask questions as to why this song was chosen. Others show short video clips that somehow pertain to the meeting. Others pass out treats to teachers or participants who answer certain questions. These can be silly questions, such as who's wearing glasses and white socks? Or even something like who knows what the initials USDA or XYZPDQ stands for? It's always a good idea for the administration to think up a few fun and creative activities that can be used to start, maintain, or end a meeting. Once this becomes policy, teachers will actually look forward to these get-togethers and they may even show up on time! The Quest Center is fortunate to have Michele Laurent as our behavioral tech specialist. When called upon, she runs incredible faculty meetings, sometimes on seemingly boring topics. For example, we recently were subjected to a three and a half hour in-service, training-marathon-session on, you guessed right - the Marzano Method. Oh what fun and games! Looks like Marzano is here to stay for a while. When I glanced at my watch I was totally surprised to see it was nearly noon and three hours had somehow magically - and ever so swiftly - passed by. How did Michele pull this incredible feat off? She ran the meeting like a class lesson should be run. Time was broken into manageable bits, with teachers being allowed and encouraged to get up and move. We had to accomplish certain tasks, as the morning training went on. Some of these objectives were carried out in small groups and involved discussion. Our responses, we either shared verbally with the entire group, or taped onto large oak tags and hung on the wall. Michele also uses a super-technique for students, (in this case us teachers), feedback.

"Did you understand this last point?" she asked. "Let me see a Fist-to-Five!"

The Fist-to-Five is a visual indicator the instructor uses to determine whether it's time to move on to the next topic. A raised fist in the air signifies that an individual didn't get the previous matter at all. Five fingers raised straight in the air indicates full comprehension. Three fingers raised means somewhere in the middle; "Yeah, I got some of it but not all, and I'd like further clarification". This maneuver is a great way to check how your students are doing before moving on to new topics. Her Fist-to-Five reminds of the Boy Scout hand signal. Whenever a Scout or troop leader needs total quiet and everyone's attention, all he has to do is raise up the Scout sign. Pretty soon, often within seconds, the entire area is as quiet as a library. Teachers and parents can devise their very own visual signal for their students or children. It can be a verbal type of "secret" code, such as a specific laugh or cough, or some sort of hand gesture. But these little techniques go a long way toward getting that important feedback, or, everyone's attention, when necessary.

One last tip for teachers and staff. This one might come as a surprise. This is especially important for new teachers: Don't take the job home. There's simply no need to. It's good to focus ahead, work on those lesson plans, and catch up on some work related ideas. But it's not necessary to spend four hours after work, on your work! In fact, I think it's counter-productive. Spending hours on work-after-work means that things are probably not going too smoothly during work time. Spending a lot of time after work, on work, also means that pretty soon, things won't be going too smoothly at home either. Once you get in the groove, then this at home after-work prep time can, and should be, reduced to an hour or less. This notion of taking the job home also can impact negatively on the quality of your home life. Stress levels rise, fighting increases between spouses, (and among the kids). It's far better to keep the after job prep time to a minimum and do something fun and positive for you and your family members.

George & The LAW

There's one more story I have to share that provides insight into Ms. Walker's unique style. It was an event that could have been orchestrated by RDK. I think these two incredible administrators are from the same mold.

To understand this particular event, I first need to tell you about George.

For two years, I held my special music program on the stage area in the school's cafeteria. George was an older African-American man, who was a teacher's aide. He had a very sweet, good-natured disposition. He used to escort the kids from their busses into the school in the mornings, and was an extra set of eyes keeping watch when they played outside. And yes, he paid his dues big time. He also helped change diapers. Every so often he'd open up the cafeteria door, peek inside, and check out the music class. I'd usually have the kids sitting in a semi-circle around me. I'd be singing some tunes and playing guitar, while the students would use their adaptive switches and assistive technology to help them participate. As time went on, his quick visits seemed to increase. He was clearly interested in what we were all about. (Either that, or he just liked listening to live music). But one day he came onto the stage and motioned to the keyboards. My assistant, Zahava, was playing on the keys, and wondered what exactly George wanted. (Zahava, by the way, is one of those unique musicians who can hear a tune and know exactly what key it's in and, more importantly, know how to play it).

"Mind if I try 'em out?" George asked us.

I gave Zahava a quick look, and seeing her nod her head, I replied "sure."

I figured, if anything, was probably gonna play that old standard "chop sticks." You know that one. You use your two index fingers to play it.

He sat down, kind of stretched out his fingers and what happened next, knocked me off my seat. He not only tickled the ivories, as they say, he blew 'em right off the board! Out came this incredible jazz! Zahava and I sat there with our mouths gaping open.

"How do you... I mean, who are you... I mean, uh..."

I couldn't get out a complete sentence. George just smiled at us, and continued playing. His hands seemed to float lightly over the entire keyboard. It was hot. George was not just a player, in the musical sense, he was top-of-the-line pro! Inside, I was kicking myself in the rear end. Why had I never invited him into my music area when he kept peeking in? Why didn't I know anything about him, even though we had been together at the Quest for some time? It was a good lesson for me. Take the time to get to know your colleagues a bit. They may just surprise you.

George didn't just surprise us. He blew us away. Turned out that in his past he had played with the great superstars in the jazz world including Max Roach, Lionel Hampton, The Count Basie orchestra, and more! We were under the same roof, and I never knew any of this! And so, after opening the door - literally - George became a frequent visitor. With him on the keys, I felt like the proverbial 5th wheel - totally unnecessary. But George had the patience of a saint, and he worked with me, teaching me various jazz chords and riffs, and how to make some feeble attempts to play along with his awesome, jazz touch. One song he loved playing was, "Somewhere Over The Rainbow." He did an amazing jazz version in the key of F. I spent many hours trying to learn the lead guitar to this sweet song.

The story doesn't end here. Enter, Ms. Walker. I got summoned to her office one afternoon, where the following conversation took place:

"Doctor," she said, leaning forward in her chair, "you don't have to do this. Just say no if you don't want to, ok?"

"Sure," I replied, not at all sure what she was talking about.

"George is going through some difficult stuff right now."

"Yeah, I know about his wife."

"Yes. Health issues. Well, he's not a well man either. They both have health problems. Serious health problems."

"He mentioned some things to me. But I didn't want to push him on it."

"Anyhow," she said, nodding her head slowly up and down. "I noticed how George is like a different person in your music room. When he's playing with you he smiles, laughs, you know, just comes to life more."

I wasn't sure where this was going, or what she was leading to.

"So, I'd like to pull him out half a day from his regular position, and put him in with you."

"With me? Half a day?"

"Now, like I said, you don't have to if..."

"George with me half a day?"

"Yes. I'd like to."

"Every day?" I asked incredulously.

"If it's..."

"Oh Ms. Walker," I said putting my arm behind my back. "Twist my arm!"

And like that, George, this awesomely talented jazz pianist and wonderful human being, became my assistant - half a day, five days a week, 'til the end of the school year!

It was only later that I reflected on what an extraordinary administrator Ms. Walker was. While most school administrators would have shown sympathy to someone like George. ("Oh, I'm so sorry for what you're going through. Stay strong. We're behind ya all the way.") Not LAW. She saw George come to life when playing piano in the music class. She understood that clearly, the music room was his place, to be, to shine, to feel open, relaxed, and momentarily, at least, free from worries. She not only recognized his needs, but acted on his behalf. I don't know if I would have the courage, the strength, and the vision to make such a move, if I was the boss. I can only hope to follow in her footsteps.

Unfortunately, George passed on after that school year ended. Meanwhile, it was truly a blessing to have been George's "5th wheel" - to have had the awesome pleasure of getting to know this remarkable person, and super-talented jazz piano master. Ms. Walker demonstrated the importance of treating others with respect and dignity, and displayed the kind of awareness it takes to help teachers find their niche, go with their strengths, and stay healthy and happy on the job. It's a lesson I will always carry with me.

TEACH ME IF YOU CAN!
CHAPTER 8

Night At The Opera — In The Real Unreal World

"A mentch tracht un Got lacht" — a person plans and God laughs

— *Yiddush expression*

O k, it wasn't nighttime. And it wasn't the opera. But it definitely could have been a scene from the Marx Brothers. Make that the "Best of the Marx Brothers." First of all, if you've never seen the side-splitting movie mayhem of the original "Fab Four," - Groucho, Chico, Harpo, & Zeppo, you owe it to yourself to pick up "Night At The Opera" — arguably their very best. Although my boys are mighty fond of Duck Soup and Animal Crackers, so, I'll leave this call to your discretion.

I was sitting in the rather luxurious seats at the Broward Center for the Performing Arts watching a wonderful performance of Nutcracker Suite. I mean, it all looked wonderful, the actors & actresses seemed professional. The costumes were top notch. The music and the singing were super. But somehow, I simply couldn't relax and just enjoy the show. Not with my Quest kiddies, who, for the time being, were actually kind of quiet. I was imagining how nice it must be to let go and kind of melt into this comfy seat, but for us teachers on duty, it was more like sitting on the edge of the seat! Tommy was having a ball and giggling so loud that approximately half of the 2400 students present could hear. The other half would turn around every so often, and wonder what the tumult was all about.

For these types of trips we had decent supervision, about one adult for every two students. Somehow, at the moment, it just didn't seem like a good enough ratio. I was the main teacher, and even with my three assistant teachers, we had our hands full. Still, in spite of the anxiety and hardships, I've always deemed these excursions out of the school and into the community to be very important. It was a chance for us to reinforce appropriate social skills. Without these practical experiences how would they ever learn how to act in public? Some school districts call these outings CBI, which stands for Community Based Instruction. It's not simply a matter of plopping your crew onto a bus and heading for the local strip mall to do some shopping. CBI can and should be, an integral part of any decent special education program. But like anything worthwhile, it takes some planning, hard work, and a good dosage of plain ol' luck.

The reasoning behind it all is quite simple. To learn how to play drums, well, you've got to eventually sit behind a drum set and play. To learn how to ride a bike, you've got to leave the dream realm and get physical. The kid has to get up on that seat, hold onto the handlebars, use some balance, and ride. Of course, the drum student is not going to turn into Ringo Star after one or two, or even 100 sessions. And little Johnny will probably start off his riding career with a set of training wheels, (as this will save a lot of elbow and knee scrapes). The game plan is to start off in small, doable increments, and to proceed ever onward and upward. The same scenario applies to students with social challenges and deficits. To learn positive social skills, they will eventually have to mingle with others in a real and meaningful way.

Community Based Instruction - Making It Work

No sense reinventing the wheel here. Kudos to autism coach Deb Kalitan & some of the Quest Center staff for putting together a checklist that's both realistic and doable. It is always checked and double-checked before leaving the safe confines of the school and heading out into the real "unreal" world. These outings into the community can be very beneficial for individuals with special needs. It's important to plan well to maximize these trips. Like the Scout motto - be prepared. My assistant principal, Mr. Abraham has taken things to a new level. His expression goes something like "be over prepared!" CBI excursions into the outside world, are definitely those times you'll want to follow the AP's wise advice.

CBI Preparation Checklist

- *CBI permission slips with emergency information*
- *Classroom preparation for site, in advance of CBI*
- *Advance notice to parents who requested it*
- *If you are the teacher supervising a site, checkmark participant names at every juncture through use of a sign out sheet, or similar documentation.*
- *CBI objectives with data sheets*
- *Communication devices, or some other communication system*
- *Visuals, or written instructions for the site*
- *Supervising Adult(s):*
- *Student(s) Attending:*
- *Site:*
- *Specific activities for site:*

It's important for parents to plan ahead when taking a child with special needs out into the real, unreal world. This may, in fact, require extensive thought in order to insure a successful experience for everyone. As with the above checklist, it's a good idea to put down on paper what the goals and objectives are for such an outing. Once the goals are set, then the parent or guardian can write down what's needed to meet these objectives, including supervision, materials & supplies, behavior modification rewards, (such as popcorn, bits of cereal, etc.), and other goodies that we simply tend to overlook. Most of us pick up on social cues and respond appropriately when "wheeling & dealing" in the outside world. But it can be a frightening and confusing place for an individual with special needs. Planning ahead will put the odds more in your favor, although nothing guarantees a successful mission.

Sitting in the luxurious Broward Center for the Performing Arts, I glanced over at Tony, one of my assistants. This solidly built African-American helper, has a great sense of humor, and has a kind of mellowing influence on my students. Whereas I tend to hype them up all the time, (tickling them, play wrestling, throwing & kicking a ball around), Tony is more on the calm side. I wisely decided to follow Tony's style at the prestigious Performing Arts Center. Still, Tony too seemed a bit on the nervous side.

"Hey Tony," I said leaning over. "Don't worry, man. We got Javi surrounded!" I patted Javi on the leg while giving Tony that, "we got the bases covered" kind of look.

I took the aisle seat. Then came Javi and then Tony. No way Javi was gonna do his "shtick" here. You see, Javi, besides being on the quite large side, (we're talking well over 250 at only 15 years old), also had the unusual habit of, well, to put it on the polite side, he liked to undress. Completely. He also paid no attention whatsoever to those silly labels like, "private" or "public." I'd seen Javi clear out shopping malls simply by tearing off his clothes and getting comfortable in his birthday suit. Javi almost always moved slowly, almost like he was stuck in a slow motion setting. It would often take me 15 minutes to get him from the top of the pool deck at the Quest to just the 2nd or 3rd step down. It wasn't that the water was cold, either. I deliberately had the school set the temperature to a warm setting, so the water experience would be enjoyable for my students. But by the time I got Javi to step #3, the period was half over and it was time to start heading him back out again. He only seemed to find that inner-speed-button when it came to undressing.

Tony flashed back the thumbs-up sign. We had poor Javi boxed in and there was no way he was going to engage in his "meshugas," (his rather anti-social behaviors). After all, we were guests of Broward County, and while a good 95% of the audience came from "regular" schools, we were one of several special education schools invited to participate and enjoy the live show. We represented the Quest Center and I was determined to put our best foot forward.

I don't know exactly what happened. More specifically, I don't know how it happened. We not only had Javi confined, but we were kind of leaning against his shoulders and arms from both sides. The first half went really well. Too well, in fact. I should have known better and not gone for the whole ball of wax. Leave well enough alone, my grandmother used to say. I mean, they had all behaved exceptionally for close to 45 minutes. After the brief 15-minute intermission we returned to our seats. The only real problem during the first half of the show was that several of the students would randomly stand up, saying two short consonants, you know, those magic letters that bring panic to any well-intentioned adult; "P.P." With this short utterance you knew that you had approximately 4.5 seconds to lead them down the aisle, (trying not to step upon every foot and ankle in the way), open up the back doors of the theatre — which, of course, immediately lets in an undesirable amount of light - and whisk them into the men's room. You prayed, often out loud, during these precarious moments, hoping that you could beat the odds and make it to the hallowed turf of the "john" in time. It was always a race against the clock. It was absolutely crucial to keep winning these races, especially since we didn't have a change of clothes for every student.

So I guess it was all about not leaving well enough alone, but who could resist not going back for the second half. First of all, we were out of the school and second of all I reasoned, it was a super learning experience. I just didn't know it was going to be a learning experience meant mainly for Tony and myself.

The second half began calmly, and in spite of Tommy's laughing out loud — he was in a good mood - all was flowing along quite smoothly. I was amazed at how the theatre was designed...state-of-the-art lighting, sound, décor, etc. The entire theatre was built at a slightly downward slant so you could see really well from any seat in the house.

Then, in a matter of less than a hair-splitting fraction-of-a-second, it simply happened...right before our totally disbelieving eyes. Son-of-a-gun, he did it! In one amazing swift motion, Javi's arm shot heavenward along with his T-shirt, which had somehow ripped from his torso. My mouth dropped open as his arm continued downward, releasing the object, and sending it flying ever downward, downward. By now the shirt had grabbed enough air that it turned into weird, slowly sinking parachute. The downward slant of the theatre was working against us. Big time. As the shirt made its way past row after row, I noticed that Tony was sinking lower and lower in his chair. I only realized this, of course, since I was more prone in my seat than him, and had a good view of what was next to me. Javi simply sat there, leaning a bit forward in his seat and in high spirits, since he had succeeded in at least becoming bare-chested. Finally, after three long seconds, (that seemed like an eternity), the shirt made a direct-hit-landing, about 25 rows down, catching some poor teenage youngster smack dab on the head. We watched mesmerized, as it gently wrapped around his head and face.

He wasn't sure what had hit him, but turning around, he knew exactly where it had come from. 2,499 students all had clothes on. But there was Javi alongside an entire clothed theatre, his bare chest standing out like, well, a large, sore thumb. Talk about a challenge! It's one thing to curse somebody out, but another matter quite entirely, to nail someone with a flying T-shirt! And it's one thing to do so privately, but a totally different situation when it's all done publicly... very publicly. About the same time that 1250 student's heads turned upwards towards us, Tony and I looked at each other and had the following conversation, both speaking at the very same time.

"Tony, you gotta go down there and tell the kid who we are and everything!"

"Laz, you gotta go down there and tell the kid who we are and everything!"

"C'mon Tony. You're the dang assistant. It's your job!"

"C'mon Laz. You're the main teacher. It's your job!"

I knew it was time for immediate action. We had a riot to prevent.

Reluctantly, I got up from my seat and made my way down the aisle, row after long row. Despite the action on stage, all eyes were focused on me. Well, let's be fair about this. Their eyeballs, and thus their head movements, went from Javi, to me, to the kid now standing, and holding the flying T-shirt in hand. Javi sat there, ever content, and somehow seemed to be watching the play. Hmmm, I muttered, I'm glad someone was enjoying the performance.

"Hey bro," I said, now standing directly in front of our teenage victim. "We're a special ed class. Real sorry, but he doesn't really understand what he's doing."

I was thinking he was gonna start swinging, but he simply put the T-shirt in my hand and said, "Don't worry, sir."

(Always a good sign when a teenager uses the word, sir).

"My older sister is in special ed too. She has autism. So it's really no big deal. I hope they're enjoying the show."

I was totally impressed with this young man's response. In front of all these people, his peers and classmates, and a whole bunch of strangers, he demonstrated tremendous sensitivity. He spoke up for my students even when it might have meant he would "lose face" in front of his peers.

"Thanks," I replied. "If you're ever looking for a teaching job, look me up at the Quest Center."

After a brief pow-wow with my assistants, we wisely decided not to push our luck any further.

"C'mon y'all," I said to the gang. "You've done a great job so far but let's hit that park outside, and relax a bit."

Javi seemed all too happy to leave the confines of his seat and head for the greener, freer pastures of the great outdoors, where to his and our liking, there were other hearty souls running around shirtless.

It takes some decent preparation, an extra set of eyeballs, and a fair amount of good fortune to make sure things flow smoothly in the real, unreal world. Students and children with special needs often flourish in a self-contained setting that's filled with understanding, warm, sensitive, and supportive adults and classmates. It can be a very different "out there" once our Johnny leaves the womb-like environment of his home or school. Even the most carefully composed plans can meet with negative results. All we can try to do is stack the odds in our favor. Sometimes, however, hope and some earnest prayers are all we have. Our trip to the mall was just such an experience. Despite extensive planning and the extra hands on deck, it was, in a nutshell, disaster with a capitol D! It truly did seem like a splendid idea since it was, after all, the winter holiday season. We're talking the music, the decorations, the festive lights and displays, all in full glory at America's wonderland - the shopping mall!

Why should our special needs students miss out on this opportunity? If it was good enough for mainstream society then it would be stimulating for my Quest students, as well. Deb urged me to bring as many extra adults as possible to help with the supervision and so, besides Deb and myself, we also brought two of my assistants along. I quickly did the math. Four adults to eight students with profound special needs. A one-to-two ratio seemed more than adequate, so we boarded the bus, eagerly anticipating a rewarding trip for one and all.

"This is gonna be awesome," I told all the adults as we boarded the bright yellow "cheese" - our small, trusty school bus. The bus felt nice and secure, as we settled into our seats.

"I might even get some holiday shopping done," I said quietly to Tony. "You know, two birds with one stone."

"Good luck, Laz," Tony smiled back. "Remember, you've got Javi! If he gets in one of those moods!"

"Yeah, I know."

"Well, if he does, he ain't moving. Unless we bring a crane. Or some backup. Like the state militia, maybe."

I laughed off Tony's last remarks not even wanting to keep those nasty images in the realm of thought. I wanted that scenario as far removed from reality as possible.

Before entering the beautiful, modern mall, all lit up for the season, we decided to split up. We figured there'd be less of a chance for a behavioral meltdown or social mishap if they couldn't pick up on one another's behaviors and start imitating one another. Deb headed down the right corridor with two students. Tony went to the left with Tommy and Mikey. Ty went straight ahead with three of our higher functioning kids, while I moved slowly on with Javi. Tony was right. It looked like I was in for a very long morning. Forget about shopping and trying to catch up on some holiday gifts. I had to remind myself that I was here for the kids, for my students, and not for my own personal needs.

After about 10 minutes, we had actually made it to the end of a long corridor that led right into Macy's. Now this was a dandy good sign indeed. Maybe, just maybe, we could get a few things done after all. But Javi wasn't paying any attention to the brightly decorated store displays that lay so tantalizingly close. Something else grabbed his attention. Straight ahead were four large, wonderfully soft couches complete with oversized, very comfortable looking pillows. He made a direct beeline to this haven. Or was that heaven? I basically knew that my shopping mall adventure was on hold. Once Javi settled in, well let's just say, neither one of us was moving too fast. I knew from my work with him in the classroom and the school pool, that he was a tough one to budge once he hit the comfort zone.

Since it was the holiday season, the mall was fairly crowded, (even though it was only around 10:30 AM). Javi settled into an empty couch while I took the spare chair. The other three couches were filled with shoppers, mostly mothers with pre-school age kids and babies. Holiday music filled the air and one didn't really have to move from this spot to see all the flashing colored lights and special effects going on. Truth be told, I wasn't all that disappointed to just be sitting in that awesomely comfortable chair. It was definitely easier than slowly leading Javi through the crowded mall corridors. "He's still getting something out of this experience," I told myself. Our only objective here was to take them to experience the sights, sounds, smells, and the entire sensory Gestalt of the holiday season. Nobody said anything about having to walk and run around to make it happen. It was, in fact, happening all around us anyhow. I didn't even become all that alarmed when Javi took off his sneakers and socks. I mean this was Miami, (which was about 75 degrees warmer than the rest of the country, this time of year). I noticed that many people in the mall wore flip-flops and clogs. No socks were the norm around these parts. The next moments, however, happened in this whirlwind blur of action and reactions, mostly consisting of flying clothes and screams of terror. I kick myself for not heeding the telltale warning sign of bare feet. In blazing speed, Javi had struck again, whipping off his shirt and pants. In what seemed like a Nano-second, he was sitting blissfully on the couch in his underwear, despite the shouting and yelling going on all around him. In less than 10 seconds, that entire end of the mall was cleared out, as mothers whisked their kids away, packed strollers and all.

But little did I know that the grand mall super-adventure had just begun. As I was getting him dressed again I began to hear yelling from the far end of the long corridor. Despite my earnest prayers that it be someone else for a change, the names started sounding way too familiar.

"No Tommy!" came one verbal outburst.

"Stop it right this instant!" came another.

"Stop him, please!" a voice yelled sounding rather desperate.

"Mikey no! Behave!"

I couldn't run to the scene to lend a helping hand because that would've meant leaving Javi alone, very unsupervised, and very willing, ready and able to take matters to the next level - the "birthday suit" stage. It took me a very long 60 seconds to get Javi dressed and ready to move. We had no trouble finding the crew members who had drawn all the attention. All we had to do was follow the noise level, which seemed to be increasing both in the number of participants and the decibel level.

Towing Javi with both hands, I came upon a scene which one doesn't see all that often in the great American shopping mall. There was Tommy struggling on the floor, while Tony was desperately trying to pin him down. Next to Tommy was a broken flowerpot of some sort. Dirt & rocks were all over the place. There was a small stand in the middle of the corridor that featured bonsai plants and trees. The guy who ran this cute little booth just stood there with his mouth open. By now an entire crowd had gathered to see what the heck was going on, and to figure out why this big adult was picking on this much younger and smaller human being. Some were yelling for him to stop, while others were yelling for the police, while Tony was yelling for Tommy to stop, while I was yelling for everyone to stop. Things were sliding out of control fast, and I had no doubt that within a minute we'd all be arrested for disturbing the peace, and perhaps, attempted kidnapping. From the outward appearance of things, it didn't look too good.

"Uh... it's okay," the guy standing behind the bonsai plants kept repeating. "It's okay. Don't worry."

I wasn't too sure what he was referring to, but my guess was the broken pot on the floor.

Then it dawned on me. Tommy was probably just in that mad search phase, looking for his fix; a nice round-shaped pebble! That's why he reached into the display area and grabbed the pot. He wanted a pebble.

Sure enough, once we put a variety of pebble choices into Tommy's hand he instantly calmed down. After a 10 second deliberation, he chucked them all aside except for one. It went straight into his mouth. He needed this oral fixation to feel comfortable and relaxed.

Once Tommy eased up, you could sense a collective sigh of relief from the ever-growing audience now crowded around the portable bonsai tree shop.

I offered to pay for the broken pot, but he simply kept uttering "it's okay... don't worry."

"Look at all the people here," I told him. "Probably the best thing that ever happened to your shop."

When crisis number two was winding down and the crowd began dispersing, we began to hear some noises from another part of the mall. No doubt about this one. It was Deb's voice rising above the humming of the lights and the undertones of a crowded shopping mall. "No," she said rather loudly and firmly. "Put that down right now!"

About four minutes later we all rendezvoused at our very secure, self-contained little haven - the school bus! Our mall trip had come to a quick and rather desperate end. "Anyone for Micky D's?" Deb asked. "Or I think better, the park. Let's take 'em to a park."

So what had gone wrong? Why this disaster instead of all the good things we had planned for and anticipated? Back on the bus, as we headed to a nearby park, we discussed what had happened. At first, it was all questions. How could this have occurred? Was it all the lights and noise and stimulation? Did we need even more supervision, like one-on-one? Should we have taken just a few kids and not the entire class? Was the venue appropriate? One question was the hardest to answer. Did we schedule this outing more for us than the students? In other words, perhaps we were all hoping to get in some extra shopping and take advantage of this "free" time.

As care providers, our first job is the safety and well being of our students and children. It takes a good deal of preparation and wisdom to pull off a happy, successful and productive outing into the "real" world. Some venues and places are simply not the best choices. In general, individuals with special needs do better in more structured environments. The loud, busy, shopping mall was probably too much sensory input for some of them to handle. The mall had become one very huge MSE, multi-sensory environment, except that they weren't allowed to touch anything. In my music room/MSE they were not only allowed to touch, but were encouraged to do so. I do my best to try to get them involved in the "outside" environment in meaningful and engaging ways. The mall was a big contradiction for them. Look and listen, but don't feel anything! It was a bad choice on our part. Later in the school year, we would discover that in smaller groups, with a one-to-one ratio, they could have successful social experiences at malls and supermarkets. Through the assistance of a professional "shadow," the students learned what was appropriate and what wasn't. That first mall trip was a learning experience for all the staff involved. We bit off more than we could chew, but we learned what it takes to make them feel successful when confronting the "unreal" world out there.

It's a slow, gradual learning process. Once they get some of the basic social skills down, then the teacher or parent can bring in another child or student. The point is to start slowly with deliberate, manageable steps. Think about what it takes to make your own visit to a shopping mall or supermarket a pleasant one. There are hundreds, if not thousands, of little steps involved. There are all the social skills that the vast majority of us learned over time, via practice and hands-on experience. Some came easy. Others came through trial & error. Here's a brief list of what it takes to be successful while shopping in public. Each general area can be broken down into about 16,000 sub-areas.

Maximizing for Social Success in The Real "Unreal" World

1) Dressing appropriately.

Just stop for a moment and think about the zillions of skills required for this one. Some special needs students are blissfully unaware of the necessity to dress when going out in public. Unless you belong to a nudist colony, it's one of those things required of us in civilized and social societies. Once this becomes imbedded in our consciousness, then other skills come into play, such as the ability to hold, grasp, and manipulate buttons, zippers, laces, Velcro, etc. This general skill also requires knowledge of what's considered socially acceptable forms of dress. Even though we consider ourselves a rather open-minded society where lots of behaviors and dress styles are ok, nevertheless, one wouldn't, for example, go out in South Florida during the month of July with a ski jacket, mittens, and a scarf. (Or go anywhere on the planet with a striped shirt, madras jacket, checkered pants, and two different shoes. They might call the psych ward on such a person). In other words, there's this unwritten, subtle form of dogma that affects how we dress in public. It's even frowned upon to wear socks that don't match, let alone distasteful clothes that are much more visible. As you can see, this skill is one that we tend to absorb and do our very best to emulate in our quest to seek social approval. Individuals with special needs may be completely oblivious to this highly important part of the public social scene.

2) Knowing how to ask for something.

In my master's degree program at Buffalo State College, we had to engage in a variety of activities that placed us in the imaginary position of having different kinds of profound challenges. Since we were all going into the field of special education, our professors felt it was a good idea for us to experience these disabilities at a gut-level. First we were covered with dark blindfolds and had to make our way to the water fountain without killing ourselves, or others, in the process. Tasks that we don't think twice about, such as making peanut butter & jelly sandwiches, became monumental challenges. At first we did these types of activities with a non-impaired partner. After a few practice runs, we attempted these "simple" endeavors on our own. I banged my knee into the wall about 43 times, got water all over my face at the fountain, and then, during the PB&J session, dropped the jar, which broke into lots of nasty pieces on the floor. My professor showed some mercy and let me clean up without the blindfold.

I now do similar activities with my university students. A popular one is to try writing numbers, letters and words while only having the ability to look in a mirror. You'll succeed real well at this one if you're a dentist and know how to work using mirrors, where the image is reversed. If this opposite perspective is not compensated for, the dentist will be working on the wrong side of that tooth of yours! But these activities give us just a glimpse into the world of an individual with dyslexia, where words, numbers, and letters all tend to be processed in reverse. Bat becomes tab. 12 is read as 21, etc. The important piece of the puzzle here is that we at least try to enter their world and see and feel things from their perspective, which is probably very different than ours.

Our next exercise was to communicate without speech. At first we were not just awkward, but like newborn infants trying to get some warm milk without being able to cry. Each of us was paired with a colleague who also wasn't allowed to verbalize, or even murmur any vocalizations. Our task was to find out 10 different facts about our partner. These could be about anything of interest, such as career, family, hobbies, etc. The first several minutes were absolutely frustrating and there wasn't a lot of understandable communication going on. But then we started using our own gestures. The 20-minute session ended with no one getting 10 facts about the other person, although a few people got five different things right. This technique has become standard practice for my college students going into special education. These kinds of exercises provide us empathy with them, even though we only get a small glimpse what they may have to deal with all the time.

3) How to find the things you need or want.

Here too, put yourself in their position as much as possible. See what it's like to express yourself when you're unable to rely on the regular means of communication that you probably take for granted; your lovely voice! Do a bit of role-playing and try it for a few minutes and then gradually increase the time. Then, when you get the hang of using communication devices in an effective manner, test yourself in the great outdoors amongst other members of the human species. See if you can do this for a complete day. Include getting gas without swiping a credit card, going shopping, and hitting your local Starbucks for an ice coffee. The next phase is to try the communication devices from a wheelchair using a knee or head switch, which if course further compounds the level of difficulty and social success.

4) How to say please and thank you at the right times.

Picking up on social cues is but one part of the social equation, but in certain social situations, we are required to think and plan ahead. This is exactly so in the case of saying "please" and "thank you." For special needs students, this cause and effect is as confusing as the mixed signals they received when asking audience members to dance at the Senior Center. Acting out social situations such as these can be very helpful. Pointing out examples of this courtesy is also helpful. One family shared with me how excited they were when their child expressed his "aha" moment by pointing to their family dog. "Look," he said, pointing to the wagging-tailed dog waiting patiently for its water. "She's saying please!" Good examples are expressed every day, we just have to help our kids tune into them.

5) How to take public transportation or how to ride in a car.

Once when I was driving home from work, I noticed one of my students named Danny, in the car next to me at the red light. I naturally beeped my horn, got their attention, and waved. Danny saw me and as his eyes lit up in recognition. He immediately reached for the door lock to get out and greet me. The adult driver quickly grabbed his hand and held him inside the car.

It's all these "little" things that are quite big and important, after all. And these are things we simply do out of habit and completely take for granted.

- Being appropriate while on the bus or in a car, such as not singing too loudly or screaming or yelling things or grabbing from others is a difficult thing to request from your special needs student or child, but after what may amount to thousands of outings, I can tell you that a certain amount of order is attainable. Rehearsing expectations by having the children verbalize things like, "I need to sit still," can help cue them in to the upcoming activity. Even better would be a rhyming jingle that brings the point home: "I need to sit still and I know I will," or "Riding is fun but I have to sit and not run."
- How to handle money and not be taken advantage of. This is a tough one for many special needs students. One parent explained that they only gave their child quarters. If the child wanted to purchase an ice cream, the parent told them that they would need 4 of their "treasure coins" and that they would not get any change back. If they wanted to get a gumball from a vending machine, they were told that they needed only one of their treasure coins. Special needs students can remember sequential numbers easier than monetary denominations such as quarters, dimes, nickels, etc. Keeping things simple will ensure better results.
- How to communicate properly and effectively. Non-verbal students or individuals

with communication difficulties can use sign language or communication devices to express their thoughts, but are often unaware of how to get someone's attention who is not looking directly at them. Teachers and parents can help them learn to ask for help in a friendly, yet polite fashion. Some parents tell their child to enter the words, "I need you," and to use them every time they need real assistance, so the parent can listen for these words, even from several rooms away.

- When and how to smile appropriately. This is often a very difficult area for individuals with special needs. Facial cues, gestures, and body language, are subtle and convey about 16,000 different messages. Is the person happy? Upset? Surprised? Flirty? Annoyed? Getting along socially in public is an area that requires constant monitoring and can be very exhausting for many people. Here too, the answer is to provide support and be a positive "shadow" as you make your way through the public arena. It's not that Big Brother is watching; everyone is watching!

All of these above areas are absolutely critical to a successful adventure into the community at large. Obviously some individuals will require more assistance than others. The responsible adult and caregiver have to know the child and what his or her strengths and weaknesses are.

My students had to practice all these skills and more when preparing to perform. Once the decision was made to end our shows with an interactive dance with the audience — usually senior citizens, we soon realized that our students simply didn't know how to deal with a "no" response. The show would usually end with something like "Let It Shine" or "I Can See Clearly Now." The keyboard player would keep the melody going, as my students and I would go out into the audience and ask someone to dance. This "asking" process was practiced for several weeks in the safe confines of the Quest Center, where we could role-play the various scenarios. Some of the more verbal students would ask the person "would you like to dance?" Others, those with less verbal ability, would hold out a card that read the same question. In this way, the senior adult could respond by saying yes or no, or shake their head in the appropriate way, (which was yet another important skill we had to practice). Sometimes these headshakes are tiny little movements up & down or sideways, and of course, each indicate an opposite desire. We reviewed these subtle body gestures over and over again, until the choir participants were totally comfortable and could perceive the proper responses.

To make matters a bit more complicated, some of the seniors would first say no, but that meant they weren't interested in getting up from their chairs. In truth, they still wanted to dance, but while sitting down. At first my students couldn't process these mixed messages. "No" to getting up and "yes" to dancing? Huh? My students would look at me or one of my assistants with a very perplexed expression. Eventually they learned that it was ok to simply hold their senior partner's hands, while he or she remained in a sitting position, and in this manner, rock to the music. Eventually they picked up these social cues on their own and became expert dance partners in the process. Fred Astaire would have been proud.

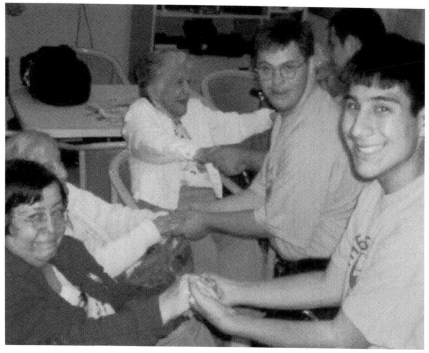

A true win-win situation. My student performers "dancing" with the adults at an assisted living facility. They had to learn a variety of positive social skills for this interaction to occur. Here they help the seniors move gently to the live music.

Let's review some of the important pieces of the puzzle to help make social outings as positive and successful as possible.

- Like the Scout Motto says — Be Prepared! Plan ahead and practice the various scenarios that might occur.

- Take a hard look at the process involved. Break down a goal into the smallest components possible. Then, when you've discovered that going to a supermarket entails about 635 steps on the ladder, keep working until you've reached step 1,635. Keep the general objective in mind, but work on these tiny, teeny, small, and attainable steps. Once a skill is mastered then, (and only then), move on to the next one.

- Reconsider the "big" trip and start off slowly. Instead of hitting a 24/7 Wal-Mart that features 14,000,000 distractions and an equal number of human bodies in perpetual motion, (and two cashiers if you're lucky), try an outing to a smaller venue, such as the neighborhood corner store. It's a quieter and more-controlled environment. But the real plus is that the storeowner probably knows you and has some compassion for your student or child.

- Do a similar process with a time factor. No need for a six-hour trip to Home Depot when five minutes might be the maximum exposure before meltdown. You know your child better than anyone. Why push him or her to the edge? Unless, of course, you enjoy living dangerously. Here too, this comfort time zone can be extended as the individual with special needs becomes more adept in the social public scene.

- Use assistive technology, such as communication devices, to help those individuals who require verbal assistance. Practice these skills in a safe, well-monitored environment, such as your classroom or home before putting them to use in the public domain. When was the last time you gave a second thought to asking for extra ketchup? Or excused yourself to use the washroom? Or asked the cook to hold the onions? All of these things and more can, of course, be programmed into a communication device, which helps enable our kids. When they can communicate exactly what they want or need, it helps turn a potentially frustrating situation into a successful experience.

- Review what went well and what didn't quite work out. It's important to take notes and write things down for future reference. You may see patterns emerge that will help you better plan more successful outings. Take the time and do some debriefing. An after-trip form should include areas that can yield valuable data. These forms should be short & sweet, otherwise teachers are hard-pressed to deal with more paperwork. A checklist format with some open lines after each question that allows the teacher or parent space to write comments, is always a good bet.

The Post Trip Evaluation Form (The long version)

- *What worked well during the trip?*
- *How did things go with transportation?*
- *Does the child need a restraining device while sitting on the bus/van?*
- *How did the child get along with others?*
- *Were there any difficulties with supervision in the store/park/outlet, bowling alley, movie theatre, etc.?*
- *Did the child require and use his or her communication device?*
- *If yes, were these experiences successful?*
- *Were any follow-up activities initiated in the classroom after the trip that would reinforce skills introduced on this trip?*

Parents, teachers, and care providers express frustration when it comes to taking individuals with special needs into the real "unreal" world. It can, after all, be a rather harsh place to succeed in. But this is one area that requires great patience and direct, hands-on supervision. Don't rely on mere "mazel" — good fortune - to see you through. Like Thomas Jefferson once said: "I'm a big believer in good luck. I find the harder I work the more I have of it." Experiencing success in the outside world is tricky business and requires hard work, before, after, and especially during the outings. Hang in there. Eventually you might say with great enthusiasm, "a fun time was had by all."

CHAPTER 9

Super (market) Lesson

> *"Much have I learned from my teachers,*
>
> *more from my colleagues,*
>
> *but most from my students."*
>
> — R. Hanina, quoted in the Talmud.

I was doing my domestic duties and shopping at our large community Publix supermarket in the Skylake area of Miami, when I was hit with that eternal question: Why do seemingly intelligent people linger at the toothpaste section? It was like some sort of giant magnet that always drew me in. Did I really need yet another super-power, magic-do-everything formula? Besides, I had been taught to brush well and brush hard. You know, get out all those little buggers wedged between the gums and the teeth. Now I was being told that, well, maybe that wasn't such a great idea after all. Seems the heavy brushing wasn't so great for the enamel on the teeth. Or the gums. The new toothpastes promised to do it; kill bad breath, whiten teeth, protect against cavities, sooth sensitive gums, protect enamel, and get you lower rates on your car insurance. Not too shabby. All was well until I decided to read the back label — the fine print, where it just happens to mention that this wonder paste should not be given to children and that adults should definitely not swallow at all. Just brush, gargle, and spit. And then rinse and spit a few more times to make sure none of this magic poison is left to do some sort of unseen damage in places where the sun don't shine. I did a double take. Now whose brilliant idea was it to create a product that smells and tastes like candy, that you purposely put inside your mouth and swish it all around where it is so dangerously close to the esophagus that it begs for some action? So, you're not supposed to swallow any? Huh? I began picking up other toothpastes from different companies, even the supposedly "health food" stuff, and they all had the same warning label. On the back it gives you the warning: Do not swallow! Right.

Lost deep in thought about this modern society bizarreness, I was suddenly blindsided by something. Hit from the behind, it knocked the wind out of me and almost knocked me over.

"Ugh!" was all I could manage to verbalize.

The person's arms engulfed around me from behind and it was not a fair attack. I was bear-hugged and couldn't even reach the mace hidden deep in my pocket. Before I attempted some defensive maneuver, I heard a voice joyously cry out "Dr. Laz!" To my surprise it was, in fact, a female voice.

Her grip loosened and I quickly turned around to see a young, attractive lady standing there — all smiles.

"Don't you recognize me?" she asked, hands now on her hips.

"Uh, no, uh sorry," I half mumbled. "But don't take it personally, I'm really bad at names."

"I was you student at JFK. You had me for three years! Math, science & social studies."

Not just one or two, but three years. And I still didn't recall her name. Oops.

"It's Theresa," she said, rescuing me. "But that was about seven years ago," she added with a laugh. "I'm almost 21 now."

"Phew," I replied. "At least I have a good excuse now. I mean you went from a girl to a beautiful young woman."

"I'll never ever forget what you taught me," she continued.

My brain went into overdrive. Three years of academic classes translates into about 43 million different facts. I was more than mystified. What was the one thing she remembered from having me for three years straight? Besides, this was Theresa — the one and only female student who could positively make a sailor blush! Back then it seemed as if every other word out of her mouth was a nice juicy curse word, not even fit for the toughest back alleys. I recalled that first day I had her and asked her some question in class. She responded with something words I can only describe with "bleeps." (Chapter 6). Today, she had something to tell me that wasn't accompanied by embarrassing words.

"I think about what you taught me a lot," Theresa said. "It really helped me all these years."

"Really?" I said still having no idea what she was talking about.

"Yeah. You taught me that I'm meant to do something good with my life."

"I taught you that?"

"Yes. It was in science class."

Again my brain was scrambling for some bit of info I could put my finger on. I kept coming up blank. Theresa then went into the whole episode:

Turns out it was a science lesson about the heart. I had brought a real cow's heart into class that I picked up at a local butcher. Since my students had various special challenges, I wanted to make the learning as real and as hands-on as possible. I was pointing out the various parts of the heart when Theresa raised her hand and blurted out a question: "Do you believe that the Jews are the chosen people?"

I was kind of taken aback and asked her what that had to do with science and the heart. She ignored my response and told me that she had been in church over the weekend and heard that from her pastor. She then told the pastor that she had a "real" Jewish teacher and would ask me about this. Her pastor thought that it was a good idea and so, she asked.

I knew that in religious matters I had to be mighty careful. This was a public school and not a yeshiva high school. This was the realm where there's a healthy separation of church & state. I wear my kippah, head covering, at work and I also sport a beard. Some of my colleagues jokingly call me King David. Still, I had to be cautious in my response. I couldn't have my students going home telling their parents about religion class today.

"In the Jewish religion," I answered, "we believe that everyone is chosen to do something important with his or her life, and that everyone is here for a good reason."

I began pointing to each student, one by one. "And that means you and you and you…"

I finished with Theresa who simply nodded her head and said "thank you."

Now, standing in the aisle of the Publix supermarket seven years later, it was my turn.

"And Theresa, I'll never ever forget what you taught me!"

"Really? I taught you something?"

"Yes. Big time. Something very powerful. And something I too, think about a lot!"

In a cute and clever twist of fate, she had forgotten this entire episode until I brought it back to life. I couldn't help but marvel at how divine providence had brought us together so we could each be reminded of these two powerful learning experiences.

My "Varying Exceptionalities" class back at JFK was a doozy and I needed something out of the norm that would motivate them. My grand prize was a scuba diving excursion if they all earned a certain amount of points. They could get these points by learning, sharing, doing their projects, working quietly during class time, etc. After a good eight weeks of some solid effort they had achieved the required number of points and it was party time! I reminded Theresa of the sequence of our dialogue back then in that JFK classroom. It went something like this.

"Okay Dr. Laz, we got the points. Let's go this weekend!"

"Sounds good."

"Let's go Saturday."

"Uh, no go. Can't do it on Saturday."

"Why not?"

"It's my Sabbath."

"So why can't you go then?"

"I don't drive on the Sabbath."

"We'll pick you up."

"No, I don't even get in a car."

"We'll take a taxi."

"It's not that. No car-like vehicles at all."

"We'll take a bus."

"No, nothing motorized. Sorry."

"Horse & buggy?"

"Nope. Not even a bike. Just walking and the beach is way too far to walk with all that gear."

My students then had a million questions all at once, and that wanted to know exactly what I did on the Sabbath.

"You go to church?"

"Yeah, well, we call it a synagogue or temple."

"What else do you do? You go shopping?"

"No. No shopping or business allowed."

"You go to the movies?"

"No. No movies."

"You listen to music, right?"

"Wrong. No iPods or radio headsets. No computers."

"No computers? Dang. How long is your Sabbath?"

"Yeah," another voice chimed in. "How long you get to sit there and do nothing?"

"Oh, it starts sundown on Friday and continues till Saturday night when it gets dark."

"How long is that?"

"About 25 hours."

"You go bowling?"

"Uh no. No bowling."

"You go to the baseball games sometimes, right?"

"Nope. Sorry."

"What about TV?" one student asked. "You watch a lot of TV right?"

"No. No TV."

"For how long?" he continued.

"For the whole Sabbath. All 25 hours worth."

"25 hours without TV," he said hitting the desk with both hands, "I'd rather die!"

"So what do you do already?" another asked. "You gotta be doing something right?" They all nodded their heads in agreement.

I was beginning to feel like I was some sort of ET who just landed from Pluto. It did, after all, sound mighty strange. It seemed like all I was saying were the things you don't do on the Sabbath and I was starting to get a bit self-conscious.

"I mean you don't just sleep right? You know, for all that time. Right?"

"Well," I said, "after temple on Friday night we come home and have this awesome meal. You know, the whole family, together. Usually other guests come too. And we sing together, tell stories, and get caught up on how our week went. You know things like that."

They ignored the quality time stuff and went straight to the real stuff.

"What do you eat?"

"Yeah, tell us about the meal!"

"Yeah, what kind of goodies?"

I then shared the basic menu for Friday night.

"First we say a special blessing on the wine and the bread. The bread is warm, freshly made whole-wheat challah. Then we have fish with all different kinds of dips and salads. Garlic dips. Humus. Cole slaw. Corn salad. Tomato and garlic dip. You know, stuff like that. Then some delicious hot matza ball soup with more salads and other dips. And then the main course begins."

"That's not even the main course yet?" they said out loud. I could see them swallowing and their mouths starting to open. A few began licking their lips.

"The main course is usually different kinds of chicken and meats, or vegetarian goodies, if you're a vegie. This course also features potato and vegetable soufflé and other kinds of salads too. And then there's the dessert. Homemade pies. Maybe a cake or two. Fresh fruit salads. Ice cream. Oh man. Delicious!"

Theresa suddenly stood up and turned around to face the entire class.

"Holy bleepin bleep!" she said out loud. "Dr. Laz got a bleepin bleepity holiday once a bleepin week!"

I was amazed as my students nodded their heads in full agreement.

Here I was, beginning to feel not only out of place but also a bit confounded. Something like, "Yeah, what do I do on the Sabbath anyhow?" I don't do this and I don't do that. It was all sounding like a bunch of no-nos, and right then and there, in that JFK classroom, I started to doubt myself. But Theresa came along to save the day and put it all in proper perspective. She taught me that my Sabbath was indeed very special. It was like having a bleepin holiday once a bleepin' week!

Theresa had gone on and graduated from high school and was in college taking business classes and working part time. She had a boyfriend and they were thinking about getting married. We thanked each other for the profound lessons and I added that I was so proud of her and what she was doing with her life.

"You know what," Theresa said before we left the store. "I think it's totally awesome, by the way."

"What's that?"

"Your Sabbath and all that."

"What do you mean?" I asked, somewhat surprised.

"I mean I think it's amazing that you totally like, get out of the rat race one day every week! No business. No running around. I started keeping more of a Sabbath too in my life. Not like you but something just to stop and relax a bit. But gotta run, Dr. Laz.
272

Awesome seeing ya!"

As I walked out of that Publix supermarket, I suddenly realized that in our 20-minute conversation I didn't hear one bleepin bleepity word from her mouth. Seven years ago at JFK who would've thought that even remotely possible? But even more importantly, was that we shared two mighty powerful lessons that had somehow been translated into our daily lives. The notion of observing a more Sabbath-like day once a week has actually gained a lot of attention in recent years, especially during these often chaotic and over-busy times. It's a chance to regroup, to step back from all the noise pollution, hustle-bustle, crazy scheduling, and multi-tasking pushed upon us by "modern" society. Kim Payne, in the increasingly popular "Simplicity Parenting," (Random House, 2009), writes about creating these special "Sabbath moments" for yourself and your family. One doesn't have to be religious, per se, to experience quieter and more relaxed times. They can be as simple as reading together, going on walks, digging in the dirt, planting a garden, and having a picnic together. The important notion here is that these times are "religiously" honored, (in the sense that they take priority and always occur on the given day). If you honor this commitment, the appointed activity will become sacred to your children or students. Payne's website features all sorts of useful information and suggestions, as well as blogs and a bookstore that offers important tips on how to get back to the real stuff of life — without all the clutter, noise, and subsequent confusion. Check out the site at: www.simplicityparenting.com. Theresa was living proof that lessons about the Sabbath experience are something beneficial for us all.

One added bonus of teaching at a community school is that I often run into my former students and we get to catch up on each other's lives. Like the quote from the Talmud at the very beginning of this chapter, we really do learn the most from our students. We simply need to stay open.

This learning can take many forms. For some, it's the lifelong lessons concerning what's really important, such as the lesson I learned firsthand from Theresa and my entire class back then. Perhaps more common is the notion that they keep us on our toes and help us sharpen our craft. They ask us a ton of questions, many of which we don't know the answers to. This forces us to examine things on a deeper level and, in this manner, increase our knowledge base. Before I took up scuba diving and became knowledgeable about these matters, one of my students once asked me about the air.

"If breathing is so important," he asked, "what's in the air that makes it so important?"

"Oxygen," I responded. "We need the oxygen to keep us alive."

I thought that was a pretty solid answer until he threw a curveball at me.

"But I saw in the nurse's office, on an oxygen tank, that it was very flammable. So why don't we all blow up when someone lights a cigarette?"

Hmmmm. Point well taken.

"So the air we breathe has gotta have more than just oxygen," I thought out loud. "Right?"

"Like what?" he asked.

So we looked it up and found out that there are all sorts of goodies in the air we breathe and oxygen is not even the main component. You'll have to take a few minutes and look this up yourselves for the details.

Students ask and say the darndest things. There's no need to feel threatened by questions that we don't have the answers to. In today's information age it's not what you know that counts. It's what you need to know. And that means knowing where to go for some answers and for more in-depth information. It's an easy process today, with just about every Sally, Dick & Jane running around with a laptop, and with pretty much every kid on the planet "hooked up" with a cell phone that gets internet. At the very least, a computer with Internet access is as close as your local library. I could have typed in "main components of air" and searched Google. That, in turn, would direct me to a zillion sources that deal with this topic. Since this incident regarding air happened in my Buffalo public school teaching days, it was also the pre-internet days, and I had to do some leg work the old fashioned way. Remember those ancient things known as encyclopedias? They took up about 14 shelves and they were jam packed with anything and everything about life. These large, very cool and intelligent looking books, were basically a physical, touchable version of the Internet, albeit a limited one at that. In practical matters, our students make us wiser.

There's another level in this student/teacher connection, however, that's deeper than simply acquiring more knowledge. Understanding and wisdom are all well and good, if used properly of course. But the Good Lord made us with more than just brains. Although many schools today focus almost exclusively on accumulating knowledge and testing to this phenomenon, our kids are a package deal. They also have hearts, imaginations, bodies, and souls. By definition, a good education means a well-rounded one; it means nurturing the whole child. Thus, every educational program should offer music, art, phys-ed, and even training in ethics. If caring adults don't offer these important components, we run the risk of our kids getting their real education from the streets.

The famous psychologist Howard Gardner (Multiple Intelligences: New Horizons. Basic Books. 2006) speaks of seven different types of intelligences, not just the usual one that involves memorization and spitting back info come test time. There has also been much discussion about emotional intelligence or a person's EQ — emotional quotient. We need to stop looking at our kids and students with tunnel vision that perceives them only as walking brains. There are many other equally valid and critical areas that also require stimulation, discussion, and nourishment. I have always felt that motivation was the central piece of the puzzle. It's not enough to give a child a skill; the motivation to use it has to be there. I've seen many students graduate from various schools with the ability and skill level to do math, or conduct a scientific experiment, or read a history book. The only problem is that many of these students don't want to do these things anymore. We've given them the necessary skills but somehow we have turned them off in the process. Skills are important, but without fanning the flames of desire and motivation, it's like giving a bird one wing to fly. A bird with one wing doesn't even get off the ground.

I've witnessed firsthand an interesting phenomenon that occurs with individuals with special needs. They may be lacking skills in some areas, but in others they have some amazing strengths, perhaps in arenas even more important than those measured by the traditional IQ. They often seem more tuned in emotionally and are more sensitive than others. I remember the first time this phenomenon occurred in my room. It was maybe two months after our daughter Devorah Leah had passed on. It was, as you can imagine, a terribly hard time for my family. I sat in the back of the room and was feeling totally sad and depressed. I turned my chair to the back wall and pretended to do some work because I didn't want them to see me crying. Three of my students with Downs-syndrome came up to me and just hugged me. For a long 30 seconds no one said a word, but their sweetness spoke volumes. It was the medicine that I needed. No doctor's pills could have done it any better. They sensed something amiss with me and their care and concern truly uplifted me.

Another time, back in my Buffalo teaching days, a 16-year-old student of mine with autism followed me home. She said that she was worried about me and wanted to make sure that I got home in one piece. I wasn't aware that she was walking behind me until the last block. She did this even though she had walked almost a half-mile out of her way. I asked her why she had done this and she told me that she had learned all about traffic lights and stop signs, and since it was kind of complicated, she wasn't sure if I knew all the critical details about crossing the streets properly. I thanked her for the escort and then, concerned of course, had to make sure that she got home safely. We walked each other back and forth like this for about four hours. Okay, I'm kidding about the last part, but in this regard we can learn lots from our students. They are often much higher up on the EQ state of affairs.

Working with individuals with profound special needs, including physical challenges and those with medically fragile conditions, has taught me another powerful lesson. Observing all that they go through, and the real hardships they face, such as needing wheelchairs to get around and communication devices to "speak" to others, has made me more aware of the truly important things in life. Like that great oldie from way back when, "Sunny Side Of The Street." My parents loved that tune when I was growing up in Buffalo, NY. The last verse in the song goes; "If I never had a cent, I'd be rich as Rockefeller — gold dust at my feet on the sunny side of the street." My students have taught me to live on the sunny side, where things like new cars, and new carpets, and all the wealth of the world doesn't hold a candle to having one's health. How can I complain about not having my shiny new Dodge Viper when I have the ability to walk and run on my own two legs? And how can I be depressed that my paycheck doesn't allow me to buy that 30-foot diving boat, when I can talk and sing and express myself without having to use one of those slow, cumbersome communication devices? My students have taught me more than any words can express or any song can convey. They continue to teach me what's truly important in life... to live, laugh, and love to the fullest measure possible. Stay open to your children and students. You might just learn a thing or two.

TEACH ME IF YOU CAN!

CHAPTER 10

Senior Moments

"And in the end the love you take

is equal to the love you make."

— *The Beatles*

"I used to be a drummer," he said with a big, almost mischievous grin.

I nodded in his direction, smiling back in return.

"I still do," he yelled above the music, thinking I hadn't heard him the first time. "I play drums. My name is Al."

I nodded again, this time with a bit more vigor. "Awesome," I managed to verbalize in between one verse and the next.

"Maybe I should run and get my sticks," he said with a laugh in my ear. "I'm a bit over 90, but I can still play." Without waiting for a response from me he headed out the door of the social hall. We were at a local South Florida assisted living facility and in the middle of a song it was rather difficult to carry on a conversation. My special needs performing group, known affectionately as Dr. Laz & The Sensations, was rockin' the crowd of close to 100 people. The audience made a rather instant connection to my students, since many watching the show also used wheelchairs for mobility. Some in the audience could be likened to my special performers, because they too, were not so good with verbal skills. For the seniors at this facility it was probably due to a recent illness such as a stroke or some form of mental dementia, rather than profound autism or Downs-syndrome.

I've always been amazed at the connection my students make with others, especially when performing. It seems to matter little whether the audience is composed of extended members of the special needs community, or those who have had little exposure. Audiences immediately embrace them. But the bond between the Sensations and seniors is quite remarkable to behold. They make a tremendous impression on individuals residing in assisted living facilities. The elderly see kids and young adults who face more challenging issues, than even their own. Yet, in spite of these difficult challenges, here they are singing with their hands, using American Sign Language, smiling, laughing, and playing instruments using adaptive switches from their wheelchairs. Some of the Sensations are amazing dancers and they love to strut their stuff in front of anyone willing to watch. Bigger hams you won't find anywhere, including X-Factor and American Idol. The seniors tend to be a rather captive audience and they start beaming with utter delight as the group begins the show.
278

Many in the audience start clapping their hands to the beat or playing along on various percussion instruments that we've passed around.

Let's be honest here, folks. Some senior centers are quite dismal and depressing places, no matter how brightly the walls are painted. It's as if society has simply put them out to pasture. Many have referred to these assisted living institutions as "God's waiting room." Next to our very own students, how seniors tend to be treated in Western — supposedly enlightened society - is number two on the "greatest waste of talent" list. It's of course a mirrored reflection of society and how we view youth as desirable and old age, (and therefore aging), something dreadful and frightening. Just pick up any magazine, or watch any TV station for a minute or two, and you're bombarded with 14 gazillion creams to get rid of wrinkles and lift up those "crow's feet." The cost for these wonder applications ranges from the generic pricing of around 10 bucks to hundreds of dollars for the really good stuff. Supposedly. All with the promise of looking younger and avoiding, for lack of a better description here, looking old. I haven't met too many people who can swear that any of these fountain-of-youth creams really work.

Not that I'm against outward appearances. Perhaps looking younger can have a psychological impact on a person, helping them act younger by smiling more often, laughing more, and engaging in fun and spontaneous behaviors, (and even perhaps, doing more physical activities). But this can probably be accomplished in all sorts of ways that don't require "reconstructive" surgery or Botox injections or magic wonder creams. Sometimes a change of outfit can do the job. Or going to a concert. Getting out more, and even dressing in something new can get those younger neurons fired up again. Wearing a simple pair of jeans and a T-shirt may offer the same psychological effects as a tummy tuck or face-lift, without the phony, stretched out look that often accompanies those crazy-expensive surgical procedures. The important thing, I suppose, is not necessarily about appearance, but about maintaining a youthful and vibrant outlook on life.

Like the expression goes: "you're as young as you feel." (Or maybe the better expression that "age is mind over matter — if you don't mind, it don't matter!") It might be just as valid to declare you're as young as you act. And play.

As previously mentioned, I've always found that music works magic in this realm. Jet was an awesome horn player that I had the pleasure of working with for many years. I would sing the horn licks that I thought belonged in a certain tune, and he would go out there and nail 'em — often on the first take in the studio! More important than his musical abilities, however, was the fact that he was an absolute pleasure to work with and to be around. Unfortunately, he passed on after a brief illness. Besides being a wonderful human being, I always figured him to be around 55 years old, maybe a bit less. Once in our studio of choice, Insane Sounds located in south Florida, Mark, the sound engineer, asked Jet his age. We were both totally floored to find out that Jet was in his 70's. I didn't believe him and made him show me his ID. Mark then shared something very insightful with me.

"It's music, bro." he said. "Keeps ya young. As long as you're not killing your brain cells and body on drugs, that is."

My suggestion is that you go back and read the chapter on music, as it contains all sorts of ideas and suggestions on how to put music to work for you, your students, your own kids, and your elderly loved ones. Better yet, go to Massachusetts and check out my sister Sharon's awesome program. Seeing-is-believing in this case, and her hands-on, creative music-engaging and arts-therapy programs are top notch. While you're at it, head south and check out the Sensations work their magic at a senior center.

A Pittsburgh Tribune-Review article entitled "Students join research to help senior citizens," by Jodi Weigand, (Nov. 28, 2011), features a story that deals with a research project involving music and seniors with mild cognitive impairments. The article describes how a dozen students from a Pennsylvania performing arts charter school will work with about 40 seniors, instructing them how to use computer software to compose music. This study, done in conjunction with the Cleveland Clinic and MIT, will determine what results may occur participants with no prior musical background. One of the research fellows from MIT, Adam Boulanger, talks about the unique effect music provides individuals experiencing cognitive impairments. "You can draw in regions, (in the brain), where music stills exists," he said, "to compensate for other areas that are shutting down." It will be interesting to see what results, if any, come from this exciting study.

My sister Sharon, as mentioned earlier, does some wonderful work with seniors in the Berkshires area of the US. She uses a variety of therapeutic techniques, such as movement, yoga, painting, and singing. "Hundreds of millions are poured into finding a cure for Alzheimer's," she told me. "Which is fine, but hardly a thing goes towards treatment. And, while there's no cure yet, the expressive arts work wonders for the elderly with physical and mental conditions." She's calling for more direct funding for intervention programs that have this proven track record. "The expressive arts may delay the onset of these horrible, mental debilitating conditions," Sharon noted. "Singing, movement, drama, visual arts, are like super vitamins for those suffering from these illnesses." Others utilizing similar techniques agree. Observations such as these suggest movement techniques offer promise and hope where there often seems to be only darkness and gloom.

We're losing out in even more important ways than simply wasting money on looking younger. It's the elder members of society that have the most experience in the job force and in life, and thus they have the most to share and teach us. Whether it's simply a desire to save money and hire younger, or a company's desire to project a more youthful face, (pardon the expression), our seniors are given the proverbial boot. This misguided approach to the elderly leads to all sorts of painful results. First, these companies have to keep reinventing the wheel. It's the seasoned veteran who knows the real "ins & outs" of the job; how to best get the job done in the most efficient manner. The elderly know the importance of working smarter not harder. In the long run all these companies lose out by forcing out their smartest and most effective workers.

The elderly lose out too, since they no longer feel productive and needed. It's this issue, in my opinion, that is often the most damaging. In Abraham Maslow's famous "Hierarchy of Needs," the need for love and belonging comes right after physiological and safety needs. In other words, if a person knows he will have food, shelter and clothing and will essentially be safe from danger, the very next basic human need is to feel loved and wanted. Without this essential component the individual feels worthless, neglected and useless, as if ultimately, he or she doesn't really matter. At this point, these elderly - yet highly experienced individuals - may hope that the Good Lord doesn't keep them waiting too long.

To be sure, some senior facilities do a better job than others. I've seen this at the various places we've gone to perform. Some actively interact with the seniors, helping them shake, rattle and even dance to our music. But all too often, I witness a rather frightening scene. The "clients" are massed into one room, many confined to wheelchairs, and they're plopped in front of a TV screen, that babbles on and on in a noisy, obnoxious fashion. While the staff is busy polishing their nails, talking on the cell phones, or watching the show, many of the seniors have their heads hanging down, their eyes long closed.

I don't blame the staff, many of who genuinely care about and often love their clients. Nor do I find fault with the individual institution. It's society at large that has created this entire system for dealing with the elderly in this demeaning, "waiting-room" fashion. We've been missing the boat here. The elderly not only have greater experience and a vast amount of knowledge, they also can be an utter delight and filled with surprises. They have much to teach and share with us about all facets of life.

There are many cultures throughout the world that have a very different approach towards aging in general, and to the elderly specifically. Western society would do well to learn from these cultures. I've noticed this perspective in many indigenous cultures, including the Native Americans, right here in the USA. I've also experienced it when visiting Arabic, Greek, and Turk villages during my travels. It is prominent within the Orthodox & Hassidic communities today. In these familial cultures, the children are taught to respect and honor the elderly. It's not just fancy words, but translates into direct, practical action. The youth are brought up to serve the elderly first, to listen closely to their words and stories, to give up their seats, if need be, and never to talk back or act with disrespect. In these cultures, the elderly are held in high esteem. Life in these and other family oriented cultures and communities, is in a constant process of growing, learning, and developing. It makes perfect sense that the elder members of these societies are the most learned and developed. It is not uncommon for these societies and familial units to have elder members who live to ripe, older ages in the same homes as their children and grandchildren, (and great grandchildren). In my opinion, these families are indeed great. The younger generations fully benefit from such wonderful, family oriented arrangements.

This treatise must be interrupted, just as my thoughts were interrupted at the Assisted Living Center when Al returned. I had been so absorbed in my ponderings that I had completely forgotten about him. He raised his drumsticks high above his head and then, to my amazement, started playing along with the band. The band consisted of me on guitar, Zahava on the keyboards, five students with Downs-syndrome communicating through sign language, Danielle operating the slideshow from her wheelchair, and Tony — The T-Man, running the bubble machine and adaptive drums from his own wheelchair. We now had us a real McCoy drummer; Al, all of 90-some-years-old, still vibrant, with it, and playing along in perfect tempo with the song!

Surprise benefit at one of our assisted living center gigs. Al joins the band as our drummer.

As a drummer, I know the importance of staying in the groove and keeping the right beat. Drummers tend to rush along a bit and kind of fade in and out of the proper tempo, either speeding up or slowing behind. It's something that can frustrate the heck out of the other band members. My drum teacher, the great John Rowland, was the head percussionist for the Buffalo philharmonic orchestra and he was a stickler for playing in the right beat and maintaining that proper tempo throughout the entire piece.

Counting was essential, and he made me play along to a loud, unforgiving, (and quite obnoxious), metronome. It had no mercy whatsoever. It provided that loud click that, unlike me, never slowed down and never sped up. He would adjust the tempo to very slow and then to very fast and somehow I was supposed to hang right there with it.

"Every time you play a beat and hit the drum pad and you don't hear the metronome clock," he told me, "well, that means you're playing in the right groove. If you hear the metronome click, then you're off. Even a hundredth of a second is off." A good percussionist, he frequently reminded me, has absolute impeccable timing that's simply absolute spot-on. When a piece calls for a few beats of a timpani drum or a hit or two on the triangle, or a quick triplet on the woodblock, the percussionist has got to be on the money and insert these sounds exactly where they belong. For my first year on the drums, I was more off than on. Al must've had Mr. Rowland as a teacher, (or he had done his fair share of practicing with that merciless metronome).

As Al played along, tapping away with his sticks on top of the table and sometimes on top of the speaker cabinet, I couldn't help but think how fortunate he was that he still had this special skill he could utilize, share with others, and simply continue using for his own enjoyment and pleasure. Our unique little performing troop was simply the vehicle that enabled him to feel a bit more needed, wanted and appreciated. We were honoring Dr. Maslow's "Hierarchy of Needs." He would have been proud. We weren't just doing Al a favor; he was helping us out too, adding something sweet and positive to our music. In Maslow's terminology, Al felt a sense of belonging, of being part of a group, and we were more than blessed to have him with us.

But the magic didn't stop here. Things were just warming up. Even bigger surprises were in store for us. I asked the audience if anyone had celebrated a birthday recently, or had one coming up. Part of our repertoire was to get the audience involved and singing along. That old school waltz beat of "happy birthday" is something probably even known to aliens from the outer realms of the universe. Several hands went up.

"Wonderful," I said into the microphone. "But before we sing to our birthday stars, let's find out who they are and how young they are." A few laughs of approval were heard from the crowd.

I pointed to one lady to my left side that had her hand raised. "Please young lady," I said. "What's your name and how young are you?"

"I'm Rose," came the first response. "And I just celebrated my 101st birthday."

Several people in the audience broke out in spontaneous applause.

"Beautiful," I responded. "That's a remarkable accomplishment indeed. Before we find out what your secret is, let's ask the other birthday superstars."

"I just turned 97," said the next person with her hand up. "And my name is Liz."

"And I'm Ruth," said another out loud. "My birthday is in a week. I will be a mere 102 years young." This elicited even louder applause.

"I'm Darcy and I'm 104," another shouted out, not waiting for any formal acknowledgment. "Ha. The others are babies! It's about time they learned to respect their elders."

This brought forth a roar of laughter, including from yours truly. No one could accuse these seniors of not having a sense of humor.

I decided to skip the happy birthday tune for a few moments to get down to more important business. Quite frankly, I couldn't recall ever meeting anyone in my life who had made this unique milestone. "Okay," I added, still chuckling a bit from Darcy's last statement. "All those at least 100 years young please raise your hands."

One more hand shot into the air.

"My name is Anna," she said with a gleam in her eyes. "I'm the baby of the group. Why I'm only 100 years young!"

I was overwhelmed with the realization that I was in the presence of four women who had a combined treasure chest of more than 400 years of life and experience. Together with the younger seniors in their mere 90's, we probably had well over 3,000 years of wisdom & wit sitting right there in front of us!

"Let's all applaud these amazing people and their even more amazing accomplishments of becoming centogenarians." It was an educated guess. If octogenarian refers to an 80 year old, then perhaps centogenarian was the proper descriptor.

We all applauded and cheered, and my brain wheels kicked in high gear.

"Now let's find out how they did this," I announced. "I mean they must have some kind of secret they could share with us. Please ladies. With your help maybe we too can make such a milestone."

"I'll go first," Anna said with a smile. "After all the baby is the one that gets spoiled by the others."

"Please, Anna. By all means. What's your special secret that helped you make it to being a centennial person?"

"One word, dear man," she responded to me. "Chocolate!"

The room filled with more laughs.

"Ah yes, indeed. Chocolate it was and chocolate it is. Any particular favorites?"

"Any and all," Anna answered.

Hollywood could not have scripted this exchange any better, I thought to myself, "so much for seniors aging into a dismal state of mental and physical deficiency." This unique group of elderly individuals had a certain spark and spunk that would rival any teenager!

"Okay Anna. Thanks for sharing your deep, dark secret with us. I will do my best to follow that path. And now, I believe Rose is next at 101."

Rose slowly stood up with the help of her walker. At first I motioned for her to stay seated and that there was no need to stand.

"Well," Rose started, "mine is not so hard to understand. It's been good friends and loving family that have all gotten me to this point in life."

"Thank you for those wise words," I said.

"I'm not quite done," she responded a bit annoyed that I had cut her off so abruptly.

"Very sorry," I apologized. "Please."

"Physical things in life are nice," she continued. "But they are not what's really important. Fancy clothes and fancy cars and expensive homes are pleasant, but they come and go. True friends and love lasts forever."

With that she sat back down to the unanimous applause of all in the room.

Having the distinct advantage of the microphone, I sang out those words of the Fab Four that Rose herself may have helped to write. "And in the end, the love you take is equal to the love you make."

"I guess I'm next," one of our centenarians — the proper term, by the way, said. "But I'll speak sitting down."

"I'm sorry but I've forgotten your name," I said with a tinge of embarrassment. Wasn't it the elderly that had these "senior moments" of memory lapse? And wasn't my pliable, flexible, younger brain power a great deal more responsive than hers?

"So what's your…"

"I'm Ruth and I'm a young 102 years."

"Okay Ruth. Please share your secret with us. How did you reach this incredible young age?"

"Men."

"Men?"

"Yes. Men."

"Men?" I was hoping the conversation would remain at least PG13.

"Yes," she said, somewhat annoyed. "Men. I avoid them like the plague!"

The room burst at the seams with uproarious laughter. Several of the women and men in the room were slapping their knees and clapping their hands. Her wonderful outrageous response nearly caused me to drop the microphone. When I finally was able to stop laughing I couldn't help but add in my two cents.

"I thank you for your secret Ruth. But I do hope, as a man, mind you, that a few ladies will stick with the love and chocolate." That statement brought more than a few nods, especially from the gentlemen in the crowd. Several shouted out loud "amen."

"Well, last but not least we turn to our youngest and wisest perhaps. None other than…"

"Darcy. I'm Darcy and approaching year number 105."

I breathed a sigh of relief that she jumped right in and offered her name.

"Awesome Ms. Darcy. Please share with us your secret to long life."

"Why young man," she said leaning back in her chair, "I have no secrets."

"None whatsoever," I asked.

"Not a one."

"Ah, so that's your secret… that you have no secret!"

"No. I keep no secrets," she said, stressing the word no.

"I'm saying that your secret to long life is that you have no secrets. You know, you have nothing to hide. So your secret is you have no secrets!"

"No. I have no secrets."

"But that is your very secret," I said playing this out, thinking I simply had to explain it more succinctly.

"No sir," she responded tapping her fingers on the arms of the chair. "I have no secrets whatsoever." As she said this, Darcy turned to the crowd and gave them a big wink from her left eye. Once again everyone roared in approval, as Darcy clearly was the winner of this little mind game. She was playing me the whole time. I applauded her sharp wit and quickly blew her a kiss from the band area.

We all need to feel engaged, like we're connected to something important and wholesome. Hands-on music helps to engage everyone, from the very young to the very young-at-heart. It's a simple, yet highly productive step to pass out all sorts of percussion goodies for folks to play on to the beat of the music. This stimulates the brain, gets the body moving and the blood flowing. It also brings smiles to nearly all involved.

But seniors don't have to be satisfied with being band members. Many seniors, particularly those with healthy mental functioning, can do a tremendous service by volunteering to help others. The Quest Center has several wonderful elderly volunteers who give of their time, love, and expertise. In this regard they not only help the classroom teachers by allowing for more individualized attention for the students, they also serve as living examples to the teachers. Ruth is one of our amazing senior volunteers. She now utilizes a wheelchair to get around, but this hasn't slowed her down one bit. I once heard a teacher express a sense of marvel about Ruth's presence in the classroom.

"How do you do it?" she asked Ruth. "Where do you get such incredible patience? I wish I had even one tenth of this quality!"

"Oh," Ruth responded, "it's nothing really. I mean, where am I going anyhow? Life rushes on so fast. Why should I rush it any faster by being impatient?"

The classroom teacher and I just smiled and continued to listen to her sage advice.

"Anyhow, kids make progress in very small steps. Especially these kids. If I'm impatient, I may just miss these steps taking place right in front of my eyes."

We need to keep the doors open for the elder members of our society. They have much to share and to teach us. Our students and children can only benefit from this wonderful contact.

The Sensations rock the senior home for a special holiday show. Performers use American Sign Language to the live music, while Danielle operates the visual slideshows using her knee switch from her wheelchair.

TEACH ME IF YOU CAN!
EPILOGUE

Some Concluding Thoughts

"I am enough of an artist to draw freely
upon my imagination."

— *Albert Einstein*

We've all heard it a million times before: "Life's a journey — enjoy the ride." This expression has been used to sell cars, vacations trips, and tickets to theme parks. Perhaps it's been used occasionally to refer to parenting, where we have this kind of built-in expectation about the joys of child rearing and creating a family. Unfortunately, it's not used too frequently when it comes to teaching. In fact, I can't recall a single time anyone ever said that to me about his or her teaching position. But it is the necessary medicine to set the wheels right and keep our focus, especially with so much of the education world gone overboard with testing, data and comparative analysis. I'm not against the notion of testing per se — after all, my doctorate is in Research & Evaluation, and I've taught graduate courses on educational analysis. So, in a sense, I'm guilty of perpetrating the very system I criticize. However, I utilize similar methods when teaching both college students and those with profound special needs; by using student-centered learning combined with an experiential and fun oriented approach — the very things discussed in detail in this book. Many of my college students who were turned-off and intimidated by the redundantly-repetitive retentive focus of college education, suddenly got excited and turned-on about research and evaluation.

It's time to bring creativity back into our homes and classrooms. We need to follow Einstein's observation quoted above, and become enough of an artist that we too can draw freely upon our imaginations. Then, there will be no limit as to what we can do as teachers and parents - and as to what our kids can accomplish.

Teaching is an awesome journey, filled with challenges, surprises, responsibilities, tears, and laughter. It's easy to stay in touch in the digital age of social networking. Please share your stories and triumphs with me and, you heard it from me right here: "Teaching is a journey - enjoy the ride!" Now go out there and knock 'em alive.

BIBLIOGRAPHY

References

Alexenberg, D. M. (2008) Educating Artists for the Future. Intellect Books.

Block, G. &. (2007) Inner Wealth Initiative: The Nurtured Heart Approach for Educators. Nurtured Heart Publications.

Bright, R. (Fall, 2011). Kids Who Can't Sit Still. Today Magazine - National   Education Association.

Campbell, D. (2006). The China Study. First BenBella Books.

De La Mater, B. (2011) Paint Memory — Alzheimer's patients speak through art. The Berkshire Eagle.

Dahl, R. (1982). The Big Friendly Giant. Trumpet Club

Fulghum, R. (1988). All I Really Need To Know I Learned in Kindergarten.   New York: Villard Books,

Gardner, H. (2006). Multiple Intelligences: New Horizons. Basic Books.

Hwang, J. (Mar 24, 2009). Music Gets Backing For Addressing Autism. The Miami Herald.

Johnson, S. (1984). The Present. Doubleday

Korman, A. (2011). Touch of home at new unit. Goal at Kimball Farms to make lives more comfortable. The Berkshire Eagle.

Lazerson, D. (1980) "I Must be Good if I can Teach" -- Peer Tutoring with Aggressive and Withdrawn Children. Journal of Learning Disabilities. v13 n3 p152-57

Lazerson, D. (1988). The Effectiveness of Cross-Age Tutoring With Truant,   Junior High School Students with Learning Disabilities. Journal of Learning Disabilities. v21

Lazerson, D. (2005). Detention home and a public school - a cooperative peer tutoring trial project. UK Journal of Emotional & Behavioral Disorders.

Lazerson, D. (1987). Skullcaps 'N Switchblades. Bristol, Rhein & Englander.

    Princeton, NJ.

Lazerson, D. (2004). Sharing Turf. Race relations after the Crown Heights riots. Ballad Productions. N Miami Beach, Fl.

Levitin, D. (2007). This Is Your Brain On Music.

Lipman, S. (1980, April 20). Talmudic Ideas Used in the Ghetto. NY Times

Louv, R. (2008). Last Child in the Woods. Algonquin Paperbacks.

Martin, D. (2011). This is a Book. Grand Central Publishing.

Maslow, A (1943). A Theory of Human Motivation - Hierarchy of Needs Chart Psychosomatic   Medicine, 1943, 5, 85-92)

Muck, S. (2011, Nov. 28). Riding program offers therapy, life-changing experiences. Washington Post

Payne, K. (2009). Simplicity Parenting. Random House.

Prager, D. (1995). Happiness Is A Serious Problem. Regan Books.

Rogers, N. (1993). The Creative Connection — Expressive Arts as Healing . Science & Behavior Books.

Sacks, D. O. (2007). Musicophilia. Vintage Books

Shlaug, Dr. G. (2009). Neuroeducation: Learning, Arts, & The Brain , Beth Israel Deaconess Medical Center and Harvard Medical School. (2009)

Topping, K. (2001). Peer-assisted learning: A practical guide for teachers.

    Brookline Books. Cambridge, MA.

Weigand, J. (Nov. 28, 2011).Students join research to help senior citizens. Pittsburgh Tribune-Review.

Web Resources

Able-Net: www.ablenetinc.com

American Art Therapy Association: www.arttherapy.org

American Dance/Movement Therapy Association: www.adta.org

American Music Therapy Association: www.musictherapy.org

CEC - Council for Exceptional Children: www.cec.sped.org

Dr. Laz: www.drlaz.com

Enabling Devices: www.enablingdevices.com

Exceptional Theatre Company: www.etcsouthflorida.org

Farm Sanctuary: www.farmsanctuary.org

International Expressive Arts Therapy Association: www.ieata.org

Kid's Gardening: www.kidsgardening.org

iObservation.com: http://www.iobservation.com/Marzano-Suite/ Dr. Morzano's Suite for Improving Teacher Effectiveness.

Laughing Matters - by Michael Coleman: www.LaughingMatters.org.

Lisa Coleman Music — Animal Stories & Songs: www.lisacolemanmusic.com

Lovewell Institute: www.lovewell.org

Mother Earth News: www.motherearthnews.com

National Association of Drama Therapy: www.nadt.org

National Parks Conservation Association: www.npca.org

Open Office: www.download.openoffice.org

Outside Magazine: www.outsideonline.com

Outward Bound: www.outwardbound.org

Farm Sanctuary: www.farmsanctuary.org

Rainbow Riding: www.rainbowriding.org

Simplicity Parenting: www.simplicityparenting.com

Scouting : www.scouting.org

The H.E.ARTS Project: www.thehealingartsproject.org

PATH - Professional Association of Therapeutic Horsemanship International: www.pathintl.org

Songs:

Beatles. All You Need is Love

Belafonte, Harry. Day-Oh.

Bennett, Tony. Fly Me to the Moon.

Bricusse, A. Put on a Happy Face.

Dr. Laz. Ain't Nobody's Fool.

Harrison, G. & The Beatles. Here Comes the Sun.

Lehrer, Tom. Element Song.

McHugh, J. Sunny Side of the Street.

Mendelsohn. Violin Concerto in E Minor.

Mitchell, Joni. Big Yellow Taxi.

Mitch Ryder and The Detroit Wheels (Performer). Devil with a Blue Dress On - Good Golly Miss Molly

Pachelbel. Canon in D Major.

Ringo & The Beatles. Octopus's Garden.

Sherman, R. B. Spoonful of Sugar.

Simon & Garfunkle. Sound of Silence.

Supertramp. Logical Song.

Menken, Alan. Under the Sea.

Vivaldi. Four Seasons.

Terms

ASL - American Sign Language

Assistive Technology - Enabling electronic devices that can be activated from wheelchairs and other locations.

Bennett High - High School in Buffalo NY

Black Lights - A form of lighting used in a darkened room to highlight whites and fluorescent colors

Broadway vs. Broad-Way Approach — Author's term for the difference between a full-fledged production and a more unstructured one.

Camp Heller - Summer Camp in the Catskill Mountains of Upstate New York

Chaver - Friend or colleague [in Hebrew]

Chavruso — Traditional method of Jewish/Talmudic learning which utilizes the peer-learning model.

Chebar - Bond or attachment [in Hebrew]

Cross Age Tutoring - Student based peer teaching or peer tutoring that involves students of different ages working together.

Davening — Prayer (in Yiddush)

DMT - Dance Movement Therapy

Dr. MLK Jr. - Dr. Martin Luther King Community School - Buffalo, NY

ESE - Exceptional Student Education

Farbrengens — Yiddush word that mean a gathering of people for positive oriented activities.

Fist-to-five - A visual indicator participants provide to indicate how much information they have absorbed.

Habilitation - Maintaining the functional skills the clients have, without trying to force them into a predetermined system - used primarily in Alzheimer's facilities

IEP's - Individualized Education Plans

JFK - John F Kennedy High School, a.k.a. Jail for Kids

Kelev — The Hebrew word for dog, which shares a linguistic connection to the following word:

K'lev - Like The Heart [in Hebrew]

Kohain - Priest

Ma'aseh — Action, even moving the lips (as when praying)

Magical Mystical Moving Movement Maneuvers — Author's phrase for a series of movements to participants

Mazel — Fortune as in Mazel Tov, which means good fortune

Medaber - The Speaker [in Hebrew]

MSE - Multi-Sensory Environment

MTM - The Most Teachable Moment

Marzano - Developer of the Marzano Casual Teacher Model (for teacher training and improvement)

Muktzeh - Things forbidden to engage in or touch on the Sabbath, such as money and business transactions.

Nez Perce - Native American Tribe

Nurtured Heart Approach - Behavior Management that highlights positive gains rather than negative behaviors

PCM - Professional Care Management.

Peer Tutoring - Cross-age-tutoring/Peer Assisted Learning (Student-based peer tutoring)

PET - Parent Effectiveness Training

PFD's - Personal Flotation Devices

Physual — Author's term derived from the two activities of being Physical and utilizing the Visual Arts

PITS - Post Irritated Teacher Stress

PPT - Power Point Presentations (slide shows)

Rule of Thirds - Start with Pizazz, Keep their interest, End with Pizazz

Ropes Course - A course that usually has various stations and activities, both low to the ground and high above the ground, that encourages individual and group challenges.

The Quest Center - Innovative center for special needs students, part of the Broward County Public Schools in South Florida.

Sponge Theory — Author's term for the "absorb and spit back" teaching method

Student Centered Process - Not teacher-driven but experiential, student-driven learning

S.W.I. T.C. H. - See What I Totally Can Handle! (One of the author's successful grant applications and projects.)

TLC - Tender Loving Care

Unadulterated - Definition: Not perverted by cynicism, sarcasm and negativity

VE - Varying Exceptionalities

Miscellaneous

As you Like It. Shakespeare, W. [12th Century Play]

Animal Crackers — Marx Bros. film

Blazing Saddles — Mel Brooks film

Dr. Laz & The Sensations - name for the author's special needs performing group

Duck Soup — Marx Bros. film

The Ha Ha Maneuver - Game to encourage interaction and laughter.

Ketogenic Diet - Special Diet for Seizure Disorders

Krupa - Drummer from the early days of jazz

MDS - Manhattan Day School

Men in Tights — Mel Brooks film

Mishkon — Former camp in upstate New York for individuals with special needs

The Music, Neuroimaging & Stroke Recovery Laboratories - Beth Israel Hospital [Dr. Schlaug's program]

Night at The Opera — Marx Bros. film

Princess Bride - film

Dr. Roland — Former head percussionist at the Buffalo Philharmonic and author's drum teacher

Ring Homestead — Ropes Course and outdoor wilderness adventure setting, about 90 minute drive from NYC.

Uncle Seymour — Author's family nickname for the television, because they always wanted to "See More."

Quotes

Alexenberg, Dr. Mel - For an artist to be truly effective in today's complex world, he or she must seek to unify the areas of art, technology, culture, and even science

Barth, Roland - The best principals are not heroes; they are hero makers.

Beatles, The - And in the end the love you take is equal to the love you make.

Bennett High School Anthem - "Bennett, Bennett, lead us onward, for the best is yet to be."

Beethoven - Music is a higher revelation than all wisdom and philosophy.

Boulanger, Adam - You can draw in regions, (in the brain), where music stills exists to compensate for other areas that are shutting down.

Campbell, Dr. - We are leading our youth down a path of disease earlier and earlier in their lives." ... "it all comes down to three things: breakfast, lunch & dinner.

Charles, Ray - I was born with music inside me. Like my ribs, my heart. Like my blood. It was a necessity for me - like food or water.

Chinese proverb - Tell me and I'll forget. Show me and I may remember. Involve me and I'll understand.

Confucius - If your plan is for one year, plant rice. If your plan is for ten years, plant trees. If your plan is for one hundred years, educate children

DMT Association - Healing through Movement

Einstein, Albert - Logic will get you from A to B. Imagination will take you everywhere.

Einstein, Albert - I am enough of an artist to draw freely upon my imagination.

Frost, Robert - I'm not a teacher but an awakener.

Gardner, Blair (teach.com) - This book (Teach Me If You Can!) is a must-read for teachers, parents and anyone interested in education. It really works — for any teacher for any student for any subject!

Hanina, R. quoted in the Talmud.- Much have I learned from my teachers, more from my colleagues, but most from my students.

Kid's Gardening.org Mission Statement - To promote home, school, and community gardening as a means to renew and sustain the essential connections between people, plants, and the environment.

Kim, Majin - Music may be effective because it compliments the cognitive abilities of people with autism, which include a strong inclination for creating patterns.

Lazerson, David - Oath of Teaching: I hereby promise not to do to my students what most of my teachers have done to me - Bore the Living Daylights out of me! I will do whatever it takes to inspire, motivate & stimulate my students to grow & learn.

Louv, Richard - Reducing the NDD [Nature Deficit Disorder] is critical because our mental, physical, and spiritual health depends on it. The health of the earth is at stake as well.

Lubavitcher Rebbe - There are several essential components of education. In order of importance they are: The warm atmosphere - the enthusiasm for learning. The connection between teacher and student. And the information and skills. Unfortunately, many schools today have turned into information factories, leaving out the very foundation - the love and motivation for learning.

Martin, Demetri - As televisions become flatter — people become rounder.

Marzano - administrative/teacher relationships are one of the most significant contributing factors to teacher growth and development.

Maslow - the need for love and belonging comes right after physiological and safety needs.

Pistoletto, Michaelangelo - artists have a unique and totally free way of understanding and analyzing society.... art can interact among all the diverse spheres of human activity that form society, and is thereby a generator for responsible transformation of society.

Prager, Dennis - We owe it to our husband or wife, our fellow workers, our children, our friends, indeed to everyone who comes into our lives, to be as happy as we can be.

Rashab, Rebbe - We should actively contemplate the education of our children for at least 30 minutes every day.

Rogers, Natalie - We do not become creative by thinking about it. We reawaken our creativity by engaging in the process of creativity.

Rosenberg, Rafi — When it comes to education, start with the advice of the medical field; First, do no harm.

Schlaug, Dr. Gottfried - Creating music is a multisensory experience, but it also involves attention networks, and the motivation and reward system." I would challenge everybody to come up with another activity that engages as much real estate in the brain as music-making does.

Sousa, David - the activities involved in making and creating music provide many more cerebral advantages than simply passively listening.

Shakespeare, William - All the World's a Stage

Topping - the benefits of peer-tutoring for students include higher academic achievement, improved relationships with peers, improved personal and social development, as well as increased motivation. In turn, the teacher benefits from this model of instruction by an increased opportunity to individualize instruction, increased facilitation of inclusion/mainstreaming, and opportunities to reduce inappropriate behaviors.

Nietzsche - We should call every truth false, which was not accompanied by at least one laugh.

Yormak, Bernie B. — FID: Frequency. Intensity. Duration. GOK: God Only Knows.

Yormak, Bernie B. - The head can only take as much as the rear end can sit

Unknown - A smile is a crooked little line that can straighten out so much

Unknown - Laughter is indeed the best medicine.

Unknown - Life's a journey — enjoy the ride.

Van Buren, Abigail - If you want children to keep their feet on the ground, put some responsibility on their shoulders.

Washington, Booker T. - Few things help an individual more than to place responsibility upon him, and to let him know that you trust him.

Walker, Ms. (The LAW)...at a faculty meeting - The rubber band is to remind us to remain flexible with students and lesson plans - flexibility is particularly important for special education. The paper clip is to remind us that sometimes the smallest thing keeps it all together. The erasable pen teaches us not to dwell on mistakes, especially the little ones - Erase 'em and move on. The Bob Marley pin encourages us to relax and know that 'Everything's gonna Be All Right,' and the Tootsie Roll is to wish us all a sweet day, week and year on the job. But it won't just dissolve in our mouths like a mint - it takes some chewing, some effort to get to all that sweetness.

Yiddish Saying - A mentch tracht un Got lacht - man thinks (plans) and God laughs.

Made in the USA
Columbia, SC
18 August 2023

21723077R00181